THE HEBRIDES
A Natural Tapestry

Fig. 1
Map of the Hebrides

− 59°N

8°W 7°W 6°W 5°W

Sula
Sgeir

North
Rona

Cape
Wrath

Butt of
Lewis

Flannan
Isles

Handa

Atlantic
Ocean

LEWIS

MINCH

− 58°N

Summer
Isles

St Kilda

Harris

Little Minch

Shiant
Isles

Monach Isles

NORTH
UIST

SKYE

BENBECULA

SOUTH
UIST

SEA OF THE
HEBRIBES

− 57°N

Canna

Rum

Eigg

MALLAIG

BARRA

Muck

Barra Head

COLL

TIREE

MULL

OBAN

Iona

Firth of Lorne

− 56°N

Colonsay

JURA

ISLAY

Gigha

Mull of
Kintyre

0   20   40   60   80 km

N

THE HEBRIDES
A Natural Tapestry

J. Morton Boyd
and Ian L. Boyd

Birlinn

This Edition published in 1996 by
Birlinn Limited
14 High Street
Edinburgh EH1 1TE

The Publisher acknowledges subsidy from the Scottish Arts Council
towards the publication of this volume.

THE HEBRIDES
ISBN 1 874744 55 6–A Habitable Land? (Book I)
56 4–A Natural Tapestry (Book II)
57 2–A Mosaic of Islands (Book III)

A CIP record of this book is available
from the British Library

Printed and bound in Scotland by Bell & Bain Limited

FOR HELEN

Stark rocks stand in the sea:
Curved islands against the sunset.
Oh Hebrides! What are you telling me?
I know wherein thy strength is set.
In thy beauty which I oft-times see
In ancient sea-girt, pillared rock beset,
By thrift and auk and cuckoo-bee.

J.M.B.

Contents

Preface and Acknowledgements

The Hebrides—a natural tapestry (H-ANT) is substantially Part I 'The Ecosystem of the Hebrides' of the HarperCollins New Naturalist volume *The Hebrides—a natural history*. The core of this book is Chapters 1–10 of that previous work and it has two companions: *The Hebrides—a habitable land?* (H-AHL) and *The Hebrides—a mosaic of islands* (H-AMI), which are respectively Parts III and II of that previous work. The three books now have independence, but their common origin in the New Naturalist volume, now out of print, give them an interdependence as a comprehensive review of Hebridean natural history. This specific book deals with the structure of the archipelago while the others deal with the human dimension of the natural history (Volume 1) and the distribution of species among the islands (Volume 3).

Morton and Ian Boyd are a father and son team, and it could be said that the work of which this is a part has been forty years in the making. Morton might never have attempted it had he not collaborated with Fraser Darling in the writing of an earlier New Naturalist volume *The Highlands and Islands* in 1964. From the inside, as it were, he could see the great advantages of having the book written by a single author, not just for style of writing, but also for the artistry of compilation of a single comprehensive work from a wide variety of sources. The alternative is to compile a book with many experts contributing one or more chapters, but the result would be very different from the types of books produced by some of the authors of classical natural history books—F. Fraser Darling, E. B. Ford, C. M. Yonge, W. H. Pearsall, Dudley Stamp, Alistair Hardy and others in the New Naturalist series. These authors were at once experts in a limited field, and naturalists of broad erudition and experience. They were able to see and describe nature in the round.

When *The Hebrides* was in its early stages of production Morton's time was taken up with his final years as the Director (Scotland) of the Nature Conservancy

Council and then, in the later stages, by the need to
conserve his energies because of an illness. Through this
he needed an assistant to help with the compilation,
primary drafting and editing of his text, the incorporation
of expert comment and the application of the judgement
and taste of a younger scientist. Morton did not require
to look further than his second son, Ian Lamont Boyd.
Ian made his first visit to the Hebrides in infancy, and
came face to face with a grey seal, the animal which was
eventually to be the subject of his Cambridge PhD disser-
tation, for the first time at the age of 19 months.
Throughout his boyhood he was continuously on foot
with his father in the Hebrides and later, like Morton,
had the benefit of a broadly-based Degree in natural
science from a Scottish University. Ian has pursued a
career in scientific research and is now in charge of seal
research at the British Antarctic Survey.

Both hardback and softback editions of *The Hebrides*
went out of print within 18 months of publication in
1990. HarperCollins decided not to reprint, but made the
book available to Birlinn for reprinting in three shorter
books. The authors, therefore, have restructured *The
Hebrides* and have provided new Prefaces, Chapters,
Bibliographies, and Indexes for all three new books. The
chapters of the original book have been reprinted
with a few amendments; it has not been possible, on
account of cost, to update the text of 1990.

The authors were faced with a vast span in geological
age, an enormous number of distinct forms of life all of
which are specially adapted to their living quarters, a
wide range of temperate maritime habitats, and a group
of human influences and impacts on the environment
rooted in Celtic and Norse cultures, and strikingly different today from those in mainland Britain. The whole
great assembly is dynamic. It is not sufficient, therefore,
to provide a snap-shot of nature and human affairs today,
but one also has to apply the dimension of history and
unrelenting change. To achieve this in three short
volumes it was a matter of, firstly, choosing how much
to include of the available knowledge; secondly, consult-
ing with specialists with knowledge about the subject of
each chapter; and thirdly, incorporating these experts'
comments.

The authors are deeply aware that the shape and content of this book and its two companions are a matter of
personal choice. It has been difficult to decide what
should be excluded; there are many studies which deserve

mention and which, in the hands of other compilers, would find a place. The fact that some works are restricted to a mention in the Bibliography does not necessarily reflect their importance in natural and human history. The authors thank the following who have provided valuable unpublished information and other special advice in the writing of this book and its two companion volumes: R. N. Campbell for the distribution lists of brackish-freshwater fishes, amphibians and reptiles in Chapter 10; A. Currie and Mrs C. Murray for revising their list of vascular plants; the Department of Biological Sciences, University of Stirling for a copy of *Mariculture Report 1988*; Professor P. A. Jewell for data on Soay sheep at St Kilda; Scottish Natural Heritage for a copy of *Agriculture & Environment in the Outer Hebrides* and, together with the Seabird Group, data from the Seabird Colony Register; Dr M. A. Ogilvie and Dr D. A. Stroud for data on wintering geese; Miss M. G. Roy for helpfully abstracting climatic data from *Scotland's Climate* (Meteorological Office, 1988). Advice on Gaelic literature and names of flora, fauna, rocks and minerals has been given by Alan M. Boyd.

The authors also thank the authors of papers in the two volumes in the *Proceedings of the Royal Society of Edinburgh* (1979, 1983) which were a rich source of material for these books and A. R. Waterston (1981) without whose efforts the natural history of the Hebrides would remain scattered and inaccessible. We also thank the following for advice and practical help; K. J. Boyd, R. D. Crammond, Miss A. Coupe, Mrs H. G. Foster, Sir Charles A. Fraser, R. Goodier, F. Hamilton, Mrs S. Hiscock, Prof. A. D. McIntyre, Dr D. S. McLusky, Dr D. H. Mills, Dr H. Prendergast, and others.

Over almost forty years, many naturalists who have not been directly involved in the writing of this book, have shared with Morton their knowledge of the Hebrides. The authors have in mind colleagues in the Nature Conservancy (1957–73) and Nature Conservancy Council (1973–85)—especially J. C. (later The Viscount of) Arbuthnott, M. E. Ball, R. N. Campbell, A. Currie, Dr W. J. Eggeling, Dr D. A. Ratcliffe, J. G. Roger, and P. Wormell; the members of the Soay Sheep research Team at St Kilda (1959–67)—especially Prof. P. A. Jewell and Dr C. Milner; the Grey Seal Research Programme at North Rona and Harris (1959–69)—especially R. Balharry, R. H. Dennis and J. MacGeoch; the Rum National Nature Reserve (1965–85)—especially Dr T. H.

Clutton-Brock and Miss F. E. Guinness; and the Sea
Eagle Reintroduction Project (1975–85)—especially
R. H. Dennis, J. A. Love and H. Misund. We wish to
take this opportunity of thanking them and saluting them
for their knowledge of natural science and their contribution to the conservation of nature in the Hebrides.

The typescripts and proofs were corrected by Mrs W.
I. Boyd and Mrs S. M. E. Boyd. The authors also wish to
thank the following who kindly read and commented on
one or more chapters of this book and its two companion
volumes—an asterisk denotes more than one chapter.
Miss. S. S. Anderson, R. S. Bailey, M. E. Ball★, Prof.
R. J. Berry★, Dr J. L. Campbell, R. N. Campbell★. Dr
T. H. Clutton-Brock, R. D. Crammond★, A. Currie★,
Dr D. J. Ellett, Dr C. H. Emeleus★. Dr P. G. H. Evans,
Dr R. J. Harding, Dr M. P. Harris, Dr G. Hudson, Prof.
P. A. Jewell, G. S. Johnstone, R. C. B. Johnstone, A. J.
Kerr, J. Lindsay, Dr R. A. Lindsay, J. A. Love, Prof.
A. D. McIntyre, H. McLean, Dr D. S. McLusky, Dr
P. S. Maitland★, Dr J. Mason, Dr A. Mowle, S. Murray,
Prof. T. A. Norton, Dr M. A. Ogilvie, Dr R. E.
Randall, Prof. W. Ritchie, Miss M. G. Roy, Dr D. A.
Stroud★, Dr D. J. Smith, Dr M. L. Tasker★, Miss V. M.
Thom, Dr P. J. Tilbrook, A. R. Waterston, Dr C. D.
Waterston, Dr R. C. Welch, and P. Wormell★.

*A fine display of
waterlillies, yellow
flags and lesser
spearworts in and
around a* dubh lochan
*at Daliburgh, South
Uist (Photo: J. M.
Boyd)*

J. Morton Boyd
and Ian L. Boyd
Balephuil
Isle of Tiree
Argyll

A detail of the natural tapestry: the lesser celandine blooms free of grazing on Dun, St Kilda? (Photo: J. M. Boyd)

Prologue
by J. M. Boyd

When I was a little boy the Garden of Hesperides, Hy Brasil and the Hebrides were in a curious way one in my mind. Two of these places are mythical; the Hebrides are real, but they reach into a legendary past and the limbo of my own mind and so, the Hebrides, however romantic they may have been in their beginnings in me, became a country which had to be trodden.

F. Fraser Darling

It is the purpose of this book to describe that reality of the Hebrides of which Fraser Darling was so conscious, and which has been experienced by many who have trodden the islands over the last few centuries. They were men and women of different philosophies and sciences, whose love of the islands and curiosity has taken them, with great energy and enthusiasm, into the remotest places. Many have left faithful accounts of their observations and experiences, though the literature can only be a minor part of the story. The remainder is held in notebooks, and in the memory of a community possessing a strong oral tradition. Every pair of eyes that has observed and every mind that has interpreted the passing scene, has been different. Naturalists have worked, alone and in groups, to produce a vast number of separate vignettes in a great natural history. Certainly, the Hebrides have been trodden!

The Soay Sound, St Kilda, looking from Hirta to Soay with Stac Biorach (73m) in the chasm (Photo J. M. Boyd)

Islands in Natural History

Islands cast a romantic spell upon people. They possess a mystique from which the pragmatist cannot escape, nor for which the scientist can find ready explanation. Nevertheless, this spell is real in island life, and engenders deep intellectual and physical responses in human beings. In the Hebrides themselves, it is an experience which many share, but which is deeply personal, and indicative of a singular, inner passion for the *ultima thule*. Charles Darwin knew it. According to Frank Sulloway (1984), Darwin raised the level of mystique of the Galapagos to that of 'enchanted islands' (which is the literal translation of *galapagos* from Spanish), in such unromantic works as biology textbooks and histories of science—so much so, that these islands have become 'the highly acclaimed symbol of one of the greatest revolutions in Western intellectual thought'. Twenty-four years were to elapse between Darwin's visit to the Galapagos in 1835, and the *Origin of Species* (1859). It is clear therefore, that his 'conversion' to the evolution theory did not occur in the heroic setting portrayed in the popular history of science. The idea of natural selection did not occur to Darwin until 1837, almost two years after he visited the Galapagos. However, the legend of a supreme, 'eureka-like' discovery by the great naturalist coming face to face with evolution in the primeval islands lives on, and has fired the imagination of generations of on-coming biologists.

The Hebrides do not occupy a grand plinth in scientific history as do the Galapagos, but, like all other archipelagos, they have their own endowment of nature and well-kept secrets to be discovered and enjoyed. The Galapagos are celebrated for their biology, but their geology (Simkin, 1984) is far less illustrious than that of the Hebrides. In studies of evolution and biogeography, the oceanic islands are unmatched by islands, like the Hebrides, that are strung along the continental edges. However, in studies of geology, ecology and animal behaviour, the continental edge is of the greatest interest. For example, the natural environment of the British Isles can be described as 'maritime', when compared with continental Europe. In greater detail, the western seaboard, including the Hebrides, when compared with the bulk of mainland Britain, is termed 'oceanic', because the communities of plants and animals there thrive in moist, mild conditions, or are greatly affected by the sea. It is this contrast of living conditions and life forms which has broadly attracted biologists to the Hebrides, while the geologists have been attracted to the Pre-cambrian and Tertiary rocks which are poorly represented in Britain south of the Great Glen. There are ample opportunities to observe how the structure of habitats changes from south-east to north-west, and also how each island has acquired its own rock base and complement of living things. Indeed, each island has its own unique and rich potential for the study of natural processes.

Island Races

Every island has a 'gene pool' and, between the islands and the mainland 'reservoir', there is a constant but usually small 'gene flow'. Each island is a unique assembly of species, which have been brought together by natural or man-assisted colonisation over long periods of time. Genetically, it is important to distinguish between 'relict' species which were present on the land before it became an island, and the colonisers which arrived after the land became an island. Small founder groups of either category possess fewer alleles of each gene than the large mainland populations from which they derive. When the founder group has grown and becomes established, the island species can have different frequencies of the different morphs than in the parent population. This is the theory anyway—in reality the situation is much more complex.

In the Hebrides, the islands became colonised from the south as the British Isles emerged from the retreating ice sheet. As time advanced more and more plants and animals arrived. Changes in sea level destroyed 'land bridges', thus isolating fragments of erstwhile mainland populations. The flora and fauna resulting from natural colonisation and physical isolation have been further complicated by man-assisted colonisation. Again in theory, many original colonisers of the north of Scotland may have been eliminated from the mainland by species which arrived later but did not reach the islands. The Hebrides, therefore, may possess relict life forms, such as the fossorial bee (*Colletes floralis*), the arctic charr (*Salvelinus alpinus*), and the plant *Koenigia islandica*. The Soay sheep (*Ovis aries*) of St Kilda is an outstanding example of a domesticated animal introduced by man to Britain in neolithic times, which became extinct as a breed (superseded by improved breeds of sheep) in all areas except the remotest and most inaccessible of islands, Soay at St Kilda.

The distribution of species in the Hebrides, therefore, begs many questions of when and how they came to be there. Analysis of pollen from peat and the beds of lochs have shown much of the time-scale and species of colonisation of the islands by vegetation; the affinities of most plant species to 'oceanic' and 'continental' biomes have been described; prob-

*St Kilda field-mouse
(Photo D.
MacCaskill)*

lems of taxonomy have arisen and identification of rare or key species has been questioned when voucher specimens and satisfactory records were lacking. However, the biogeography, taxonomy, and genetics of the Hebridean flora and fauna is still a wide-open field for research. This work is closely linked to the need for more information on the invertebrate fauna—and, with new techniques such as 'genetical fingerprinting' in the revision of existing information on the entire biota.

The flora and fauna of the Hebrides are rich in distinct island taxa: the St Kilda sub-species *hirtensis* and the Rum sub-species *hamiltoni* of the field mouse (*Apodemus sylvaticus*), (Delany, 1970); dark Hebridean forms of the dark green and the small pearl-bordered fritillaries (*Argynnis aglaia* and *A.selene*), the common blue (*Polyommatus icarus*), the grey mountain carpet (*Entephria caesiata*), the twin-spot carpet (*Perizoma didymata*), the mottled beauty (*Alcis repandata*), and the lesser yellow underwing (*Noctua comes*). Distinct forms of the bumble bee *Bombus jonellus* and the dragonfly *Sympetrum nigrecens* occur in the Hebrides. Amongst birds, the St Kilda wren (*Troglodytes t. hirtensis*) is distinct from that of the Hebrides (*T.t. hebridensis*), and in fact more closely resembles the Fair Isle wren (*T.t.fridariensis*), which in turn is distinct from the Shetland wren (*T.t.zetlandicus*). Starlings (*Sturnus vulgaris*) from Shetland and the Outer Hebrides are thought to be distinct from the race occupying the rest of Britain.

Professor R. J. Berry (1979, 1983) has examined the genetical and evolutionary significance of the Hebrides, where in his own words 'genes and geography meet'. He concludes:

The physical tides that have caressed and pounded the Western Isles have biological parallels: waves of animals and plants have beaten on the islands and formed their biological environment in the same way that the waves of rock, ice and water have determined their geographical limits. And just as the physical waves have laws which must be obeyed, so the interactions of drift, migration, and selection have forged the genetical constitution of the island races; and as the incoming tide cleans the sands and rocks over which it passes, but leaves unexplained features in secluded eddies, so the biological tides have left us with many genetical puzzles. The scientist believes as an article of faith that these eddies can be explained as knowledge accumulates, though some will remain as statistical anomalies of history.

Grand Relationships

We have used the example of genetical evolution and change to set the islands in the light of scientific discovery. We see the Hebrides not simply as the beautiful physical shapes they are, but as complete little worlds in themselves—each a unique repository of life. But there are also the rocks and the puzzles *they* hold. We try to interpret the genesis of the Hebrides from the Geological Record and find, in the great span of geological time, that part of the earth's surface which was destined to become the British Isles, moved northward across the surface of the globe from tropical to temperate latitudes. Having done so, and assumed its present geographical stance, the crustal plates parted and the British Isles were formed. This is a spellbinding story captured forever within the rocks of Ireland and Western Scotland, including the Hebrides. The disentanglement of the rocks on the north-west seaboard of Scotland, which plumb the depths of 3000 million years, is a wonderful achievement, and now part of classical geology of world-wide significance. The dynamic, three-dimensional perception of geological processes over such long periods of time, punctuated as they were by upheavals of the earth's crust

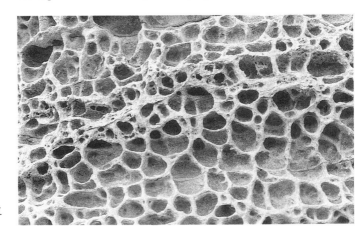

Looking like a living tissue, the Jurassic sandstone at Elgol, Skye has been eroded by the sea into this delicate, pale yellow, lacunary web (Photo J. M. Boyd)

such as the Grenville and Caledonian orogenies and the Moine Thrust, are so complex as almost to defeat lay presentation.

The coral islands of tropical seas display a biological process in which living corals extract lime from the sea water and build enormous reefs which, following changes in sea level, become raised islands or coastal platforms. In the Hebrides, there is at work a similar grand relationship between sea, land, and air, in which marine invertebrates and algae provide a vital link in the accretion of shell sand. Since the end of the last ice age, about 10,000 years ago, vast quantities of lime have been extracted from the sea-water by countless generations of shell-forming animals, whose remains have been ground in the surf and cast up by sea and wind upon the rocky shores. Spacious coastal platforms of dunes and machair (Hebridean maritime grass-land) have been formed in the southern Outer Hebrides, Tiree and Coll, enriching both the natural and human ecology of these islands. The whole process is supported by untold numbers of animals and plants of many different kinds. A thimbleful of shell sand, spread and magnified, will reveal the fragmented shells of a host of humble creatures, each of which makes its tiny but vital contribution to the grand scheme.

Islands for Science

The Hebrides, therefore, have a potential for research in fundamental, natural processes, and none have been used more than Rum and St Kilda for this purpose. In the 1950s, both of these islands were recognised as outstanding for their unique flora and fauna. They have concise temperate/maritime eco-systems and classical geology, and are laboratories for long-term ecological research. Accordingly, they were made National Nature Reserves in 1957 and have been centres for research ever since.

Studies of the fundamental biology of large herbivores—the red deer on Rum and the Soay sheep on St Kilda—have been central research endeavours, which have provided an understanding not only of the animals themselves, but of the ecology of their whole island. The research on the red deer on Rum has been done in controlled conditions, which would be hard to obtain among wild deer on mainland deer forests. This has revealed the precise structure and dynamics of the deer population, and the behaviour of stags and hinds, through entire life-spans. At St Kilda, the mechanism of natural control of numbers of a free-ranging (unmanaged) population of Soay sheep has been studied over thirty years. These sheep have survived in their island home for probably over 1,000 years, and the mechanism of control of numbers seems to protect them and their habitat from degradation through overpopulation and inbreeding.

Twenty-two species of seabird breed in the Hebrides. St Kilda alone has fifteen species and possibly holds over a million seabirds in summer. The oceanic seabirds—petrels, auks, gannets and kittiwakes—have the mystical beauty of all truly wild creatures. They live most of their lives far upon the face of the wide ocean, and in summer they gather in their thousands

for a great carnival of nesting. The beauty and excitement of
the birds wheeling and darting in the splendour of sunlit cliff
and chasm brings awe and rapture to the dullest of hearts. For
those who brave the benighted tops of Rum or the cliff terraces
of the outliers there is a contrast equally as moving—the weird,
dark world of the night-flying petrels.

The study of the seabirds poses physical as well as intellectual problems. Simple routines of counting the birds and
interpreting the census data are difficult to achieve with any
degree of consistency between counts. Nonetheless, in the past
thirty years, marine ornithologists throughout the world have
greatly improved census methods of many species which
present different technical problems. For example, gannets
and fulmars nesting in the open require different techniques

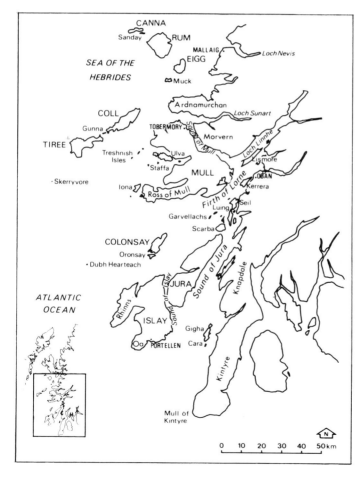

Figs. 2 *a* & *b*
*Location maps of the
Outer and Inner
Hebrides*

The south-east face of Sula Sgeir showing the northern limits of the gannetry in 1962 (Photo J. M. Boyd)

from burrowing puffins, and both are different from night-flying petrels. To detect changes in the size of the populations, a sustained census effort is required over decades, and this needs forward planning and the handing on of the techniques to successive workers.

The seabirds of the Hebrides are a major part of Britain's heritage of wildlife, requiring study for its own sake. However, the status of the seabird populations can also be an indicator of the health of their environment. Through the food chain which starts with the microscopic life in the sea and passes through invertebrates and fish, the seabirds can become the repository of pollutants such as polychlorinated biphenols (PCB's) and heavy metals. Such pollutants are likely to affect the breeding performance of the seabirds and the golden eagles and sea eagles which feed upon them in the Hebrides. In the case of a Chernobyl-like nuclear fall-out in the north-east Atlantic, St Kilda might prove an invaluable nuclear sensor. The great puffineries are rich in marine organic debris gathered from a wide area of ocean. They are grazed heavily by sheep which could become contaminated. The concentration of radio-active material in the individual seabird might be very small, but that in the bone marrow of the lambs may be much greater. Is it too imaginative to see the seabird-sheep islands as future sensors of the marine environment?

Geology

CHAPTER I

What happens to us
Is irrelevant to the world's geology
But what happens to the world's geology
Is not irrelevant to us.
We must reconcile ourselves to the stones,
Not the stones to us.

Hugh MacDiarmid

Natural history starts with the elements of fire, earth, air and water all of which long pre-date life on the face of the Earth. No clear understanding of the origins and nature of life can be obtained without knowledge of the rocks, weather and conditions of the seas and freshwaters. It is on the interface between these elements that all life has sprung and been maintained throughout aeons of time, and nowhere is this truth more explicit than in an archipelago. There, among the islands, the grand relationship between land, sea and sky is obvious and makes a deep appeal to the human mind. Islands are a source of inspiration and happiness; their beauty is enshrined in a multitude of native island cultures all over the world and appreciated by historian, artist and scientist alike. The Hebrides are no exception. In them it is possible to trace the connections between these base elements and the lives of the wild creatures and human beings that spring from them, and to see the islands as one large system with its own in-built stops and balances in terrain, weather and ocean. Let us start with the rocks.

The span of geological time represented in the rocks of the Hebrides is almost as great as anywhere in the world. Though we know that planet Earth is some 4,600 million years of age, in human terms, the Lewisian gneiss formed some 3,000 million years ago is as old as time itself, while on the beds of the sea and the deep lochs the rocks of the future are being formed from

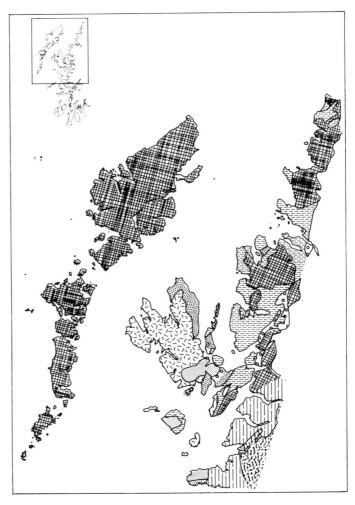

from the erosion products of by-gone glaciers, rivers and the
sea. The cycle of regeneration and decay of hard rock seems
timeless when compared with the timespan of human life.

In this vast interval of time, that part of the crust upon which
the Hebrides now stand underwent a gradual transposition
from tropical to temperate latitudes. Some ages of peace and
tranquility are marked by the depositions of the sedimentary
rocks: the Torridonian sandstone eroded from a range of
mountains and deposited in predominantly desert conditions,
1,000 to 800 million years ago; the sandstones, shales and limestones of Cambro-Ordovician/Dalradian age, 600 to 450 million years ago; and the limestones and mudstones of the

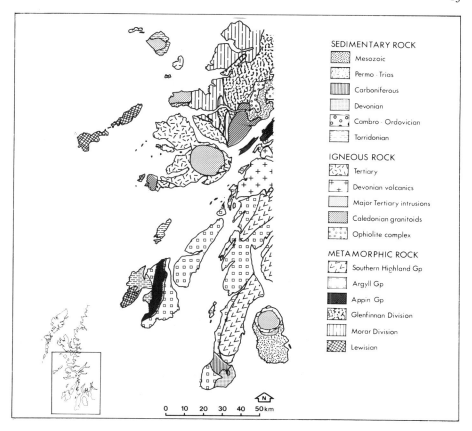

SEDIMENTARY ROCK

- Mesozoic
- Permo - Trias
- Carboniferous
- Devonian
- Cambro - Ordovician
- Torridonian

IGNEOUS ROCK

- Tertiary
- Devonian volcanics
- Major Tertiary intrusions
- Caledonian granitoids
- Ophiolite complex

METAMORPHIC ROCK

- Southern Highland Gp
- Argyll Gp
- Appin Gp
- Glenfinnan Division
- Morar Division
- Lewisian

0 10 20 30 40 50km

Jurassic, deposited in shallow lacustrine or estuarine conditions *c.* 150 million years ago (called not after the island of Jura, but the Jura Mountains in France).

Between these periods of quiescence there were periods of profound crustal movement as blocks of continental crust fractured, jostled and were transported on plates of underlying crust, though the first of these hardly touches the Hebrides. During the Grenville mountain building about 1,000 million years ago, rocks which were probably the equivalent of the Torridonian strata far to the east of the present outcrops were compressed, deeply buried and heated in the crust, baked and altered to form the schists and metasandstones of the Moine Supergroup. These metamorphic rocks together with unaltered Torridian in turn formed a land surface on which were deposited limestones, shales and sandstones of Cambrian and early Ordovician age.

The second great upheaval was the Caledonian mountain

Fig. 3 *a* & *b*
Geological maps of the Outer and Inner Hebrides (Smith and Fettes, 1979, Craig (ed) 1983)

building, 650 to 400 million years ago, when the rocks of the
mainland were again folded and altered to form the rocks of
mountains now occupying Scandinavia, Scotland and eastern
USA. Moine rocks were heated and altered again, while Cambrian strata became the schists of the Dalradian Supergroup.
Into the folded and refolded rocks, huge masses of molten
crust were emplaced as granite, now widespread in the
Highlands and represented in the Hebrides in the Ross of

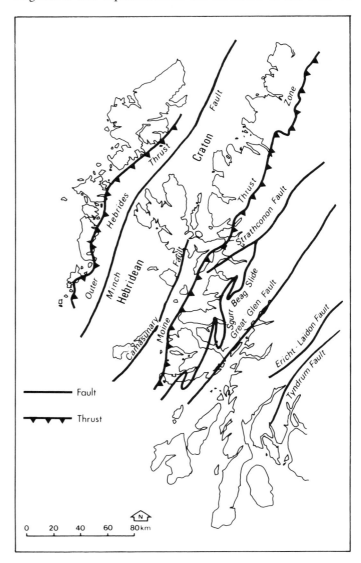

Fig. 4
*The main geological
faults of the Hebrides
and West Highlands
(Craig (ed) 1983)*

Mull. Along the western seaboard, however, rocks of the metamorphic mountains were thrust upwards and outwards in a dislocation of up to 80km. This is known as the Moine Thrust which runs on the land surface from Loch Eribol to the Point of Sleat in Skye. To the west of the Thrust, the Lewisian, Torridonian and Cambro-Ordovician rocks are in unmoved (and unaltered) sequence; to the east of the Thrust, within the Caledonian mountain belt, lie the Moines of Sleat and western Mull and the Dalradian of eastern Mull, Jura and Islay.

The mountains formed from this orogeny were subsequently eroded to form the Old Red Sandstone (ORS) *c.* 350 million years ago, a vast continental fluviatile and lacustrine deposit. Orkney is composed almost entirely of ORS but only small outcrops occur in the Hebrides—sediments in Kerrera and Seil, and lavas at Loch Don in Mull.

The third upheaval was the rift of the European and Greenland continental plates which created the British Isles, the continental shelf and the Hebrides, but not as we know them today. This rifting, which began 70 million years ago and still continues today, was accompanied by much volcanic activity, the thrusting up of masses of gabbro and granite, the outblasting of vast quantities of dust, ash and cinder and the outpouring of basalt lavas. These are the Tertiary volcanic complexes of Arran, Mull, Ardnamurchan, Rum Cuillin, Skye Cuillin and St Kilda, with associated plateau lavas in North Skye, Canna, Eigg, Muck, West Mull and Morven. They are related to other such centres in Ireland (Giant's Causeway), Faeroe Islands and Iceland, where the volcanic activity still continues. The islands as we know them today have been evolved through a northward drift of the crustal plate(s) of the planet from which the British Isles were formed, from a latitude of 30°S to the present latitude of 55°N. Throughout the drift, the palaeogeography was also continuously transformed by mountain building of the type described above, erosion, sedimentation, and volcanic activity. The genesis of the British Isles throughout geological time has been described simply by J.P.B. Lovell (1977).

Geological Framework

The solid geology is shown in Fig. 3 and Table 1.1. The Hebrides lie at the south-eastern margin of a crustal plate which included much of the material which forms Greenland and eastern Canada (Fig. 5). This plate broke and the parts drifted away from each other, 'floating' for tens of millions of years on the plastic sub-crust. The great trough between the parts now holds the Atlantic Ocean. This common basement between the Old and New Worlds contains some of the oldest rocks known to science, *c.* 3,000 million years old, from which younger rocks such as the Torridonian sandstone have been derived, and upon which the sandstones and other younger rocks are placed. In the Outer Hebrides, Tiree, Coll, Iona and Sleat in Skye the gneiss forms the present-day land surface— all the younger rocks have been removed by epochs of erosion. Elsewhere, the basement is covered by an array of younger rocks, or has been penetrated or pushed aside by great intrusions of magma and covered by extrusions of lava.

Era	Period	Age (m.y.)	Rocks	Islands
Pre-Cambian		+3000–600		
	Lewisian	+2800–1200	acid & basic gneisses, granites, limestones	N. Rona, Lewis, Harris, Uists, Barra, Coll, Tiree, Skye, Raasay, S. Rona, Iona, Islay
	Torridonian	1000–800	sandstones	Handa, Summer Isles, Raasay, Scalpay, Skye, Soay, Rum, Iona, Colonsay, Islay

Rocks east of the Moine Thrust affected by the Grenville Orogeny, *c.* 1000m.y.

	Moine Supergroup	1000–700	schists, granulites	Skye, Mull
Palaeozoic		600–230		
	Cambro-Ordovician	600–500	piperock, serp. grit, Durness limestone	Skye

Rocks east of the Moine Thrust affected by the Caledonian Orogeny, 500–400m.y.

	Dalradian Supergroup	+600–500	quartzites schists	Lismore, Kerrera, Seil, Garvellachs
			limestones, slates	Luing Scarba, Jura, Islay, Gigha
	Silurian	440–400	none	none
	Devonian	400–350	conglomerate	Kerrera, Seil
	Carboniferous	350–270	lava, sediments	Jura
	Permian	270–225	sandstones, conglomerate	Lewis, Raasay, Mull

Era	Period	Age (m.y.)	Rocks	Islands
Mesozoic		230–65		
	Triassic	225–180	sandstones, conglomerate	Lewis, Raasay, Skye, Rum, Mull
	Jurassic	180–135	sandstones, limestones	Shiants, Skye, Raasay, Eigg
	Cretaceous	135–70	sandstone	Skye, Mull, Eigg, Raasay, Scalpay, Soay
Cainozoic		70–0		
Tertiary		70–1		
	Eocene	70–40	basalts, granites, syenites, gabbros, dolerites, rhyolites	Shiants, Skye, Raasay, Rum, Eigg, Canna, Muck, Mull, Treshnish Is., Staffa, St Kilda, Oigh-sgeir
	Oligocene	40–45	erosion pdts	widespread
	Miocene	25–11	erosion pdts	widespread
	Pliocene	11–1	erosion pdts	widespread
Quaternary		1–Present		
	Pliestocene	0.6–0.013	erosion pdts	widespread
	Holocene	0.013–0	erosion pdts shell sand	widespread widespread

Table 1.1   The distribution and age in millions of years (m.y.) of the rocks of the Hebrides.

The major faults in northern Britain run from south-west to north-east (Fig. 4). The Southern Uplands Fault and the Highland Boundary Fault do not affect the Hebridean shelf; the Great Glen Fault (GGF), the Moine Thrust (MT), the Camasunary–Skerryvore Fault (C–SF) and the Outer Hebrides Thrust (OHT) all have an important bearing on the Hebrides. The GGF runs from Shetland to north Ireland, passes between Lismore and Kingairloch, through south-east Mull and just to the north of Colonsay; to the east there are the

Tertiary basalt pavement showing hexagonal jointing on Heisgeir (Oigh-sgeir) off Canna (Photo J. M. Boyd)

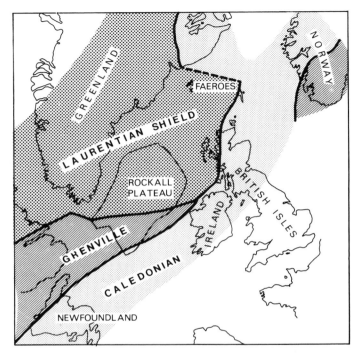

Fig. 5
*The tectonic provinces
of the North Atlantic
prior to continental
drift (Smith & Fettes,
1979)*

Caledonian granites with the Dalradian schists, slates and
quartzites; to the west there is the Moine Supergroup of
schists, bounded in the west by the Moine Thrust and interrupted in the south by the Tertiary complexes of Mull and
Ardnamurchan. The only terrestrial sections of the GGF in
the Hebrides are from Duart Bay to Loch Buie in Mull, which
is an area of great interest with faulted Liassic sediments folded
in Tertiary times around the Mull volcanic centre.

The MT runs from the west of Shetland, entering the Scottish mainland at Loch Eribol and traversing the north-west
Highlands roughly parallel to the coast, through Kylerhea and
the Sleat peninsula of Skye and possibly through the Sound of
Iona. To the west are the northern Inner Hebrides where the
gneiss basement is evident in Tiree, Coll and Iona and is interrupted in Skye, Small Isles and St Kilda by massive
emplacements of Tertiary lava, granite and gabbro. The Moine
and associated thrusts occur from Loch na Dal to the Point of
Sleat, and as far west as Broadford and Beinn an Dubhaich.
The MT may just clip Rum at Welshman's rock. To the east
there is gneiss; to the west there is Torridonian sandstone and
Durness limestone. Under the Sea of the Hebrides and the
Minches, there are trenches in the gneiss basement filled with

much younger sedimentary rocks. These have been derived from bygone mountains and are akin to the New Red Sandstones around Broad Bay in Lewis and to sedimentary strata of the wider shelf to the west of the Hebrides and around Orkney and Shetland, which may hold oil and gas. The C-SF, running from the Loch Scavaig in Skye through the Rum and Tiree Passages to the Skerryvore, is the western limit of a Mesozoic basin extending southward from Strathaird under Eigg and Muck to Mull.

Lastly, the OHT runs from the North Minch to beyond Barra Head along the east coast of the Outer Hebrides. It defines the main mountain chain of Barra and the Uists but northwards, in Lewis, it splits into a number of discontinuous planes before finally reaching the sea just north of Tolsta Head. To the east there are the sedimentary rocks in the submarine trench, while to the west is the Lewisian platform, interrupted in Harris and West Lewis by massive blocks of granite of Lewisian age.

Pre-Cambrian and Palaeozoic Rocks

These are mainly the Lewisian gneisses and granites, most of which were in existence 3,000 million years ago. In this vast span of time they have been changed. The granites, found mainly in Harris and west Lewis, are locally sheared and reduced to mylonite. South Harris is banded south-east to north-west with all the major rocks of the Lewisian series: gneiss, granite, gneiss veined with granite (all of acid character), metamorphic intermediate and basic igneous rocks, metasediments and anorthosite at Rodel. Metasediments are formed by the recrystalisation of sedimentary rocks, and occur at the north tip of Lewis, the south tip of Harris, and in the Uists and Benbecula. Substantial bands of mylonite (a slaty rock formed from crushed material along the OHT) occur in south-west Lewis and on the east coast of South Uist.

There were two distinct periods of metamorphic change, named after the districts of Sutherland where the original studies were done. The Scourian, 3,000 to 2,500 million years old, was followed by the Laxfordian, 2,500 to 1,400 million years old, and were separated by a period of crustal tension forming fissures into which a swarm of dykes were intruded. These are the Scourie Dykes which serve as distinct time-markers, separating Scourian from Laxfordian events. The Laxfordian period is marked by large-scale folding of the rocks. It concluded with the injection of the granites and pegmatites, 1,750 million years old, in Harris and Lewis, and the OHT, which

A quarry face in South Uist showing a section of Lewisian gneiss with characteristic banding of the minerals (Photo British Geological Survey)

was reactivated at the time of the Caledonian orogeny about 1,200 million years later, i.e. 400 million years ago (Smith and Fettes, 1979). None of the Torridonian, Moine, or Cambro-Ordovician rocks, which are well represented in the Inner Hebrides and the West Highland mainland, are present in the Outer Hebrides. The only sedimentary rocks are sandstones and conglomerates of Permian or Triassic age, 225 million years old, around Broad Bay in Lewis.

Among the Inner Hebrides the Pre-Cambrian rocks are widespread. The Lewisian complex occurs in Islay, Coll, Tiree, Skye, Raasay, and South Rona. Research on Rona has played a part in the elucidation of the Lewisian complex, and has revealed the oldest rocks in the British Isles — gneiss containing zircons older than 3,200 million years (Bowes *et al.*, 1976). As in the Outer Hebrides, there are metasediments among the predominant gneisses in Coll, Tiree, and Iona. These include garnet and graphite gneisses and marbles. Torridonian sandstones occur in Handa, Summer Isles, Raasay, Scalpay, Skye, Soay, Rum, Iona, Colonsay, and Islay. These sandstones and shales lie unconformably upon the Lewisian gneiss to the west of the Moine Thrust, have their greatest development in Wester Ross, and continue in a band some 150km long and 15km broad south-east from Skye, under the sea, to the west of Coll and Tiree. There are several different

groups of Torridonian characterised by their colour, grain-size and degree of deformation—'Sleat', Skye (3.5km thick), 'Torridon', Raasay (7km), 'Colonsay' (4km), 'Bowmore' Islay (4km), and 'Iona' (500m). Moine schists of similar age occur in Skye and Mull. Late Cambrian rocks, *c.* 550 million years old, are restricted to outcrops of pipe rock (quartzite with 'pipes' of worm burrows), serpulite grit and limestone in south-east Skye. Dalradian schists, which dominate the West Highland mainland south of the GGF, appear in the southern Hebrides. Quartzites, schists, limestones and slates occur in Islay, Gigha, Jura, Scarba, Garvellachs, Lismore, Luing and Seil. So far, no rocks of Silurian age have been found. Only small outcrops of Devonian (ORS) occur in Kerrera (130m thick) and Seil (5m) with contemporaneous lavas at Loch Don, Mull. The sole possible representatives of the Carboniferous period are lavas and sediments on Glas Eilein, Jura. Similarly, the only possible representative of the Permian period in the Inner Hebrides is a small pocket of boulder sediment on the Oa, Islay. New Red Sandstones in Skye, Raasay, Rum, and Mull are thought to be Triassic, but these continue under the sea and may include rocks of Permian age. Summary accounts of both the Pre-Cambrian and Palaeozoic rocks of the Hebrides are given in studies by Smith and Fettes (1979) and Anderton and Bowes (1983).

Torridonian sandstone eroded by the sea into freakish, dinosaur-like shapes on the north-west coast of Rum (Photo J. M. Boyd)

Mesozoic Rocks

The Triassic, Jurassic and Cretaceous periods are well represented in Raasay, Skye, Eigg and Mull with lesser outcrops in
Rum, Scalpay, Pabay, Soay and the Shiants, which, though
geographically part of the Outer Hebrides, are geologically
part of the Inner Hebrides (Fig. 6). These Mesozoic rocks are,
however, the exception rather than the rule in the Hebrides,
which, paradoxically, adds to their importance for two reasons:
firstly, they are a vital link in the geological history of the
islands, joining the distant Palaeozoic period and the much
more recent Tertiary era; secondly, they are predominantly
lime-rich rocks which have a marked effect on the ecology of
the islands in which they occur. The outcrops above sea-level
generally are set unconformably upon the Pre-Cambrian-
Paleozoic basement, and are overlain by the Tertiary volcanic
rocks. Under the North Minch and the Sea of the Hebrides,
these mesozoic rocks now fill deep basins, and are much more
extensive than on the islands, which may hold only thin fringe
outcrops on the margins of the submarine basins. Much of the
research data from these potential oil-bearing basins is unpublished. However, the labelling of the Stornoway Beds as
Permo-Triassic leads to the conclusion that these basins probably hold a New Red Sandstone series.

It is impossible to say whether or not the well-separated
Mesozoic rocks on the various islands are the surviving parts of
one continuous basin, or of separate basins, though the lateral
continuity of the Great Estuarine rocks from Muck in the south
through Eigg, Strathaird, and Raasay to Duntulm on the north

*Calcareous concretions
like cannon balls
exposed by marine
erosion of the Jurassic
sandstones at Bay of
Laig, Eigg (Photo
British Geological
Survey)*

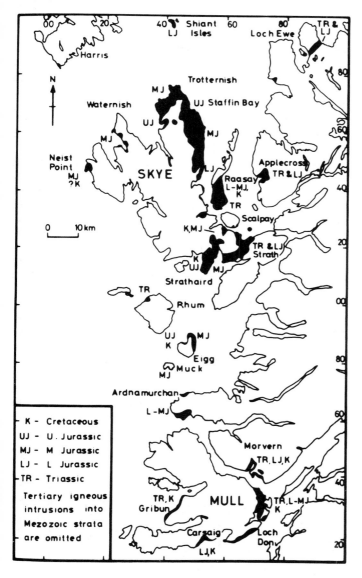

Fig. 6
Map showing the distribution of the Mesozoic rocks in the Hebrides (Hudson 1983)

point of Skye, is highly sustained. The most complete succession from the Triassic up through the Lower, Middle and Upper Jurassic to the Cretaceous occurs in Raasay and Trotternish (Fig. 6).

The Triassic rocks are mainly sandstone and conglomerates derived from riverine and lake-bed deposits—fossil soils indicate periodic inundations in a semi-arid climate. The Jurassic rocks are by far the most extensive of the Mesozoic series above sea level. They are mostly sandstones, shales and limestones in that order of importance. However, the sandstones and shales often contain carbonate concretions which are eroded out like great cannonballs from the softer sandstone. The beds are generally fossil-bearing allowing precise correlation between strata at different sites using ammonites. The lower levels are marine and fine-grained, the middle is riverine, estuarine and deltaic in character, and the upper is again marine and fine-grained. These are the finest fossil beds in the Hebrides, and have attracted geologists since Hugh Miller so graphically described his collecting foray in Eigg and Skye in *The Cruise of the Betsey* (1858) (p. 321). Fossil sharks' teeth and the bones of Pleisosauri and crocodiles have been found on Eigg; there are specimens of these and other Hebridean fossils in the Royal Museum of Scotland in Edinburgh. Lagoon beds were covered with mussels (*Praemytilus*) and other indicator species include brachiopods, oysters, and ostracods. Ammonites and belemnites abound in the shales and sandstones of Skye and Raasay. The Mesozoic series is capped locally with thin beds of upper Cretaceous sandstone in Skye, Raasay, Scaplay, Soay and Eigg. These have a maximum thickness of 25m but are usually less than 10m. They represent deposits in a shallow sea during a short interlude of erosion between the end of the Jurassic and the onset of the Tertiary volcanic epoch, when the Mesozoic rocks were buried under several hundred metres of lava and ash beds and cut by sills and dykes. A summary account of the Mesozoic in the Hebrides has been given by Hudson (1983), and the Jurassic and Cretaceous sediments in Scotland is reviewed by Hallam (1983).

Tertiary Rocks

During the Eocene commencing 60–65 million years ago, Europe and Greenland began moving apart. This crustal movement created the wide rift now filled by the North Atlantic, and was accompanied by much volcanic activity along the line of parting, from the south of England through Wales, Ireland, western Scotland, the Faeroes, and Iceland to Greenland. The whole segment of the earth's crust is known as the North Atlantic or Thulean Igneous Province, of which the Hebridean Province, stretching from Ailsa Craig to St Kilda, is a part. The main centres of volcanic activity were in Arran, Mull, Ardnamurchan, Rum, Skye, St Kilda, and the submarine Blackstones Bank, all of which hold the magma chambers of large volcanoes (Fig. 7). Most of these and other islands— Treshnish, Staffa, Muck, Eigg, Canna and the Shiants—

The Sgurr of Eigg (387m) is a pile of Tertiary rocks. A layer of pitchstone on the summit ridge lies unconformably on basalt lavas (Photo British Geological Survey)

contain fragments of the laval flows and ash falls from these Eocene volcanoes. The sources of these outpourings are uncertain. One view is that they emanated from the above centres; another is that they issued from long fissures in the earth's crust above, and stretching away from, the centres, much as occurs in the 'shield' volcanoes of Iceland today. The country rocks of many islands are also intruded by dykes and sills. These trend south-east to north-west and consist of both basalt and its coarser-grained relative, dolerite (p. 40). C.H. Emeleus (1983) has reviewed the geology of the Tertiary in Scotland and C.H. Donaldson (1983) has provided a useful summary account of the Tertiary in the Hebrides.

There are two distinct types of igneous rocks—the fine-grained which have cooled quickly on or close to the earth's surface, and the coarse-grained which have cooled slowly at depth in the crust. Basalts, rhyolites and pitchstones are of the former; gabbros, dolerites and granites are of the latter. In the main centres, i.e. the magma chambers of the great volcanoes, granites and gabbros predominate. The granites are rich in silica and feldspar and are grey or pink; the gabbros are dark, rich in iron, magnesium and calcium and poor in silica. Of the fine-grained volcanic rocks, basalt is by far the most important. It is a dark, fine-to-medium-grained analogue of the gabbro. Basalt is the stuff of the plateau lavas of north Skye and west Mull, and the terraced tablelands and columnar scarps of Durinish (Macleod's Tables), Canna, Rum (Bloodstone), Eigg, Muck, Treshnish Isles, Staffa (Fingal's Cave), and The Burg (MacCulloch's Tree) in Mull. The Sgurr of Eigg is a layer of pitchstone overlying a conglomerate-filled valley in the basalt flows. The rock called Heisgeir off Canna has a hexa-gonal pitchstone pavement—a miniature Giant's Causeway (p. 31). Probably basalt of over a kilometre thick was extruded

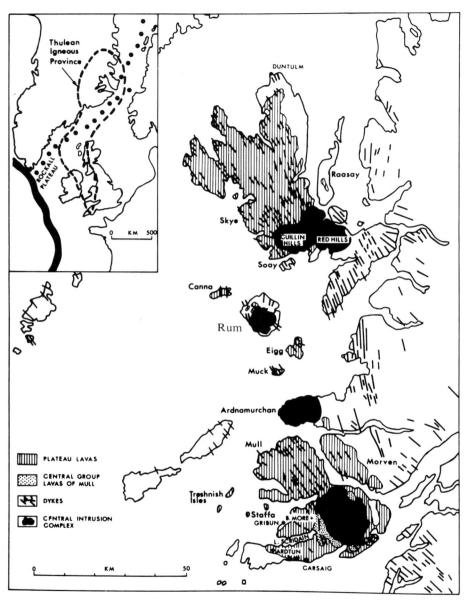

Fig. 7
*Map showing the
Tertiary volcanic
centres and swarms of
dykes in the Hebrides
(Donaldson 1983)*

over the crustal area now occupied by the Inner Hebrides. Much of this has since been removed by erosion, but the thickness of the existing basalt plateau reaches 1800m in central Mull and 600m in Skye and the Small Isles. The maximum thickness of individual flows is about 30m with the average about 8m, and the most extensive known flow stretches over 22km. An impression of the depth and extent of the Hebridean lava plateau in the late Tertiary (15 million years ago) can be obtained today in the Faeroe Islands, where a magnificent basalt plateau persists throughout most of the archipelago.

One of the salient features of the main Tertiary centres, particularly well-displayed in central Mull, is the formation of calderas caused by crustal ring fractures. Within these fractures — which were superimposed upon each other over millions of years — the solid rock sank, and the space was filled by upwelling magma. This has caused the fairly sharp juxtaposition of great masses of granite many cubic kilometres in extent with even greater masses of gabbro. The plane of fracture is a shatter zone in which fragments of the dark gabbro became embedded in the upwelling granite, or *vice-versa*, to create a breccia. This is well seen in the sheer cliff of Mullach Mor at St Kilda, where the eucrite (gabbro) to the west marches with the granophyre to the east, and is deeply veined by it. (A more detailed description of the magma-chambers of Rum and St Kilda is given in Chapters 6 and 7, H-AMI.)

The enormous explosive forces of these volcanoes resulted in the cracking and fissuring of the crust. The geological map shows Skye, Mull and Arran like the points of strike of bullets on a pane of glass, with the systems of cracks running roughly north-west to south-east. The cracks range from a hair's breath to over 30m thick and they have been filled with dark dolerite and basalt dykes (vertical) and sills (inclined). The swarms of Tertiary dykes from Skye, Mull and Arran traverse the crust from Lewis to Loch Linnhe, from Coll to Yorkshire and from Colonsay to Ayrshire respectively. The Inner Hebrides are riven with basalt and dolerite dykes which are usually 1–5m thick. These often become hard ridges among softer rocks like those in the Jurassic limestones on the shores and cliffs of Eigg, and trenches in harder rocks such as the gneiss on the shores of Tiree and Coll. The Camus Mor dyke on Muck is a striking example, which slices through the limestones and lavas and has a broad vertical exposure on the sea-cliff. Sills often occur in the bedding planes between lava-flows and sedimentary rocks and, like the lava, have columnar jointing. There are good examples of sill complexes to be seen in northern Skye and the Shiant Islands and, being composed of a hard coarse-grained dolerite, they often form a break of slope or escarpment edge in the basalt country. They play an important part in the composition of the landscapes of Raasay, Skye, and Mull.

The earthquakes which accompanied these episodes of

cracking and fissuring must have been enormous, certainly greater than any that happen in the world today. Another type of circular fissuring occurs as a result of great crustal explosions within the roots of the volcanoes, which split the existing igneous complex in a nest of conical cracks several kilometres in diameter at the present land surface. Sometimes they are several metres wide and are filled with basalts and dolerites— these are called cone-sheets. All the Tertiary centres possess them, and they are exceptionally well displayed on the Oiseval and Conachair cliffs at St Kilda and at Gribun in Mull.

Quaternary Features

In the last 18,000 years Scotland has endured a glaciation, and a period of emergence from the ice and the recovery of life. In the Devensian period between 18,000 and 11,000 years BP, the ice-age gradually declined leaving an arctic habitat with receding valley glaciers and seasonally exposed land and sea surfaces. The effect of the ice on the land was enormous, gouging and planing the uplands and depositing the detritus on an array of downstream surfaces ranging from large boulders to fine muds. About 13,000 BP, the summer temperatures must have been about 15°C, judging from the insect remains recovered from contemporary sediments, which, in Skye, also contain the pollen of birch, hazel, grasses, sedges, clubmosses, sorrel and others (Birks and Williams, 1983). By 12,000 BP, however, the insect evidence suggests a drop in summer temperature to 3°C, and there was a re-establishment of glaciation between 11,000 and 10,000 years BP. This is thought to have been caused by a sweep of polar water southward along the west coast, based on evidence of arctic Foraminifera and dinoflagellate remains in contemporary marine sediments off Colonsay. The main ice accumulation was in the West Highlands from Wester Ross to Loch Lomond and the episode is known as the Loch Lomond Readvance (LLR). It had a limited effect in the Hebrides, creating scree slopes on the mountains of Mull, Rum and Skye.

The disintegration of the ice sheets and the disappearance of the valley glaciers in the islands brought to light a great number of glacial and fluvio-glacial features; landslips, raised beaches, and accumulations of shell sand, dolomite, and peat. The end of the permafrost brought with it the collapse of many escarpments and cliffs and the shattering of rock-faces, resulting in a range of postglacial sheets of scree and stoneshoots, in which the islands abound and which are particularly well developed in the Cuillins of Skye. Landslips on a vast scale

occurred at the Storr and Quirang in Skye, and below the
northern ridge of Eigg. Fields of giant boulders were
created—some as large as a house, with a cap of soil and vegetation, as in upper Guirdil in Rum. Solifluction terracettes and
stone polygons related to the LLR are present on the summits
of Mull and Rum.

The relationship of the wave-cut benches along the coasts
and raised beaches to the glacial structures is not fully understood. The changes in sea level which accompanied the disappearance of the ice during the Quaternary period, resulted
from two related factors—the melting of a great part of the
polar ice caps which served to raise the sea level, and the isosta-
tic raising of the land released from the superincumbent load of
the ice sheet. The interplay of the two factors and the rewor-
king of coastal and marine deposits by the sea at different levels
is highly complex. The heights above present sea level of the
raised beaches in the Hebrides are grouped around 8m and
30m, and on the west coast of Jura these two levels are well
developed in the same system. Enormous drifts of even-sized
quartzite pebbles are placed in steps above the waters of Loch
Tarbert. J.B. Sissons (1983) has reviewed the Quaternary in
Scotland and J.D. Peacock (1983) has given a useful summary
account of it in the Inner Hebrides. Recent (Holocene)
sediments and sedimentation, which include the dominant formations of shell sand and peat mentioned in later chapters of
this book, are summarised by G.E. Farrow (1983).

The rocks of the Hebrides have therefore a dramatic story to
tell. Those who have an eye for country can read the geology of
the islands from their architecture, often at a great distance.
The shape of the granite and quartzite hills is distinct from the
gabbro, and both are distinct from the basalt. In Skye the granites of the Red Cuillin are cheek-by-jowl with the gabbros of
the Black Cuillin; the former are smooth paps and the latter are
a jumble of serrated peaks and ridges. The same is seen at St
Kilda; viewed from North Uist on a clear day, the smooth granite cones of Conachair and Oiseval are flanked by the peaked
gabbro of Dun, Mullach Bi and Boreray. The basalt islands, of
which Canna, western Mull and northern Skye are typical,
have stepped landscapes with beetling, horizontal scarps,
terraces, tablelands, and galleried sea-cliffs several hundred
metres high—the eroded basalt gives the Treshnish Isles the
look of a fleet of dreadnoughts. The ecological effects of the
country rocks is usually masked by wind-blown sand, a blanket
of peat, or by agricultural improvement. However, the greenery
of hill and wood in Raasay, Strath and Ord in Skye, Gribun and
Loch Don in Mull, Lismore and around Ballygrant in Islay
strongly suggests the presence of limestone.

CHAPTER 2

Climate and Hydrography

Climate

The weather puts demands enough upon coastal and rural communities in mainland Britain, but in the Hebrides the demands are much greater. Weather continuously prompts forethought of action, and in many fishing communities it still carries a sense of impending danger, damage and even tragedy. Island life is fashioned by the weather — the health and spirit of individuals and whole communities are all linked to it, just as are the intuitive and physiological responses of animals and plants.

The Weather System

The British Isles lie on a climatic frontier between moist oceanic air to the west and dry continental air to the east. These air masses differ in character and are in continuous interaction in a storm-belt which stretches for much of the time along the western seaboard of Ireland and Scotland to Scandinavia. This storm-belt has successions of depressions which course from mid-Atlantic to the Norwegian Sea. They are vigorous over the Hebridean shelf but, by the time they have reached the Norwegian coast, they have lost much of their strength.

In the Hebrides there can be periods when the islands are possessed by dry, calm continental air from the east which brings warmth in summer and frost in winter, instead of the usual wet and windy weather from the ocean. However, on the shorter time-scale there are the more rapid changes, which often occur in a matter of hours, particularly in the oceanic systems. Then fast-moving depressions bring active fronts sweeping across the Hebrides. These fronts are boundaries between warm and cold air, the warm rising over the cold at the warm front, and the cold undercutting the warm air at the cold front. Both are usually areas of cloud and rain. If a deep depression passes to the north, then high winds occur, at first southerly or south-westerly as the warm front approaches, then south-westerly in the warm sector, and eventually westerly or

north-westerly behind the cold front. Several hours of continuous and often heavy rain are usually followed by an easing in
the warm sector. The clearance at the cold front may be rapid
and accompanied by heavy rain, or it may be gradual with little
rain. Behind the cold front there may only be a few showers,
but at other times, particularly in autumn when the sea is still
warm, the showers are heavy and frequent. There is little
respite before the next frontal system moves in. On other occa-
sions the depression may pass eastward through the Hebrides
giving easterly winds to the north of its track, and the more
usual sequence (above) to the south.

The view to the west is of a vast sky and seascape upon which
the weather forecast is often vividly written: squally troughs
may already be visible, with slanting shafts of rain which will
arrive in an hour or two's time; or there may be the prospect of
an afternoon or evening of unbroken sunshine. More subtly, in
a few hours a frontal depression may bring high winds and continuous rain over the horizon. The warm front is heralded by
cirrus cloud (mare's tails) grading westward to cirro- and alto-
stratus; the 'watery sun' in the alto-stratus casts a weird light
upon the sea and islands before the wind and the rain. Boats

An approaching warm front with a 'watery sun' shining a veil of cirro-stratus with bands of alto-stratus and strato-cumulus cloud over Ben Hynish and Traigh Bhaigh, Tiree (Photo J. M. Boyd)

run for shelter as the storm strikes, and livestock stand in the lee of stonedykes. Following the incessant rains of the warm front and the clearance of the cold front, the drenched islands emerge once more into bright sunshine.

The oceanic air may come from any latitude in the North Atlantic, but it is generally divided into southern or tropical Atlantic air from the Azores, and the northern or polar Atlantic air from Greenland and Iceland. Likewise, the continental air may come from central and Mediterranean Europe or from Scandinavia and Siberia. In the Hebrides the oceanic air dominates with long periods of changeable weather, particularly in autumn and early winter. When strong anticyclones develop over Scandinavia in winter, the cold easterlies on their southern flank may develop troughs which bring blizzards to the east of Britain, but these have usually lost their burden of snow over the mainland before they reach the Hebrides, which remain comparatively snow free.

Ecological Effects

The range in mean monthly temperature in the course of the year is about 9°C, but the growth of vegetation is slow because of the sluggish rise of temperature and slow drying-out of the soil—even in well-drained loams it is not usually possible to plough until early April. Crops grow slowly even in areas of high sunshine due to wind-blast, high rates of transpiration and low day-time temperatures. Moreover, the low islands have occasional summer droughts; a month's drought with bright windy weather in May and June will result in light crops of potatoes, grain and hay. Although the climate is generally mild, the combined effect of the elements makes it severe on plant growth, livestock and wild animals. Cattle and red deer lose heat rapidly in high winds and this is increased by driving rain, mist and snow. A wet, windy and cloudy summer can therefore retard the growth of pasture and increase the loss of body heat from animals on the hill. This means they will enter the winter in relatively poor condition and, in the case of stray sheep and red deer, may succumb in winter snow. Supplementary feeding of livestock against the energy deficit caused by normal Hebridean summer weather near sea level is similar to that prescribed at an altitude of 300m on the hills of Perthshire.

The loss of heat by the human body in days of strong winds and rain with temperatures around 10°C is enough to drive all but the fittest of people indoors. The draw-down in levels of physical energy and work-rate of those who work out of doors

is greater than one might expect by looking at the data. It is for this reason that the crofting way of life is regarded by the outsider as desultory and anachronistic, when it is a naturally reactive style of living related to a punishing and highly changeable climate.

Wind-blown shell sand has drifted over the ruins of the village on Mingulay, Barra Isles which lost its people earlier this century (Photo J. M. Boyd)

The two most obvious effects of weather are on tree-growth and blown-sand seen among the ruins of Mingulay. Wind, salt and water-logging reduce colonisation by trees in the Hebrides, although conditions vary from the exposed western rim of the Outer Hebrides and Tiree, to the more sheltered east-facing slopes of the Inner Hebrides. However, trees do grow in the more wind-blasted islands, naturally as at Allt Volagir on the lower western slopes of Beinn Mhor in South Uist, and as plantations at Northbay, Barra, but usually in defiles or sheltered hollows. The scrub woodlands on the islands of Loch Druidibeg, South Uist, show that willow, rowan, birch and juniper will grow in high wind exposures beyond the reach of salt spray, provided the ground is ungrazed and unburnt. On Rum, experimental plantations show what can be achieved by a variety of native species growing in the

A willow-birch-gorse thicket in a fenced plot on the west side of North Uist in the 1950s, typical of the natural wind-blasted woodland which would develop without grazing (Photo J. M. Boyd)

Hebrides in different exposures to prevailing winds and at different altitudes. It is clear from these and many other small scattered woods in the outer islands, that if man did not burn the ground and graze it with his sheep and deer, the Hebrides would possess a scrub forest today as in the past.

If it was not for shell sand drifting against the weather face of the islands and being carried by the wind several hundred metres inland, many fertile islands like Tiree and the western coastal plains of the Uists and Benbecula would be as barren as their rocky and peaty interiors. The scourge of the wind is softened a little by its burden of beneficent sand which buffers the acid of the peat, gives porosity to the soil, and supports agriculture.

In ecological terms, precipitation is considered together with the combined effects of evaporation and transpiration (evapotranspiration) to provide an assessment of water-balance in soils, ground water and loch and stream systems. Physiological water-balance is also involved in the initiation and maintenance of growth in plants and animals. A potential water surplus leads to waterlogging and a large deficit to drought, and the point of balance between these extremes is seldom reached in the Hebrides—though they have, on average, a surplus of rainfall over evapo-transpiration every month—crofters therefore speak of 'wet' and 'dry' summers (June to August).

The latter occur when very little or no rain for several weeks is accompanied by sunshine and warm south-easterly winds, which rapidly draw moisture from the land. The water-table falls, shallow lochans and streams dry out and crops on sandy soils wilt for want of water. Occasionally, water deficits have occurred in February and March, when dry easterly winds have prevailed, usually with high evapo-transpiration and low rainfall. It is during these periods of drought that moorland fires occur and spread easily.

Humidity and Temperature

Evapo-transpiration potential relates to the relative humidity of the air, which is the ratio of the actual vapour pressure to the saturation vapour pressure at the same temperature, expressed as a percentage. This is important to plants and animals, as it affects physiological processes such as the opening of buds, seed capsules and sporangia, and the olfactory communication and stimulation of insects and mammals. The mean range of water-vapour pressure at 1.2m above ground in the Hebrides is 8 to 13 millibars which is similar to the rest of Britain. However, because of the low summer temperatures, the mean relative humidity in daytime in summer, when plants and animals are most affected, is 82%, compared with 67% at Edinburgh and 58% at London Airport (Heathrow). Anticyclones sometimes bring periods of very high relative humidity; in brilliant sunshine and calm conditions the islands become swathed in sea fog which curls over the lower slopes leaving the top bathed in sunshine. In such weather St Kilda lies shrouded in feathery mist, showing a sparkling array of sunlit humps and spires above. Sadly, it was at such times of poor visibility that the islands were so dangerous to low-flying aircraft during the Second World War; St Kilda alone had four airwrecks.

The North Atlantic Drift and the prevailing winds from the south-west dominate the weather picture and play a major role in determining the temperature regime—on Tiree we once found a whole coconut complete with green husk, presumably having come all the way from the Caribbean, and saw it as a symbol of the benign influence of the great ocean drift. The mean annual temperature at Tiree, 9.1°C, is only 1°C lower than southern England. The seasonal range is much less however: 8.5°C at Tiree compared with 11.6°C in Glasgow and 14°C in southern England. The maritime influences also reduce the diurnal range, which in July is only 5°C. The extremes of temperature recorded at various sites are: Stornoway 25.6–12.2°C; Tiree 26.1–7.0°C; Rum 27.9–9.5°C. To obtain these values for

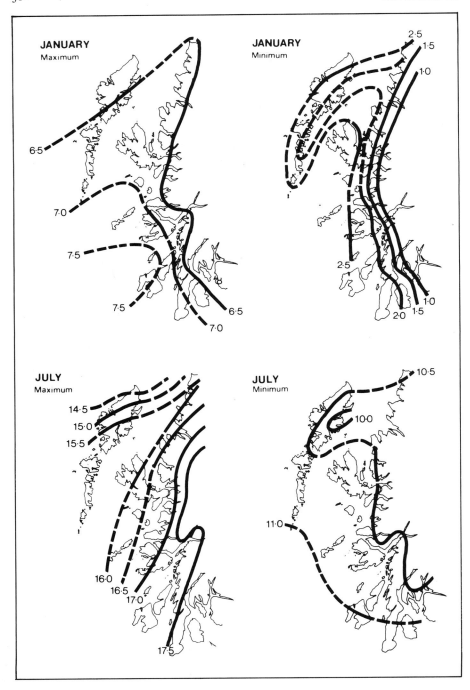

summer maxima, quiet unbroken sunshine with light south-easterly winds over several days are required—conditions like these have given a maximum at Benbecula of 27.2°C. These figures cover the period of observation up to the present. Winter minima occur on calm, clear nights with a fresh covering of snow. The oceanic character of the weather is most accentuated in the low, small islands; the weather in the interiors of the high, larger islands has a wider range of temperatures caused by shelter, altitude and distance from the sea, although we have very few observations to characterise these areas. Average monthly maximum and minimum temperatures from Tiree on the outer rim of the Hebrides and Perth in Scotland are shown in Table 2.1

| Station | | | | | | Month | | | | | | |
	Jan	Feb	Mar	Apr	May	Jun	Jul	Aug	Sep	Oct	Nov	Dec
Tiree Max	10.3	9.9	11.0	13.7	17.2	19.7	19.6	19.3	17.7	15.5	12.7	11.2
Min	-2.2	-2.8	-1.2	-0.2	2.2	5.2	7.3	7.0	5.2	3.2	0.1	-1.2
Perth Max	11.3	11.1	13.1	17.6	21.6	24.4	24.8	23.7	21.1	17.5	13.8	11.9
Min	-8.4	-8.0	-4.6	-2.5	0.3	3.7	5.2	4.0	1.6	-1.3	-5.2	-6.6

Table 2.1 The average monthly maximum and minimum temperatures from Tiree and Perth over the period 1951–80 from *Scotland's Climate—Some Facts and Figures* Meteorological Office (1989).

The growing season may be defined as the period in which the soil temperature is above 6°C and in the Outer Hebrides it lasts on average 245 days, similar to that near Stirling. It extends from early April to early December. The intensity of the season can be measured by the sum of day-°C, which, in Tiree averages 1,505, a figure which is similar to those obtained for lowland Scotland, but higher than for the Outer Hebrides. The inner islands, therefore, have an advantage in temperature over the outer islands, but this advantage is diminished by the inner islands having a higher rainfall, except in Tiree, Coll, Iona and Colonsay.

Soil Climate

The soil has a climate of its own which is related to, but different from, the atmosphere. Moisture content, temperature and the physical stresses of freezing and thawing are all important in the function of the soil. The effects of waterlogging on plant life, which cause the formation of blanket peat, are to be seen everywhere in the interiors of the islands, but on the other hand the effects of drought are often seen in dry

Fig. 8
The mean daily maximum and minimum temperatures (°C) for January (above) and July (below) 1951–1980, from Scotland's Climate—Some Facts and Figures, Meteorological Office, *1989)*

summers on sand dunes, bare hill slopes and hill-top gravels. Between the two, there are the semi-natural and cultivated loams in which the balance of the physical and biological features produces fresh machair, fields of sown grass, wheat and barley.

In summer the top 10 centimetres of soils near sea level are on average warmer by 3°C than the air above, whereas in winter they are 1°C colder. These figures are for bare ground such as a field ploughed and harrowed. Under tall grass cover, for instance, the temperature of the soil may be slightly cooler in summer and warmer in winter than the air immediately above. Therefore, the machair and stubble swards, which are generally closely grazed exposing the soil surface, will have temperatures close to those of the atmosphere, and subject to atmospheric fluctuations. Continuous cover of vegetation is therefore a great advantage. It not only reduces erosion but also extends the growing season in autumn—a point which seems to be missed in many crofting townships with extensive heavily-grazed dunes and machairs.

The difference of summer and winter soil temperatures is an important factor in the length and quality of the growing season. On the summits and ridges of high islands there are solifluction features caused by the incessant freezing and thawing of the land surface in winter. This 'frost heave' is seen well on Sgur nan Gillean, Rum, but nowhere in the Hebrides have we seen these features as well developed as on Hoy, Orkney and North Roe, Shetland.

An example of local variation is the comparison of temperatures recorded at two stations in Barra, Craigston and Skallary, over ten years in the 1930s and 40s. Craigston is on the exposed western side of the island about one mile from the sea; Skallary is on the sheltered eastern side about half a mile from the sea. Daytime temperatures at Craigston were above those at Skallary. The minimum temperatures at Craigston on clear nights fell slightly below Skallary, but the gain by day was greater. Overall, the daily temperature range at Craigston was greater than at Skallary and the growing season was longer. However, temperature is not the only factor to be taken into account. Rainfall at Skallary was affected by the hill of Heaval (367m), and it received much more rain and less sunshine than Craigston, but Craigston was windier. In the interval of days the climatic differences are small, but they are significant when considered together over the months from sowing to harvesting in the full span of pasture growth for grazing animals. They help to explain why the harvests generally begin earlier in the sunnier, drier and more exposed parts of the islands than elsewhere in the Hebrides.

Rainfall and Sunshine

In Britain the variation of rainfall with altitude is very variable, depending not only on the local topography but also on whether the major rain-bearing winds have already passed over hills or mountains where much of their moisture has been shed. As might be expected, the increase of rainfall with height is much greater on the west-facing slopes on the Inner Hebrides and the north-west Highlands than it is in the east, for example in the Cairngorms, and, on the annual basis, may reach about 450mm per 100m.

The maximum rainfall often occurs not at the top of a mountain, but just in the lee side of the summit. On small mountainous Rum comparisons can be made of the rainfall assiduously recorded over a number of years at seven sites. Near sea level on the windward west side of the island, the average annual rainfall is about 1,500mm (59 inches), on the north coast away from the highest mountains it is about 1,900mm (75 inches), while on the leeward side, still close to the mountains, it is about 2,500mm (98 inches) only 7km (4.5 miles) away from the driest part of the island.

Fig. 9
The average daily duration (hours) of bright sunshine in December and June 1951–80. In December, to the left of the line is 1+, to the right 1− from Scotland's Climate — Some Facts and Figures, Meteorological Office, 1989)

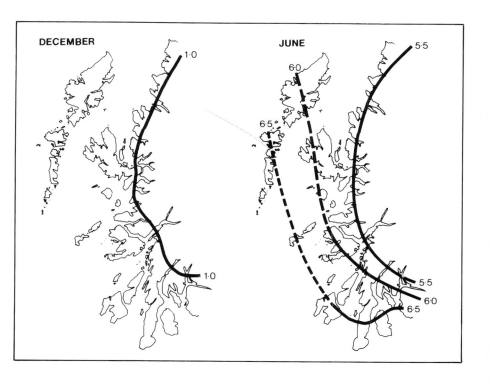

The meteorological records are mainly obtained from stations manned by persons in the line of duty such as at airports, lighthouses and nature reserves or by volunteer recorders. Together, the records give the climatic character of each station and of the whole Hebrides, but they do not show the detail of local variations, such as those provided by a network of stations on Rum, let alone the microclimates of soils, grasslands, heaths and woodlands which determine rates of growth and productivity of plant and animal populations. The monthly and annual average rainfall for Hebridean and mainland stations are compared in Table 2.2.

Station	Alt(m)	Jan	Feb	Mar	Apr	May	Jun	Jul	Aug	Sep	Oct	Nov	Dec	Year
Stornoway	15	115	77	80	66	62	67	72	74	103	126	129	125	1096
Benbecula	5	129	86	89	62	65	76	83	83	119	139	140	132	1203
Tiree	9	120	71	77	60	56	66	79	83	123	125	123	123	1106
Skye*	27	182	116	129	93	91	104	113	118	170	204	203	210	1732
Mull (Aros)	37	210	116	142	97	96	109	120	133	199	208	203	220	1853
Islay#	21	139	85	92	70	67	74	93	93	128	139	149	149	1278
Perth	23	70	52	47	43	57	51	67	72	63	65	69	82	738
Edinburgh+	26	47	39	39	38	49	45	69	73	57	56	58	56	626

*Portree   #Eallabus   +Royal Botanic Gardens

Table 2.2   Monthly and annual averages of rainfall (mm) from six stations in the Hebrides and two on the Scottish mainland for comparison in the period 1951–80, taken from *Scotland's Climate—Some Facts and Figures*, Meteorological Office (1989).

Weather recording began at Stornoway Castle in 1856, continued at various sites around the town, and later moved to the Coastguard Station at Holm Point. An average annual rainfall of 1,266mm (49.6 inches) was published in *British Rainfall* from period 1881–1915. In 1942 the station was moved to the airport on the drier east side of the town, and from observations after 1942 a calculated average of 1,003mm (39.5 inches) for 1916–1950 was estimated. For the latest standard period (1941–70), the average was 1094mm (43.1 inches). This compares with 1,204mm (47.5 inches) in Tiree for the same period. Similar calculated averages for 1941–70 are: Tiree, 1,204mm (47.5 inches); Vatersay (Barra), 1,174mm (46.2 inches); Butt of Lewis, 1,100mm (43.3 inches); Back (10km from Stornoway), 1,100mm (43.3 inches). In such a windy climate as that of the Hebrides, the exposure of rain gauges is very important to ensure that rain falls in the gauge and is not blown over the top, so natural shelter or the construction of a turf wall is required, and exposure to sea spray must be avoided. Some of the apparent differences between sites may be due to problems of exposure, and there may also be significant differences in the averages between different recording periods. Taking this into account, it may be stated that the annual rainfall near sea level on the outer wester rim from Tiree to the Butt of Lewis is about 1,200mm, rising to about 1,400mm in Harris where the mountains are close to the sea. As has already been mentioned, large variations in sea level values of rainfall can occur due to the effects of local topography such as on Rum.

Thunderstorms are infrequent and of the 'one-clap' variety mostly in autumn and early winter, when rapidly-moving heavy showers come in from the west off a relatively warm sea. They can be accompanied by giant hailstones, such as fell in the Uig

A towering cumulo-nimbus over Benbecula with the church and manse caught in a shaft of bright sunshine, typical of a north-westerly airflow over the islands (Photo J. M. Boyd)

area of Skye in 1986. The thunderstorms, though short-lived, can be very violent, with cloud to earth discharges resulting in heathland fires. This is thought to be the source of charcoal layers in peat in north-west Scotland which antedate human occupation.

The temperate, oceanic climate has few days of falling snow, and this very rarely settles. It is unusual for the maximum temperatures near sea level to remain below freezing point for long, though long spells of freezing weather can occur on the high hills of Jura, Mull, Rum, Skye, South Uist and Harris. The weather stations near sea level at Stornoway and Tiree have recorded respective averages of 35 and 16 days of air frost annually. Similar averages of 10 and 4 days respectively of lying snow have been recorded. In exceptional winters, such as in 1946–47, the total at Stornoway rose to 31 days of lying snow with the snowfalls outlasting the midday thaw. At Kinloch Castle, Rum, the average for days of snowfall during 1948–80 was about 20 and that for Prabost, Skye 30. The averages for snow lying at these two stations were 10 and 24 days respectively. Comparative figures for Derry Lodge in the east Cairngorm for a similar period give an average of 85 days per year on both counts.

Because of their high latitude the Hebrides have some of the highest measurements of sunshine in a single day in Britain, daylength being much longer than further south. Sunshine measurements are made by using a glass ball as a lens to concentrate the sun's rays on a specially treated card, and measuring the length of the burn. The average monthly durations of sunshine in the period 1951–80 for Hebridean stations compared with the mainland are shown in Table 2.3. Because of the clarity of the air, the start and finish of the burn in the morning and the evening are often earlier and later, respectively, in the Hebrides than they would be where the atmosphere is less clear, as it is in most other parts of the United Kingdom.

Station	Alt(m)	Jan	Feb	Mar	Apr	May	Jun	Jul	Aug	Sep	Oct	Nov	Dec	Year*
Stornoway	15	1.2	2.5	3.6	5.2	6.0	5.9	4.2	4.4	3.6	2.5	1.5	0.8	1256
Benbecula	5	1.3	2.5	3.7	5.8	6.5	6.5	4.6	4.9	3.8	2.5	1.6	0.9	1361
Tiree	9	1.4	2.4	3.7	5.8	6.9	6.6	5.1	5.2	3.9	2.5	1.5	0.9	1400
Skye#	67	1.3	2.7	3.5	5.2	6.0	5.8	4.1	4.3	3.3	2.3	1.5	1.0	1243
Perth	23	1.4	2.3	3.2	5.1	5.7	6.0	5.5	4.3	3.7	2.7	1.8	1.1	1309
Edinburgh+	26	1.5	2.4	3.2	4.9	5.7	6.1	5.5	4.8	4.0	3.0	2.0	1.3	1351

*Average annual total (hours) of bright sunshine;   #Prabost;   +Royal Botanic Gardens

Table 2.3 The average duration of bright sunshine in hours for four stations in the Hebrides and two on the mainland, in the period 1951–80, taken from *Scotland's Climate—Some Facts and Figures*, Meteorological Office (1989).

Measurements of solar radiation on a horizontal surface have been made at Stornoway since 1983. These show maximum daily values which are as high as anywhere in the British Isles, despite the fact that the sun is at a lower elevation than further south.

Wind

The Hebrides are attractive to tourists who enjoy the challenge of changeable weather. Wind dominates everything. Yachtsmen can seldom make firm plans for more than six hours ahead; from their sheltered moorings on the mainland coast, they make cautious advances upon the Outer Hebrides and St Kilda with an ear to the weather forecast and an eye on a quick retreat to havens such as Castlebay, Canna and Tobermory, or the many safe little anchorages like Geometra, on the storm coast of Mull, and Loch Skipport, Rodel and Loch Shell on the leeward coast of the Outer Hebrides. St Kilda is an

A storm at St Kilda with the islands under a shroud of nimbostratus with continuous rain and a high wind from the south-west. The view is from Boreray (left) and Stac an Armin (right) looking to Stac Lee (centre) and Hirta (Photo J. M. Boyd)

ultima thule for many yachtsmen; its exposed position to heavy seas, which we describe more fully in Chapter 16, is a special challenge.

In the last decade wind surfing has become popular. The best conditions are obtained in spring and autumn when strong to gale-force winds are accompanied by high tides and huge breaking seas. Sand yachting has also been tried on spacious beaches like Traigh Mhor in Tiree, but has not become as widely popular as wind surfing. The 'hardy annual' visitor sees the weather as a game of chance — runs of warm sunny days are a 'jackpot'. For the occasional visitor, especially those who are accustomed to the well-wooded or well-paved mainland environments, the Hebrides can bring highly contrasting reactions. Those whose brief visit coincides with bad weather may never return, but those who have savoured the islands in their various moods of weather, tend to return again and again.

Both the wind and sea in the Hebrides have enormous power which at some time in the near future will be harnessed. Experiments with wave and wind generators are already in existence. Prototype wind generators in Orkney and 'wind farms' in other countries show the vast scale to which windmill development must be taken before it can contribute significantly to the national energy budget. However, wind generators on Fair Isle point the way to the local use of wind as an alternative to diesel engines in the Scottish islands. The Hebrides are one of the windiest places in Europe, so there is a great amount of wind energy waiting to be harnessed. This is shown in comparing the wind data of Tiree with that of Glasgow Airport on the west mainland (Table 2.4). The seas to the west of the outer rim of islands from Islay to the Butt of Lewis also possess enormous amounts of wave energy. With the progressive exhaustion of fossil fuels and the dangers which attend nuclear power generation, there are promising prospects for alternative technologies such as wind and wave power, and the Hebrides have great potential for such power. However, when it comes to be harnessed, the greatest care must be taken to safeguard the welfare and culture of the people, and to conserve the fragile environment of the islands.

Station	Jan	Feb	Mar	Apr	May	Jun	Jul	Aug	Sep	Oct	Nov	Dec	Year
Tiree	6.9	3.7	3.4	1.4	0.5	0.3	0.3	0.5	1.6	3.3	4.7	7.2	33.8
Glasgow Apt	1.2	0.4	0.4	0.2	0.1	0.2	0.0	0.0	0.2	0.2	0.4	1.0	4.3

Table 2.4   Monthly and annual average number of days with winds of gale force and over during the period 1951–80 at Tiree, compared with Glasgow Airport, taken from *Scotland's Climate—Some Facts and Figures*, Meteorological Office (1989).

Climate in the Past

Analysis of pollen from the beds of lochs and peat bogs shows a succession of climatic periods experienced by north-west Europe since the ice departed from Britain 10,000 years ago. The Hebrides were on the edge of the ice-sheet at the maximum of the Quaternary glaciation, but some islands like St Kilda may have been beyond the edge of the ice with small ice caps of their own. There is evidence from pollen in the soils which suggests that plants survived the ice-age in the Hebrides and some land was always free of ice in the arctic summer, possibly on nunataks, which are rocky islands protruding above the ice.

Through the ice-age and in the early phases of its retreat, the ecology would be arctic with stocks of plants and animals similar to parts of Greenland today. However, the change of the climate from arctic to temperate was not uniform. In the Boreal period, 10,000 to 7,000 years ago, immediately following arctic conditions (Preboreal), the weather was drier and warmer than today. The ice retreated and the conformation of the coastlines changed with changes in sea level; land animals, distributed widely by the ice-bridges, bergs and floes, became isolated in newly-created islands. There then followed two warm periods which took place between 7,000 and 3,000 years ago. These Atlantic and the Sub-Boreal periods were of about 1,000 years each with wet and dry conditions respectively. It was during the Atlantic period, about 6,500 years ago, that man first came to the Hebrides from the south, as a hunter-fisherman, and from thence to Orkney. During the wet Atlantic period, the birch-hazel woods of the new Boreal forest, which graded westward from the high forest on the mainland seaboard to low scrub on the islands, changed their character with an increase in the amount of alder and moss.

The terrain was probably well vegetated, reducing erosion on the lower ground, but chemical leaching of nutrients from the young soils probably stunted tree growth through nutrient deficiency. Added to this, there was waterlogging and growth of *Sphagnum* moss. Soil conditions must have ameliorated to some extent in the warm dry conditions of the Sub-Boreal, but a decline recurred in the cooler, wetter Sub-Atlantic which prevails today, and this natural decline in soil fertility has been accelerated by man's use of the land in the past 2,500 years.

There have been three minor fluctuations from the normal conditions of the Sub-Atlantic: between 1,000 and 1,200 AD the climate was on average 2°C warmer; the arrival of St Columba preceded this change and the weather was probably similar then to the present day; then came amelioration during the Viking occupation when, in both ecological and economic terms, the islands were more clement.

The effects of weather pervade the entire natural system on land and at sea. It affects the sea's surface and the penetration of light, heat and gaseous exchange at depth. Climate is all-embracing, having as great but different effects in the south on Gigha as on North Rona; on sheltered Lismore as on exposed St Kilda; on large Lewis as on small Colonsay; likewise on high Mull as on low Tiree. The great physical forces of atmosphere and sea on the North Atlantic seaboard are highly variable, but imposed upon this is local variation caused by the position and character of the individual islands each of which can be a little world unto itself.

Hydrography

We have described the mellowing effect of the sea on the climate in the Hebrides which means that snow rarely lies for more than a few hours except on the high mountains. The water masses around the Hebrides have about the lowest degree of annual variation in temperature of any area around the British Isles, a fact which owes much to the complex nature of the water masses which mix out to the west off the contintental slope. Subsurface waters of low salinity moving from the north-west into the eastern North Atlantic basin, plus deeper saline outflow from the Mediterranean, mean that the density gradient between surface and mid-depth waters is lower than normal. This has an important consequence because it means the slightly cooled surface waters in winter descend to greater depths, resulting in deep overturning of the water column, bringing warmer water to the surface. David Ellett of the Scottish Marine Biological Association has likened this to a large capacity storage heater. The idea that the Gulf Stream is implicated as a major factor in the warming of the British climate is now doubted by some, but there are still many reasons for considering that the heat energy contained within this northerly moving water mass is a significant proximate source of energy leading to climatic warming.

Some 3 to 6 million tons of water per second flow northward through the Rockall Channel to the west of the Outer Hebrides. This, the Atlantic Current, then breaks east towards Shetland. West of the southern Hebrides, it forms a large clockwise gyre. Another recently discovered current, the Slope Current, also moves north along the line of the continental slope off the Hebrides, bringing with it about one million tons of water per second. It sends fingers of dense, saline oceanic water into the Hebrides to mix with the fresher, less dense waters of the northward moving Coastal Current. This current is much affected by local tidal and climatic conditions, but it will deliver 40 to 100 thousand tons of water per second into the Sea of the Hebrides. It forms from the outflow of the Irish Sea which wends its way round Kintyre, the Mull of Oa and the Rhinns of Islay before debouching into the channels between the islands of the Hebrides. Much of the coastal current moves north, squeezing through the Little Minch and then The Minch. South of Skye, part of the Coastal Current breaks off to move clockwise along the east coast of the Uists and Barra, around Barra Head and then northward again along the west side of the Long Island.

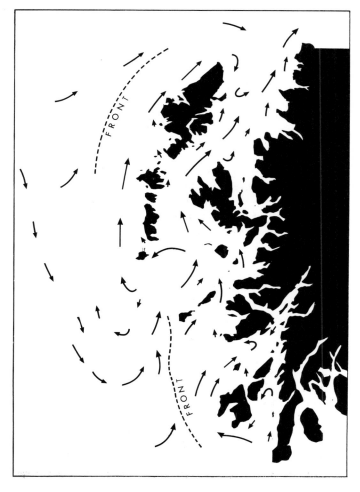

Fig. 10
Surface circulation in the sea to the west of Scotland in summer (from Ellett, 1979)

The oceanic water west of the Hebrides is a stratified water mass with a fairly constant gradient of salinity with depth. This is in contrast to the coastal water, which is mixed by tidal currents and the weather, and abuts onto the oceanic waters in places, such as west of Islay, to form fronts. The coastal waters also contain the run-off from rivers causing brackish conditions in the inner recesses of some lochs. The single largest source of freshwater is the Firth of Lorne through which drain much of the Glengarry, Lochaber, Lorne and Morvern catchments. The total run-off for the coast from Kintyre to Cape Wrath varies from 11–25 cubic km per year which is approximately 11–25 billion tonnes of water per year.

The influence of the coastal current and run-off on salinity

Fig. 11
Surface salinity of the sea, o/oo, 11–19 November 1977 (lower), and 2–12 February 1978 (upper) (from Ellett, 1983)

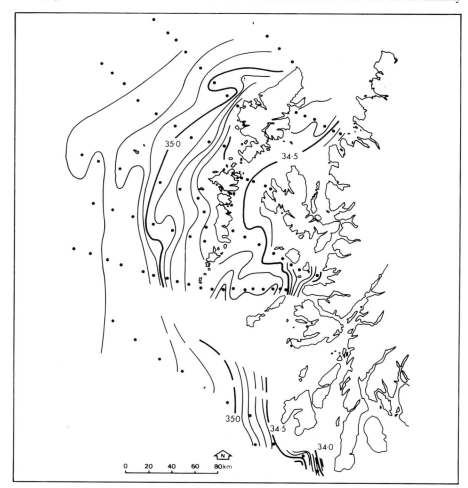

is well illustrated by the large salinity gradient on the western fringe of the Hebrides in summer, although in winter some of the deeper parts of the Hebridean seas are invaded by cold, dense tongues of oceanic water. The coastal current and run-off also cause a general lowering of summer surface temperature by about 2 to 3°C from an Atlantic maximum of 13°C. There is a similar pattern in winter when Atlantic waters stay at about 9°C while coastal waters dip to 6–7°C.

Allowing for tidal currents, the actual flow rate of the coastal current as it pushes through the Tiree passage between Coll and Mull can reach 18km per day in winter but is commonly 1–5km per day in summer. Further offshore, the slope current, at the rim of the Hebridean shelf, can run at 15–22km per day, but 2–9km per day may be more normal. The flow of these currents can be about half the surface flow rate near the bottom.

Radioactive caesium, released from Sellafield into the coastal current before it leaves the Irish Sea, has been a useful if dangerous marker to follow the progress of this water mass through the Hebrides. It has illustrated the sharp contrast between the unpolluted oceanic waters and the coastal waters, and has also helped to chart the velocity of the coastal current over long distances. An overall rate of flow from Islay to the Pentland Firth of 1.5km per day has been calculated.

The most immediate hydrographic feature of island archipelagoes is often their tidal races, and the inner sounds of the Hebrides often have considerable rips. At Corryvreckan,

The Gulf of Corryvreckan, the sound between Scarba (left) and Jura (right) which has whirlpools and overfalls in the tidal race (Photo J. M. Boyd)

between Scarba and Jura, there is an extreme example, while in the Lismore Passage overfalls give rough passage to yachts entering the Sound of Mull from the Firth of Lorne. The Corryvreckan rip arises from a one metre difference in sea level over 5km between the waters of the Sound of Jura and the Firth of Lorne. Currents of 8.5 knots are generated where the friction of the sea bed opposes the levelling flow of the water. In the main channels currents of 1–2 knots are normal, although they will reach 4 knots in the North Channel. Unusual tidal currents occur on the shelf at St Kilda which also affect the Sound of Harris. During summer neap tides, the stream running southeast flows all day, while in winter it flows all night, and vice-versa for the north-west flow.

Tidal amplitude in the Hebrides is not unusual by British standards. There is a point between Kintyre and Islay where the tides of the shelf, the North Channel and the Sound of Jura meet. Here, the tidal range is 0.5–1m. Around Skye and The Minch it is 1.6–4.5 metres at neaps and springs respectively, but there are no areas with extreme tidal ranges.

All this movement of water takes place over a varied submarine topography which plays an important part in mixing or separating the upper and deep waters. The glaciated landscape above sea level continues below with deep-graven rock basins such as the sea-lochs of Skye and Mull. Drowned fjords occur west of the Rhinns of Islay. There are also isolated trenches, many over 100m and some over 200m in depth in the Firth of Lorne, east of Barra Head and around the Small Isles, and the deepest at 316m off the north-east coast of Raasay. The water and communities of organisms in these deep waters are different from the mobile upper waters, and there is limited exchange between the two levels. The Raasay Deep, lying in the shelter of Skye, has been attractive to those who require deep water for construction of oil/gas production platforms and for naval research and tests.

Soils

Soils are formed from mixtures of minerals derived from rocks, and by microbial action on organic material in the presence of water and air. The soil type is dictated by the relative proportions of these components, particularly the types of minerals present, and the way in which they are organised from the soil surface to the base rock. Hebridean soils do not generally lend themselves to cultivation on a large scale; they are usually too wet, occasionally too dry, or are susceptible to being eroded by the wind. Even where there are extensive areas of cultivable land, the land surface is commonly uneven and rocky and so highly restrictive. Besides being the substrate of agriculture, the soils provide a range of habitats for plant and animal communities, foundations for houses and roads, and domestic fuel. Water for the tap is filtered through the soil, and water derived from peat accounts for the distinctive taste of the malt whisky of Islay, Jura and Skye.

Throughout the Hebrides there are signs, some recent and some ancient, that man has been at work with the soil. Soils are one of the few elements of the physical environment which man can actively modify for his own benefit, but in the Hebrides this is a continuous and arduous process. Through the centuries land has been progressively claimed from the hill or bog by drainage, to improve the grazing for livestock. Over many years, drains have become blocked, but some have recently been re-established in the Integrated Development Programme and the Agricultural Development Programme in the Outer and Inner Hebrides respectively, which provided grant aid for agricultural improvement, *Feanagean* (spade cultivation in ridges sometimes called 'lazy beds') were dug on the thin wet soils, and long-derelict furrows are still seen corrugating the hillsides of Skye and Mull, Rum, Harris and the Barra Isles. Even the outlying islands of North Rona and St Kilda have their old lazy beds. Seaweed, always a plentiful commodity in the Hebrides, was applied to land as a fertiliser and this practice still continues. Sadly, it has been widely displaced by artificial fertilisers, with the consequent changes in the soil biomass affecting the ecology of the croftlands. Liming of the soils was rare, mainly because there is little

Feannagan *or 'lazy beds' in Glen Harris, Rum. The thin soil was raised in parallel ridges by spade-cultivation, fertilized with seaweed, and planted with oats, barley, potatoes and kale (Photo J. M. Boyd)*

limestone in the Hebrides, but since the last war calcareous shell sand has been added to the moorland soils by grant-assisted schemes in the Outer Hebrides. This has the same effect as liming by improving rough grazing land and even increasing the area of tillage; it effectively adds a small amount of material of high carbonate content to another of low carbonate content to improve its agricultural potential, though a compound fertiliser is also added, together with a clover-grass seed mixture. Over the centuries, man has had a hand in the development of many of the Hebridean soils.

Soil development is slow and may involve a gradual movement of material transported from elsewhere by wind or water and then deposited over the existing soil or bedrock. Transient periods of occupation or cultivation by man can be distinguished as layers, or horizons, in this sequence of accumulation. This is especially obvious where subsequent chemical alteration or natural mixing of the soil components is slight, such as in the regosols (immature soils) which underlie the machair. Occupation horizons have been identified in the machair soils of Rosinish in Benbecula, Northton in Harris and Udal in North Uist. They are characterised by greater accumulation of dark organic material than in the intervening horizons. Horizons may also depict changes in the climate or vegetation.

Hebridean soils have evolved within the last 10,000 years, and every soil has a parent material from which it has been derived to varying degrees. In some cases, the bedrock upon which a soil has developed may have contributed directly to the parent material, or it can influence the properties of the soil as it develops. However, most parent materials owe their origin to the deposition of the eroded fragments of the Tertiary and the pre-Tertiary rocks of western Scotland by glaciers and then by rivers and the sea.

The Soil Survey of Scotland recognised six different parent materials in the Hebrides, and each one of these has a range of soils developed within it depending on such factors as rainfall, topography, the nature of the bedrock and the level of biotic activity associated with them. These were: glacial till, morainic drift, outwash and raised beaches, colluvium, aeolian sand and montane frost-shattered detritus.

Glacial Till with Brown Forest Soils

The Quaternary ice sheet covered most of the Hebrides, and its great erosive power ground the underlying rock to powder. The resulting soils tend to be compact and lack surface boulders. This glacial till is found in many parts of the Outer Hebrides, where it is often positioned in the lee of hummocks in the bedrock of Lewisian gneiss, and therefore indicates the direction of movement of the ice sheet. Most of North Uist and Benbecula are covered with this kind of till, where it lies deepest on the northwest side of the rocky hummocks. Further south around Lochboisdale, the till lies on the west side and to the north of the small ice-cap of Harris and south Lewis, and is on the north of the hummocks. Further north on the line from Stornoway to Shawbost the hummocks fade out and a flat plain has developed where the till lies up to six metres deep over the gneiss. The flat topography and fine texture of this till restricts drainage, which leads to waterlogging. Peat, up to four metres deep in central Lewis, has accumulated on top and now forms a soggy featureless landscape. This till probably formed partly from plateau basalt rocks which could have overlain the gneiss in a thin layer, and which has now been completely removed by ice erosion. Such basalts are rich in many minerals required to form productive soils.

In the Inner Hebrides, the till deposits are sporadic and their composition reflects the rocks from which they were formed. On Skye the main sources of material were the plateau basalts and soft Jurassic shales. Other Mesozoic strata, much of which is now submerged below the sea, gave rise to tills on Islay, Colonsay, Tiree and the Ross of Mull. Where drainage is good, glacial till forms the basis for most of the productive cultivated land in the Inner Hebrides, the largest such area being on Islay. Tills derived from Jurassic rocks also provide productive croft

Brown calcareous soils at Torrin, Skye with a crop of potatoes and a rowan tree growing from the pile of stones cleared from the field. Blaven (913m) stands behind. (Photo J. M. Boyd)

land on Tiree and Coll, and at Glendale and Staffin on Skye, while tills from Mesozoic rocks give good grazing land on the Ross of Mull, north-west Islay and Colonsay.

Morainic Drift with Peat and Gleys

Morainic drift is formed from the rock debris of the retreating glaciers. It has a very wide range of particle sizes, from minute individual crystals to large boulders the size of a house which can be left perched on hilltops or bare hillsides. It forms the hummocky terrain on the floor of glens of the Inner Hebrides. In the Outer Hebrides it occurs around the shores of Loch Seaforth, west Loch Tarbert and along the western seaboard of North Lewis from Shawbost to North Dell. In the Uists and Barra it occurs at Balivanich, from West Gerinish to Dali-burgh, and on the slopes of Heaval, Barra. Although these soils are normally fairly permeable to water, a hard impermeable consolidated horizon, thought to be a relict showing the upper extent of the permafrost until 10,000 years BP, often impedes drainage. This, and the high rainfall over much of the Inner Hebrides, has caused the development of peaty soils (gleys) on these moraines. Peats are formed typically in areas of high rainfall and poor drainage, and where the soil temperature is cool, thus preventing microbial action which would normally break down the organic material from dead plants. Such conditions are common throughout the Hebrides.

Outwash Fans and Raised Beaches

As the glaciers receded they released water which fed torrential rivers and streams. The land, free at last from its enormous burden of ice, began to flex imperceptibly upwards, causing a raising of the post-glacial shorelines to form present day raised beaches. The glacial torrents re-sorted many of the tills and moraines left by the retreating ice, transporting and re-depositing their loads of gravel, sand and silt. The rivers flowed fastest near their source and were able to carry most of the glacial debris, but as the gradient of their course declined, they lost their power to move large fragments. By this process, fragments were sorted according to their size. Coarse materials were dropped in outwash fans and most of the fine colloidal clays and sand ended up in the sea. Where steep gradients continue all the way to the coast, as is often the case in the Inner Hebrides, boulders also ended up in the sea.

The debris deposited by this process is now often seen as terraced outwash plains of sand or gravel, the particles of which are rounded by impact against one another caused by the action of the water. Their extent is mostly limited to the low ground and river valleys and in some localities part of the deposit has been removed by the sea to form the pebbled and cobbled raised beaches found mainly in the Inner Hebrides. The value of the soils developed on these sands and gravels varies. At one extreme are stretches of unvegetated cobbles which may be piled to a depth of several metres on raised beaches which are

The calcareous sandy loam of the raised beach platform at Barrapol, Tiree being made ready for a crop of potatoes (Photo J. M. Boyd)

scenically magnificent but relatively lifeless. At the other
extreme are the fine gravels and sands. These are highly permeable to water and, because of this and the wet climate,
leached soils known as podzols have often developed on them.
Humic acid, from decaying organic matter in the upper horizons, mixed with the downward draining water, causes leaching of minerals from the upper part of the profile, and a distinct
white mineral-deficient horizon develops. However, the top
horizons of most of these podzols have been mixed by tillage,
causing the upper horizons to be obliterated. Such podzols
form the nucleus of many crofting areas in the Inner Hebrides.
Where the climate is most favourable, they form some of the
best agricultural land in the Hebrides. Their value is limited by
their local occurrence but, unlike soils in many other parent
materials, they usually occur in relatively flat sheltered areas
such as near the mouth of Glen Brittle on Skye. The most
notable of these podzolic soils are on the shores of Lochs Gruinart and Indaal, Islay, and on much of the cultivated land on
Tiree. (St Columba also chose a small patch of this soil on Iona
on which to found his early mission.) One problem with these
soils is that valuable nutrients can be quickly washed away. The
close proximity of the Dalradian limestone on Islay has meant
that limestone could be burnt and the resultant lime used to
enrich the soils, and on Tiree, wind-blown shell sand has
caused the same effect.

Colluvium and Shallow Drifts with Podzols

Areas of bare rock left after the retreat of the glaciers have
subsequently been subjected to weathering by wind, rain and
freeze-thaw conditions. The products of this form a soil parent
material known as colluvium or shallow drift. The nature of the
soil which develops from these drifts is highly dependent on
the rock from which it forms. For example, basalts give loamy
soils, quartzites stony acid soils and slates give silty soils. Colluvium occurs on slopes at most altitudes and this in itself may
influence the evolution of the soil. Those at low altitudes can
form rich loamy brown forest soils, but subalpine and alpine
colluvial soils are formed at high altitudes. These are often
podzols because of mineral leaching and are shallow and
exposed to frost action for much of the year on the peaks of
Mull, Skye and Rum. Peaty soils usually form at intermediate
altitudes.

   The landscape associated with soils developed in colluvium
or shallow drift is variable, but the countryside is often rocky
and undulating with small lochans in ice-gouged rock basins,

peat flats and steep, occasionally terraced, slopes. The rocky
nature of these soils means that they have little agricultural
value and provide good or poor hill pasture. Apart from the
high mountains, examples of colluvial soils are found on the
Ross of Mull, eastern Jura and at Trotternish on Skye.

On the Dalradian limestones of Islay and the ultrabasic
rocks of Rum, brown forest soils have developed in colluvium,
but cultivation of these is usually restricted by the steep, rocky
slopes. The extinct communities, at Dibidil, Harris and
Papadil on Rum have left cultivation ridges, indicating that it
was once feasible to cultivate these remote areas. Now, only red
deer and feral goats exploit the lush herb-rich vegetation on
these soils. Shallow drifts, derived from the Tertiary basalts,
have also produced brown forest soils on Eigg, Muck and along
many of the sheltered shorelines of Skye and Mull. They
support some arable land on Skye and Mull, but steep slopes
often restrict their use to pasture for livestock. They often also
support mixed deciduous woodlands such as those at Loch
Don, Loch na Keal, Loch Buie and near Craignure on Mull,
on Skye, and Eigg and Jura. These are biologically rich soils
and, even with high grazing pressures, they support a diverse
flora and fauna of importance in nature conservation.

Aeolian Sand with Regosols

One of the most important soil-forming materials in the
Hebrides is wind-blown, or aeolian, sand. Much of this sand is
formed from the crushed remains of shells of marine molluscs
and crustacea and is widespread in the Hebrides. The soils
formed from this parent material are poorly evolved, differing
little from the parent material itself. The landscape formed by
these soils is machair, (the character and extent of which is
discussed in Chapter 6), and the largest areas are on the
western seaboard of the Outer Hebrides from Harris to Vatersay, with small pockets on other islands. These regosols are
easily eroded by wind when the turf is broken and dune blow-
outs then form. Some of those nearer the coast are continually
on the move, being cut by the wind and pushed inland. Heavy
grazing by livestock, or rabbits on some islands, of the rich
semi-natural grasslands of the machair, tends to encourage
this instability. They are also dry soils, because the wind causes
water removal by evaporation and water drains away easily to
ditches and, via the water table, to the sea. Some trace nutrients
such as cobalt, which are necessary for the health of grazing
livestock, are lacking in the vegetation on these soils because
the high pH does not favour their release to plant roots.

*A section of untilled
machair soil at The
Reef, Tiree, showing
the present-day sandy
loam (top), a dark band
of peaty soil from a past
period of flooding
(middle), and the base
of shell sand (bottom)
(Photo J. M. Boyd)*

Despite their rudimentary form, machair soils are fertile and
provide good quality grazings. In the Uists they are tilled and
planted on a considerable scale. Elsewhere, cultivation is
patchy and carries with it a risk of erosion.

Montane Detritus

Like aeolian sands, soils formed from frost-shattered detritus
are poorly evolved. The screes of the Red Hills of Skye and the
boulder fields just below the summits of Askival and Hallival
on Rum are detritus formed from the freezing and thawing of

water percolating through cracks in the rock. This gradually splits the rocks along lines of weakness, and the resulting debris tumbles downhill. Although this process is still continuing in the higher mountains of the Hebrides, many of the screes were formed during the later stages of the Quaternary glaciation. In the sub-arctic conditions of immediate post-glacial times, the cycle of freezing and thawing was particularly severe, especially on the peaks of Jura, Mull, Skye and Rum. The senescence of the glacial period was not a continuous process in western Scotland. The glaciers retreated, advanced a little and then retreated again. Like the cobbled raised beaches, the screes are usually unvegetated and the steepness of the slopes means that they are unstable and may move downhill. They are prone to erosion by rivers and eventually end up as components of outwash fans, thus contributing to the formation of other parent materials.

Human communities have relied on the soil as much as on the sea to produce food, and there was a time when the wealth of an island was based mainly upon the richness of its soils. Political turmoils like the collapse of the Lordship of the Isles or the transition from the clan to the feudal system of government associated with the landed lairds have, without doubt, revolved around the productivity of the land and the ability of the workers of that land to squeeze the goodness from its soil. It was probably no coincidence that the power base of the Lordship of the Isles was on the comparatively rich agricultural system of Islay which could compare favourably with those on the mainland and Ireland. We refer to the recent occupational history of the Hebrides in later chapters.

CHAPTER 4

Life in the Sea

Sir Maurice Yonge was an inspired marine biologist who enthralled his students by his lectures on 'The Seas'. He transferred his own sense of the infinite to young minds and described the enrivonment of the deep, the 'marine pasturage', with rare passion and enlightenment. He had an immense understanding of how so many forms and functions of life had evolved in one vast interconnected system, and as the course proceeded, so the sense of wonder grew of a world which, by its nature, is closed to human beings but which, by technology, has been partially revealed. What is unseen is imagined—the angler-fish (*Lophius piscatorius*) with its lights twinkling in the abyssal depths, the tiny shrimp (*Eurydice pulchra*) in the everlasting sandstorm of the breakers. The course of scientific exploration is driven on by that sense of awe engendered as the student comes face to face with the unknown, the fearsome, the bizarre and the beautiful.

Our knowledge of life in Hebridean waters comes mostly from fishermen and fishery research, though in the last ten years there has been a small but growing effort in the survey of the coastal seas for the purposes of nature conservation. The main communities of organisms are situated in the different parts of the hydrographic system; ocean depths, continental slope and shelf with sublittoral platforms in the shallow seas immediately around the islands. None are self-contained and all are connected by currents. Many species of fin-fish move from one to the other to feed or breed and others, such as copepods, arrow-worms, sea-gooseberries and the egg and larval stages of a diverse fauna, move passively in the plankton. The waters around the Hebrides possess a rich phytoplankton; this is the 'vegetation', which fixes gaseous carbon and nitrogen, and which is grazed by the zooplankton. The zooplankton are then eaten by other animals and thus the food-chain is begun. The large devour the small and so on up to the large carnivores—the large gadoid fish, seals, whales and seabirds. The glaring exception to the rule is the basking shark (*Cetorhinus maximus*). This is the second largest fish in the world and the largest in the Hebrides and yet its food consists only of plankton.

Fish

The communities of fin-fish are described as 'demersal' or bottom-living, and 'pelagic', which includes fish which live between the bottom and the surface. Both groups are well known because of their commercial value.

English	Scientific	Gaelic
Cod	*Gadus morhua*	trosg
Haddock	*Melanogrammus aeglefinus*	adag
Whiting	*Merlangius merlangus*	cuiteag
Spurdog	*Squalus acanthias*	gobag
Saithe	*Pollachius virens*	piocach
Hake	*Merluccius merluccius*	falmaire
Ling	*Molva molva*	langa
Skate	*Rajidae*	sgait
Angler-fish	*Lophius piscatorius*	carran
Plaice	*Pleuronectes platessa*	leabag-mhor
Lemon sole	*Microstomus kitt*	leabag-chearr
Megrim	*Lepidorhombus whiffiagonis*	—
Witch	*Glyptocephalus cynoglossus*	leabag-uisge
Dab	*Limanda limanda*	—
Sand-eel	*Ammodytidae*	siolag
Conger	*Conger conger*	as-chu
Halibut	*Hippoglossus hippoglossus*	leabag-leathann
Tusk	*Brosme brosme*	—
Turbot	*Scophthalmus maximus*	turbaid
Lythe	*Pollachius pollachius*	liubh

Table 4.1 Demersal species in the Hebrides which have commercial value

Most species have spawning grounds on the Hebridean shelf. The adult fish move back to deep water after spawning but the eggs and infant fish either remain in local nursery grounds where hydrographic conditions favour a settled life, or they drift north-east to waters around Orkney and Shetland and into the North Sea. Cod, whiting, saithe and plaice probably remain inshore for the first two years of life, often in sea-lochs and then, as recruits to the adult population, they move to the main feeding grounds further offshore. Surface trawling north and west of Orkney, at the outflow of coastal currents from the Hebrides, has netted sufficient numbers of young cod, haddock and whiting to suggest movement of these species from the Hebrides to the North Sea, while tagged cod, haddock and plaice from the North Sea have been caught on

*Haddock (Photo
Crown Copyright)*

the Hebridean shelf, showing that there may be a passage of adult fish from east to west. Spurdogs are viviparous and there is evidence of a concentration of fish giving birth off north-west Scotland in summer.

In the period 1953–67, Bennet Rae (*et al.*) made lists of rare and exotic species of fish recorded in Scotland. Table 4.2 shows those found on the west coast.

English	Scientific	Gaelic
Blue shark	*Prionace glauca*	boc-glas
Six-gilled shark	*Hexanchus griseus*	—
Frilled shark	*Chlamydoselachus anguineus*	—
Long-finned bream	*Taractichthys longipinnis*	—
Black sea-bream	*Spondyliosoma cantharus*	—
Deal fish	*Trachipterus arcticus*	—
Boar fish	*Capros aper*	—
Sturgeon	*Acipenser sturio*	stirean
Pilchard	*Sardina pilchardus*	geilmhin
Ray's bream	*Brama brama*	—
Red mullet	*Mullus surmuletus*	—
Snipe fish	*Macroramphosus scolopax*	—
Black scabbard-fish	*Aphanopus carbo*	—
Red band fish	*Cepola rubescens*	—
Sunfish	*Mola mola*	—
Electric ray	*Torpedo nobiliana*	craimb-iasg
Pilot fish	*Naucrates ductor*	—
Opah or Moonfish	*Lampris guttatus*	—
Angel-fish	*Squatina squatina*	sgait-mhanaich
Eagle-ray	*Myliobatis aquila*	—
Bogue	*Boops boops*	—
Stone-bass	*Polyprion americanus*	—

Pearl-fish	*Echiodon drummondi*	—
Black fish	*Centrolophus niger*	—
Blue-mouth	*Helicolenus dactylopterus*	—
Tunny	*Thunnus thynnus*	—

Table 4.2   Rare and exotic fish recorded on the West Coast of Scotland

Pelagic fish feed in the surface- and mid-waters. They occur in shoals, feeding on plankton and the young pelagic stages of other fish.

English	Scientific	Gaelic
Herring	*Clupea harengus*	sgadan
Mackerel	*Scomber scombrus*	rionnach
Sprat	*Sprattus sprattus*	—

Table 4.3   The main species of pelagic fish in the Hebrides

The main food of the herring are tiny copepods, including *Calanus finmarchicus*, a key species of the zooplankton upon which depend pelagic fish and possibly the infant stages of some demersal fish. Copepods, in turn, feed on even tinier diatoms and dinoflagellates in nutrient-rich waters flowing northward along the continental shelf.

The plankton have a diurnal rhythm within the photic zone, where sunlight penetrates. During the day, the main biomass

Herring (Photo Crown Copyright)

may be 10m below the surface but, at night, it is much nearer
the surface. At night, therefore, plankton feeders are also near
the surface and within reach of many types of net operated on
the surface. In the Hebrides herring were traditionally fished
with drift nets by small boats, but now, when fishing is allowed,
the pelagic fish are caught by mid-water pair trawlers and
purse-seiners.

Surveys of herring larvae in the plankton show that herring
spawn from late August to early October. The spawning
grounds are mainly within 20–30 miles of the coast, eggs are
demersal, and the herring is rather unusual in that it deposits
its eggs on a carpet of gravel. This localises the spawning
grounds and, because of the large numbers of gravid adults
which congregate in these restricted areas, this has meant that
the herring has been easy to over-exploit. Spawning areas are
smaller in the Hebrides than in the northern North Sea and
occur east of the hydrographic fronts on a line which follows
the western shore of the Outer Hebrides, but east of St. Kilda.
There are also spawning grounds close inshore to the west and
north of Tiree. After hatching, the larvae become pelagic and
disperse slowly until they enter the frontal zone when they are
transported north with the currents. This takes them both into
the sea lochs of the Minch and Skye and into the North Sea.
Here they mature for about two years and they then migrate
back to their natal spawning grounds to be recruited as adults.

Mackerel have a wider diet than herring and can be caught
by lures on short-lines in summer from the inner sounds and
sea-lochs to St Kilda. They also occur on the surface, making

*Mackerel (Photo
Crown Copyright)*

the sea boil with a ripping sound as the shoal breaks the surface
and changes direction in the same instant. They feed on
macro-plankton and small fish, and there appear to be two
stocks which move to and from their spawning grounds in the
North Sea and south-west of Ireland respectively. The western
stock seems to predominate in the Hebrides and probably con-
stituted most of the catch in the prolific Minch fishery.

There is little known about the distribution of the sprat on
the Hebridean shelf. It occurs inshore in winter in the sea-
lochs of the mainland and in the Minch and disperses offshore
to spawn and feed in spring and summer, small numbers
having been recorded off St Kilda and Skerryvore. Surveys of
eggs and larvae have shown that large numbers of sprat spawn
occur in June in the north Minch and north of the Butt of
Lewis. The Norway pout (*Trisopterus esmarkii*) also occurs in
the north Minch and on the shelf to the west of the Hebrides in
water 100–200m deep. Unlike the sprat, the Norway pout is not
found in the inner sounds and sea-lochs; it is a bottom-living
fish which inhabits relatively deep areas with a mud substrate.
Research ships have recorded stocks similar in density to those
in the north North Sea. In the Minch, main concentrations
occur between Tiumpan Head, Lewis and the Clash Deeps off
Sutherland. Sand eels (mainly *Ammodytes marinus*) shoal on the
shelf from the inner sounds to waters around St Kilda. Until
recently, this species, which is important feed-stock for predatory fish and sea birds, has been disregarded by the fishing
industry, but it is now recognised as a profitable source of oil
and meal.

Benthos

The rocky bed of the Hebridean shelf is masked by sediments
deposited by past glaciers and past and present rivers flowing
westward from the mainland plateau. It is sorted by sea-
currents and the activity of benthic animals and man. In the
most sheltered areas there are muds, and in the most exposed,
bare rock and pebbles; in between there are grades of muddy
sand, coarse sand, shell- and 'coral' sand and gravel.

Mud-dwellers like the Norway lobster *Nephrops* and the red-
band fish *Cepola rubescens* live in burrows, as do the sea-pens
Virgularia mirabilis and *Pennatula phosphorea*. Off the east coast
of Rum, mud is present at a depth of 20m and this contains the
large sea-pen *Funiculina quadrangularis* and the cup coral
Caryophyllia smithii. The characteristic community of the
muds and sandy muds at over 100m contains many bivalves,
including the smooth artemis *Dosinia lupinus*, the small razor

Phaxas pellucidus, the basket-shell *Corbula gibba*, the striped venus *Venus striatula*, trough-shell *Spisula elliptica*, *Nucula* spp. and *Abra* spp., plus echinoderms including the heart urchin *Echinocardium cordatum* and the brittle stars *Amphiura* spp. Worms which are present include the proboscis worm *Phascolion strombi*, peacock worms *Sabella pavonina* and *Owenia fusiformis* and the crustaceans *Nephrops* and *Calorcaris macandreae*.

The sand-dwelling community is characterised by bivalves; the razor shell *Ensis arcuatus*, trough shells *Spisula elliptica* and *Abra prismatica* the heart urchin, the worm *Lanice conchilega* and sand-eels *Ammodytes* spp. Bivalves are also found in the gravels, such as the oval and banded venuses, the dog-cockle *Glycymeris glycymeris*, the banded carpet-shell *Venerupis rhomboides*, the rib-saddled oysters *Monia patelliformis* and *M. squama*, the small scallop *Chlamys distorta* and the horse mussel *Modiolus modiolus*. Gastropod snails include, *Colus glacilis*, the cowrie *Trivia monacha*, the grey top shell *Gibbula cineraria*, the whelk or buckie *Buccinum undatum* and *Calliostoma zizyphinum*, plus the sea urchins *Echinus esculentus* and *Psammechinus miliaris*, the starfish *Asterias rubens* and the brittle stars *Ophiothrix fragilis* and *Ophiopholis aculeata*. Crustaceans include barnacles *Balanus* sp. and *Verruca stroemia*, Cup coral, brachiopods, bryozoans and hydrozoans, and the encrusting algae *Phymatolithon calcareum*, *Lithothamnion glaciale* and *L. sonderi* are also present in the gravels.

Among extensive beds of pebbles and boulders off the west and north coasts of Tiree, the community is dominated with *Lithothamnion*, barnacles *B. crenatus*, the sponge *Mycale rotalis*, the colonial squirt *Botrylloides leachi*, vast beds of brittle stars *Ophiocomina nigra* and *Ophiothrix fragilis*, the sea cucumber *Neopentadactyla mixta*, and the banded carpet shell.

The solid rock habitats are well represented in the exposed islands, with near-vertical walls and extensive shelving. Many of these surfaces are swept clear of rock debris and form the walls, floors and ceilings of submarine caves and tunnels, all encrusted with marine growth. This is a world which is shut to all but the most daring of divers in settled weather.

In 1988, Susan Hiscock dived under the plummeting cliffs of St Kilda and found them descending below as above the sea 'with vertical drop-offs to 40m and beyond, huge arches and sheer-sided tunnels'. She found the water exceptionally clear with very good light penetration. Sloping terraces held luxuriant forests of *Laminaria*, and vertical walls were festooned with sea anemones, sea firs (hydroids), sea mats (bryozoans), and sponges. The white anemone *Sagartia* spp., the dahlia anemone *Tealia felina* and the tiny jewel anemone *Corynactis viridis*

were abundant, the latter being the most beautiful, with a brilliant fluorescence. In deeper water, the white trumpet anemone *Parazoanthus anguicomis* hung in clusters from overhangs with its rosettes of tentacles in full display to catch passing plankton. The mosaics of anemones had patches composed of animals of identical colouring, representing clones which had developed from off-buds from a single coloniser. Small pink and purple sea slugs and small bright red scorpion fish were also caught in the beam of the diver's torch, which illuminated an underwater wonderland remote from man.

Queen scallop (Chlamys opercularis) with a commensal sponge (Suberites sp.), starfish (Henricia sp.), and brittle stars (Ophiocomina nigra) (Photo Crown Copyright)

The meeting of the oceanic and coastal waters in the Hebrides brings together two different biotas. The Hebridean biota contains southern, or Lusitanian, species in a predominantly Boreal or Atlantic system. Many marine species are at their northern limits, such as the sponge *Ciocalyta penicillusthe*, anemone *Aureliania heterocerathe*, paper piddock *Pholadidea loscombiana*, the cotton spinner *Holothuria forskali*, the bryozoan *Pentapora folicea* and the algae *Bictyopteris membranacae* plus four others. On the other hand, northern species such as the anemone *Protanthea simplex* and the soft coral *Swiftia pallida* are at their southern limits. There are rarities to the British biota such as the anemone *Arachnanthus sarsi* and the alga *Erythrodermis allenii*. The large sea urchin *Echinus* is abundant in the Hebrides and feeds on sessile organisms, locally reducing the diversity of the sea-bed communities. A comprehensive survey and classification of the varied habitats of the marine benthos of the British Isles is required as an essential prerequisite of nature conservation in British waters. This is already under way, but needs much more research.

Commercial species occupy a wide range of sea-bed habitats: the Norway lobster *Nephrops*, which forms the basis of the popular dish 'scampi', lives in mud; scallops live on sandy gravel; lobsters and edible crabs on the rocky sea bed. *Nephrops* is a burrow-living predator found in fine, sticky mud in the Minch and well into sea-lochs, around Skye and the Small Isles, Mull, Colonsay and the east coast of Islay. Scallops are filter-feeders often lying recessed in the sand, opening the upper valve to feed and breathe, or sometimes swimming freely by clapping of the valves. They occur in depths to 50m. Lobsters and edible crabs are powerful predators, mostly on hermit crabs *Eupagurus* and molluscs. The edible crab is more widely distributed than the lobster. It excavates sandy pits to a depth of 20cm in search of tellins *Tellina* spp. and razor-shells. Lobsters and crabs are caught in depths down to 60m throughout the rock-sand transitions of sea bed, and they thrive in the fringes of the kelp forest. The spiny lobster *Palinurus elephas*, which is at the northern limits of its range in the Hebrides, feeds on echinoderms and molluscs and is present in small

Norway lobster inhabits burrows in seabed mud (Photo Crown Copyright)

numbers to depths of 20m on inshore reefs, often interspersed with steep rock faces and swept by strong tidal currents, off Skye, Raasay, Mull and in the Firth of Lorne.

Squid *Loligo forbesi* migrate inshore in late summer and early autumn preparatory to spawning from December to March. They are taken incidentally in trawls and seine nets and when abundant they are fished directly by trawl and jig and most of the catches are exported to the Mediterranean. Another squid, *Todarodes sagittatus*, is sometimes abundant and taken in trawls. The octopus *Eledone cirrhosa* is taken in lobster creels and *Nephrops* trawls. The shrimp *Dichelopandus bonnieri* is also taken in *Nephrops* trawls and the squat lobster is taken in *Nephrops* creels; the latter lives in sandy muds and gravels close to the mud beds of *Nephrops*.

In 1953 about 100 tonnes were landed in the Inner Hebrides, mostly as incidental 'take' in white fish trawling and seining, whereas in 1979 about 6,800 tonnes, with a market value of £9 million, were landed in the same area as the result of direct fishing. This was 53% of the Scottish shellfish landings of *Nephrops* for that year. Scallops are fished now as much by skin-divers as by dredges. In 1972 a peak was reached when, at Stornoway, 141 tonnes fetched £33,000, while in 1976 the peak was 2,561 tonnes from Inner Hebridean grounds. Stocks of clams in the Hebrides are small compared with other parts of Scotland. In 1980, for example, of the market value of just over £1.1 million, only £15,000 (1.5%) accrued to the Inner Hebrides, with little more from the Outer Isles. Unfortunately, fishing for shellfish can have a severe impact on the sea bed because of the methods used; frequent trawling and dredging of fine muds scarifies and denudes the bottom of the sea.

Plankton

We have spoken of the fish and plankton and the interconnected web of life which knits them into one whole creation. A silk drogue drawn through the surface waters of the Minch at midnight in summer will produce a wonderful display of winking lights. Under the microscope, the washings from the drogue are alive with a diversity of shapes; diatoms, medusae, shrimps, flagellates, eggs, arrow-worms, bizarre larvae of crabs and sea cucumbers. Among them is a copepod, *Calanus finmarchicus*, which is extremely abundant and is the food of the herring, the basking shark and other gill-feeding fish. *Calanus* itself is an efficient feeder with a filter mechanism which retains organisms for ingestion ranging in size from 20–30 microns. Almost all diatoms, flagellates and other single-celled green creatures can be utilised. *Calanus* occupies a crucial position in the food chain, channelling much of the fixed energy of the sun to a diverse range of other animals.

Marine Mammals

Records of whales in British waters have been reviewed by Peter Evans from strandings and sightings. Waters around the Hebrides are thought to be under-represented due to lower coverage of reporting than elsewhere. Nonetheless, 20 species of whale have been recorded from the shelf between Connemara and Cape Wrath, including the North Channel and Hebridean waters (Table 4.4).

English	Scientific	Gaelic
Minke whale	*Balaenoptera acutorostrata*	muc-mhara-mhionc
Fin whale	*B. physalus*	muc-an-sgadain
Sei whale	*B. borealis*	muc-mhara-sei
Blue whale	*B. musculus*	muc-mhara-mhor
Humpback whale	*Megaptera novaeangliae*	—
Right whale	*Balaena glacialis*	—
Sperm whale	*Physeter macrorhinchus*	muc-mhara-sputach
Bottle-nosed whale	*Hyperoodon ampullatus*	—
Cuvier's whale	*Ziphius cavirostris*	—
Sowerby's whale	*Mesoplodon bidens*	—
White whale	*Delphinapterus leucas*	—
Porpoise	*Phocoena phocoena*	peileag
Common dolphin	*Delphinus delphis*	deilf
Bottle-nosed dolphin	*Tursiops truncatus*	muc-bhiorach
White-sided dolphin	*Lagenorhynchus acutus*	*
White-beaked dolphin	*L. albirostris*	deilf-gheal-ghobach
Killer whale	*Orcinus orca*	mada-chuain
False killer whale	*Pseudorca crassidens*	—
Pilot whale	*Globicephala melaena*	+
Risso's dolphin	*Grampus griseus*	deilf-Risso

* deilf-chliathaich-ghil   + muc-mhara-chinn-mhoir   — no Gaelic name

Table 4.4   Whale species recorded from the shelf between Connemara and Cape Wrath.

The porpoise and the white-beaked dolphin appear to be the most common cetaceans in the Hebrides followed by white-sided and Risso's dolphins; minke whales, killer whales, pilot whales and bottle-nosed dolphins are less common but regular in summer. Bottle-nosed whales and common dolphins are

uncommon and mainly found offshore, while all others on the
list are only rarely seen. Most species occur between April and
October. Occurrences of large whales such as the blue, fin and
bottle-nose are related to the annual latitudinal migrations,
whereas others such as the porpoise, killer whale and the dolphin are resident in narrower latitudinal limits although they
can move great distances in search of prey. The large whales
breed in low latitudes and probably follow the progressive
growth of plankton and shoals of plankton-feeding fish, northward along the continental edge in spring and early summer.
The smaller whales, including the pilot whale, killer whale,
white-beaked whale and Risso's dolphin, move inshore in
summer and autumn, probably following inshore feeding
movements of fin-fish and squid.

The porpoise is much more common in the Hebrides from
August to October than in other months, and more so on the
west coasts of Britain than in the North and Irish Seas and
English Channel. This may be due in part to pollution and disturbance by shipping, since chlorinated hydrocarbon residues,
similar to those found in fish, seabirds, seals and marine
sediment, are found in the fat of porpoises from the North Sea.
Hebridean waters are comparatively low in such pollutants,
and numbers of porpoises are high. They feed on pelagic fish
of less than 25cm in length, mainly herring and whiting, but
they also take a variety of other species including mackerel, cod
and hake. Salmon are too large a prey for porpoise and records
of them taking salmon are probably cases where the identity
has been mistaken for the bottle-nosed dolphin with which the
porpoise sometimes associates. It also associates with minke
and fin whales while feeding on shoals of sprats and sand-eels.
Schools of about 10 porpoises are usual but over 100 are occasionally seen together; Fraser Darling saw 'two or three hundred' in the Badentarbat Sound, Summer Isles in 1939 and 150
were seen off Harris in October 1973. Porpoises are born in
June; one baby porpoise was found in Loch Hourn in June 1975.

The killer whale is easily identified by its prominent dorsal
fin and pale markings behind the eyes, dorsal fin and hind
flanks. Killer whales are most surely and frequently identified
than most other species of whales although they are sometimes
confused with Risso's dolphin because of its large dorsal fin,
though the latter may be distinguished by its grey, speckled
body. A school of killer whales is an awesome sight; like sharks
they have a bad name from their aggressive carnivorous habit of
chasing and savaging their prey, particularly other smaller
whales and seals. One observer, P. Taylor (Evans, 1980)
described a kill by a school of one male, two females and a
juvenile:

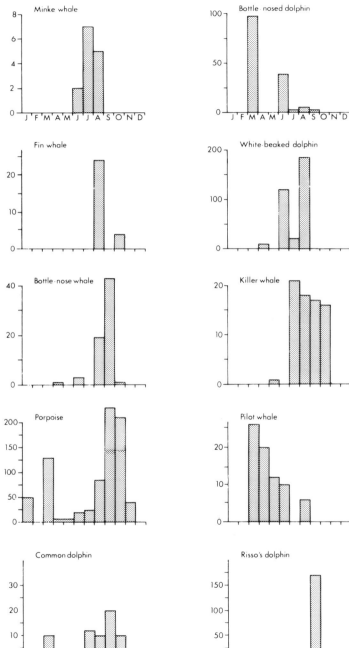

Fig. 12
The seasonal occurrence
of the main species of
cetaceans in Hebridean
seas (adapted from
Evans, 1980)

the herds followed close to the cliffs occasionally making high-pitched squeaks, and then suddenly united and dashed for a seal which was making for the rocks. On capture, the male took it in his jaws and carried it out to deeper waters where the others appeared to queue up and play with the seal before dividing it up.

Currie (1988) reported a pod of six or seven killer whales feeding on seals at the Flannan Isles. The behaviour of killer whales in the wild does not seem to fit the same species that provides such a show of gentleness and affection to its fellow creatures when tamed in a dolphinarium!

Little is known about the breeding of killer whales. They may be polygamous but with stable matriachal social groups. Schools of about 5–10 adult females plus immatures of both sexes with one adult male are often seen—excess young males form bachelor groups. More males become stranded than females. Killer whales disappear from the Hebrides in October and reappear in May; it is thought that they move into distant offshore waters to mate and give birth. Recent research on killer whales off the Pacific coast of Canada has shown that they live in stable family groups of closely related individuals with a high degree of fidelity to a particular home range.

Killer whales have been seen with white-beaked dolphins and diving gannets among herring shoals. They eat porpoises, dolphins, seals, seabirds, large squid, salmon, cod, sand-eels and halibut. Little is known about the false killer whales in the Hebrides, but a herd of six small whales off north-west Scotland in November 1976 resembled this species, and at least one school of false killers has been identified west of the Outer Hebrides in recent years.

The white-beaked dolphin is most frequently seen in the Hebrides in June to September. Herring, mackerel and haddock are reported as important prey and in August large numbers of white-beaked dolphins are seen off the coast of Sutherland, keeping company with Risso's dolphins and gannets. Like other dolphins, small family groups unite to form large ephemeral schools when migrating or when gathered round a prolific source of food. The breeding season is probably between July and September and coincides with the spawning of herring off north Scotland.

Risso's dolphin is relatively frequently recorded, possibly because it occurs inshore in summer and is more easily identified by its grey body and high recurved dorsal fin. In September 1971, a herd of 100–200 was seen off the Outer Hebrides. Because of their ease of identification, some behaviour patterns which are common to many species of whale are attributed solely to Risso's dolphin: 'bottling' like seals, repeated breaching, head-slapping, tail-slapping of the sea's surface and swimming in unison with touching flippers. They probably breed between April and July in deep waters to the south-west and west of Britain, moving into waters around the Hebrides, Orkney and Shetland from June or July to November.

The pilot whale appears in the Hebrides from March to September, but in smaller numbers than in Orkney and Shetland between September and November. This is the species that is hunted so inhumanely on the Faeroe islands. Pilot whales feed mostly on large squid, but cod, turbot and horse-mackerel (*Trachurus trachurus*) have also been recorded. They are often associated with bottle-nosed dolphins and have been seen with large flocks of Manx shearwaters and gannets. It is thought that pilot whales breed in deep waters north of Britain mainly in early spring though births probably occur during most months. In March 1976 a herd of 25 recorded off Lewis included very small calves. There is a correlation between catches of herring and occurrences of pilot whales which suggests that pilot whale numbers in the Hebrides are either directly or indirectly linked to pelagic fish numbers. Common dolphins, white-sided dolphins and bottle-nosed dolphins all feed on squid and a selection of fin-fish including herring, mackerel and salmon. Whitebeaked dolphins also take haddock, plaice and dab while bottle-nosed dolphins feed mainly inshore and in estuaries taking mullet and occasionally 'rounding-up' salmon.

D'Arcy Thompson, whose papers on Scottish whaling 1908–27 are a key to our understanding of the status of cetaceans in Scottish waters this century, recorded small numbers of sperm whales off western Ireland and the Outer Hebrides. Strandings have been from June to August and all have been males; female sperm whales do not migrate as far north as males and are therefore not found in the Hebrides. A juvenile was stranded in the Outer Hebrides in June 1955 and a large bull at Gortantaoid, Islay in summer 1985. Sperm whales probably move northwards in deep water off the edge of the Hebridean shelf in quest of their staple food, squid.

Turning to the baleen whales, the minke, or lesser rorqual, is more common in the Hebrides, Orkney and Shetland, than elsewhere in British waters. It is sometimes seen amongst shoals of sand-eels in company with porpoises and auks. The minke will also take young herring, mackerel and cod, and probably follows spawning concentrations of these species. The fin whale, or common rorqual, occurs in the Hebrides in late summer and autumn, moving along the continental shelf edge. Following the whaling of the 19th and early 20th centuries, this species, amongst others, went into a decline from which it has not yet recovered. In 1974, the population of the North Atlantic was possibly less than 5000. The fin whale feeds on euphausid shrimps and copepods but also forages in deep waters off the Outer Hebrides for herring spawn in September and October. Like minkes, fin whales are usually sighted singly or in pairs. No young fin whales have been seen in British waters and probably the young remain in lower latitudes.

The largest living animal in the world, the blue whale, grows to a length of 30m and weighs up to 150 tonnes. It used to be common, but has become increasingly rare, and is now protected in the North Atlantic, where, until 1955, hunting continued by Norwegian, Faeroese and Icelandic whalers. British hunting ceased in 1928, but earlier, small numbers were landed each year at the Bunaveneadar station, Harris. Two years of whaling in 1950–51 (Maxwell, 1952) yielded six blue whales. In 1974, the population in the North Atlantic was probably less than 2000, with less than 500 in the north-east Atlantic. The huge blue whale feeds mainly on the microscopic euphausids and probably follows the flushes of these and other plankton on the upwelling waters on the continental slope.

The humpback whale is another species that declined because of whaling and, like all other whales, it is now completely protected. Small numbers were landed in Harris but none after 1920 and, though the North Atlantic population may be less than 2000, there are signs of recovery, on the American coast at least. It feeds on plankton swarms, small squid, and young of herring and mackerel. Between 1904–14, 91 Biscayan or right whales were caught just inside the shelf and landed in Harris, but only three were caught after 1918. Even though this species has been totally protected since 1946, there are still no signs of recovery, and the North Atlantic population was assessed in 1974 as 'low hundreds'. Spending the winter in the Bay of Biscay, the right whales, in a similar way to fin and blue whales, probably move northwards and perhaps remain in the Hebrides through the summer. A white whale was seen off Soay, Skye in 1950.

Peter Evans (1982) has also looked into the associations of whales and seabirds. The sea going naturalist in the Hebrides might detect the presence of whales by observing the behaviour of seabirds feeding on similar prey to that of whales, or scraps of whale food or on whale faeces. Cormorants and shags have not so far been recorded in attendance with whales, but being mainly inshore species this is perhaps not surprising. Among the whales the most common seabird associates are minke and pilot whales, common dolphins and porpoises, and among the birds, gannets and kittiwakes. Though whales may be guided to prey by birds, the birds would seem to gain more by following whales which may drive prey species near to the surface and within striking depth of diving birds. During sea passages to the Outer Hebrides, particularly in late summer when gannets are feeding young, a sea-watch of gannets may bring the unexpected sighting of a pod of minke whales or common dolphins.

The Hebrides hold populations of grey seals (*Halichoerus grypus*) and common or harbour seals (*Phoca vitulina*). These are of outstanding interest and are described in Chapter 3, H-AMI. The otter (*Lutra lutra*) is mainly a marine species in the Hebrides, and is described in Chapter 5.

Turtles

The loggerhead (*Caretta caretta*) and leatherback (*Dermochelys coriacea*) appear occasionally. Loggerheads have been reported from Vallay (North Uist) and Dunvegan (Skye), and a leatherback was reported from Tiree in 1985. Kemp's loggerhead turtle *Lepidochelys kempi* was found at Kinlochbervie, Sutherland.

The Sea Shore

The sea shore is the meeting place of sea and land. It is for that reason the most fascinating and the most complex of all the environments of life.

C.M. Yonge

The Vivid Frontier

The realms of sea and land are worlds apart, governed by an entirely different set of physical principles and having their own separate relationships with the atmosphere. However, they are interdependent and face each other across a worldwide frontier of which the shores of the Hebrides form a small but nonetheless wonderful part.

The rocky coast of North Rona exposed to the full force of the Atlantic holds surf-adapted communities, including the grey seal in autumn (Photo J. M. Boyd)

Set in a tempestuous climate and exposed to the full force of the Atlantic's temperate waters, the islands present a front ranging from the high, west-facing, vertical, rocky ramparts of St Kilda to the low, east-facing, silty flats of Loch Spelve in Mull, with all manner of variation and permutation in between: from exposed to sheltered shores, rocky to sandy, and sunlit stretches to sunless recesses of sea caves.

To add to this variety, the habitat is covered by the sea and exposed to the air twice each day. The highest and lowest parts of the shore are covered and exposed by the sea respectively at spring tides once a month—the very highest and lowest perhaps twice a year, at the exceptionally high vernal and autumnal spring tides. Above the full flood of the tide, there is a spray zone which fades further from the sea; conversely, immediately below the full ebb there is a zone of turbulence which fades as the water deepens. The zonation of upper, middle and lower shore is arbitrary and not observed by shore-dwellers, but it serves nonetheless as a useful frame of reference in describing the limits of settlement of species and communities. (The interactions of land and sea which fashion the shore are described by Yonge in Chapter 5 of *The Sea Shore* in this series and is summarised in Fig. 13, taken from that work.)

Fig. 13
Shore levels in relation to tidal changes. In the labelling A = average, E = extreme, H = high, L = low, M = middle, N = neap, S = spring, T = tide, W = water (from Yonge, 1949)

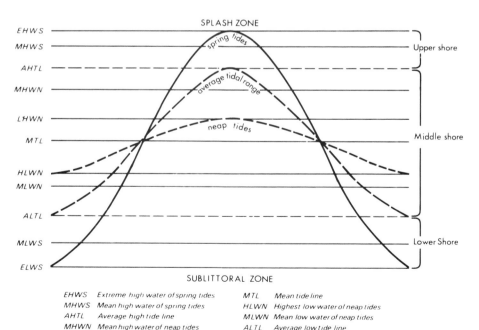

SPLASH ZONE

EHWS
MHWS ———————————————————— Upper shore
AHTL
MHWN
LHWN
MTL ———————————————————— Middle shore
HLWN
MLWN
ALTL
MLWS ———————————————————— Lower Shore
ELWS

spring tides
average tidal range
neap tides

SUBLITTORAL ZONE

EHWS	Extreme high water of spring tides	MTL	Mean tide line
MHWS	Mean high water of spring tides	HLWN	Highest low water of neap tides
AHTL	Average high tide line	MLWN	Mean low water of neap tides
MHWN	Mean high water of neap tides	ALTL	Average low tide line
LHWN	Lowest high water of neap tides	MLWS	Mean low water of spring tides

ELWS Extreme low water of spring tides

The character of Hebridean shores is dominated by the
stark contrast between the hardness, darkness and angularity
of the rocky shores and the smoothness, lightness and elegant
curvature of the sandy beaches and wide expanses of tidal flat.
An aerial view of South Uist shows this contrast well; the west
coast is of the latter and the east coast of the former type, with
an entirely different shoreline.

Boulder, pebble and shingle beaches abound in the
Hebrides with sometimes banks of all three present on the
same shore. The surf has enormous power — at full-strength
with a force of over 20 tonnes per m^2, the sea can move large
rocks. However, normal surf, with five breakers a minute, will
soon reduce the pebbles to shingle and the shingle to sand. A
break-point is ultimately reached when the particles become so
small that, when wet, each grain has an aqueous coat maintained by capillary action, causing them to slide across one
another. Thus the energy of the sea is eventually dissipated
upon sandy beaches with little or no physical change to the
beach sand and the islands have a beautiful shield from the fury
of the Atlantic.

The thrust of the surf up the beach has the effect of building
storm-beaches, sometimes of massive boulders like the one at
Village Bay, Hirta, but more usually with a bank of large pebbles, which in many of the Inner Hebrides lie about 10m below
the post-glacial raised beach. The backwash has the function
of shifting and sorting the pebbles into uniform bands, the
smallest being carried furthest. With sand of uniform grain-
size, the minerals of low specific gravity travel furthest. Thus in
the pale shell-sands of Tiree, the heavy dark minerals are left
behind (the same principle is involved in panning for gold) and
in the dark basalt sands of Mull, the light shelly material travels
furthest. In sunshine this dark streaming sand is like polished
lignite. Pebbles of a kilogram or more on the floor of the offshore Laminarian forest, are floated up from the sea bed by the
massive growth of weed attached to them, and cast ashore. In
time offshore banks of loose small pebbles are transported in
this way to the upper shore by storms.

Each year vast quantities of beach material are moved by surf
and tide. In summer, sand moves from the shallow offshore
shelf onto the beach only to be sucked back into the sea by
autumn and winter storms and tides. The sandy beach at Village Bay, St Kilda almost disappears in winter, and over many
years we have seen the huge oscillations of sand on Traigh Bhi
where we live on Tiree. Strong cross-currents carry material
along the beaches in one season and return them in another.
Onshore winds, with many hundreds of miles of a 'fetch' across
the ocean, pile tides high on the islands; conversely — and with

less effect—offshore winds tend to diminish the tide and swell of the ocean and take long veils of spindrift from the top of the breakers.

Each tidal pool is a microcosm with an ecology of its own—not simply a detached particle of the vast ocean. For example, the changes in temperature, salinity, oxygen and carbon dioxide content are much greater than in the open sea, and competition for space and resources between the inmates is also far greater than on the sea bed. The higher on the shore the pool is situated, the greater are the environmental changes in it between tides; exposure to sunshine and shadow affect photosynthesis; wind and shelter affect aeration of the water.

In the Hebrides the tidal pool may lie in the rounded surf-smoothed, sculpture of pink and blue-grey Lewisian gneiss; in rough, brick-red sandstone; among the broken, dark purple pillars of Tertiary basalt and slabs of pink granite; or in the splintered shelves of pale yellow limestone. The shores of Skye possess all these rocky substrates and these, combined with a 360° front to sea, make that island particularly attractive to the naturalist.

In this world of variety, the flora and fauna have adapted to meet the needs of life, each to its own niche with its own formula for survival. Almost all the invertebrate groups have found a place on the shore. There are shore fish, vast numbers

An exposed rocky shore community on Lewisian gneiss with barnacles, mussels, limpets, whelks, anemones, sea squirts, bread-crumb sponges and encrusting algae (Photo J. M. Boyd)

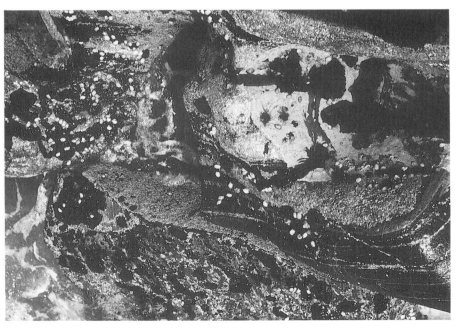

of seabirds and waders feed on the rich pickings of the tideway, and Hebridean shores also have seals and otters. The seaweeds have different sensitivities to turbulence, exposure to air and changes in salinity, and this results in a distinct banding of the shore by different communities of weed, each well settled within the strict limits of its own tolerance to surf, wind and freshwater.

Therefore, the shore is both a fine training ground for the life-scientist and a joy to the naturalist. However, apart from birds and insects, few naturalists have a knowledge of even the most common animals and plants of the shore: molluscs, crustaceans, worms, starfish and sea urchins, sponges, sea squirts, hydroids, medusae and algae, and very few organisms have popular names. Accordingly, we shall select from the assortment of shore communities in the Hebrides, those which are readily recognisable and which possess well known species.

At low tide, the rocky inlets on the east coast of Benbecula show at a glance the pronounced zonation of the seaweeds, characteristic of sheltered shores of the Hebrides. The bevelled sides of the creeks are like a garment woven in various bands of brown and yellow and the shallow, sea-filled lagoons are a mass of tangle moving to the rhythm of the gentle swell. An expression of the same in an entirely different setting is found in the sea caves of St Kilda, exposed to the full force of the Atlantic: the walls are near vertical and their surfaces resemble plasterwork in vivid bands of blue-green, emerald and pink algae above a sea made turquoise by the droppings of countless seabirds. While we attempt to describe the zonation of the shore, therefore, we must stress that no two shores are alike.

Upper Shore

The upper shore is the area above average high tide. In the Hebrides the rocky upper shores are dominated by the chan-nelled wrack *Pelvetia canaliculata*, the flat wrack *Fucus spiralis* and the barnacle *Chthamalus stellatus*. A more detailed examin-ation, however, will reveal the two small periwinkles *Melaraphe (Littorina) neritoides* and *Littorina rudis*. The former reaches well above the highest tide into the spray zone, which is also marked by the grey (*Lecanora* spp.), orange (*Ramalina* spp.) and black lichens (*Placodium* spp. and *Verrucaria maura*) in descending order. The thick top-shell (*Gibbula lineatus*), a true middle-shore snail, just reaches the upper shore. All the upper shore seaweeds (except *P. canaliculata*) and periwinkles (except *M. neritoides*) are found in the middle shore, but none of the

The mixed sandy and rocky shore typical of the shell-sand islands (in this case Tiree), with seaweed beds and rock-pools cheek-by-jowl with sand and pebble beds (Photo J. M. Boyd)

middle or lower shore species mentioned below, appear in the upper shore.

In the uppermost limits of the rocky shore there are often deposits of weed and other jetsam which harbour large populations of the sand-hoppers (amphipods) *Orchestia gammarella* and *Talitrus saltator*. The former was found in North Uist and Barra over 100m from the sea and from west to east coast in South Uist through Loch Bee. The same banks of rotting weed are habitat for swarms of the fly *Clunio marinus*, the bristle-tail *Petrobius maritimus* under pebbles and jetsam, and the seaslater *Ligia oceanica*, which is also abundant under jetsam and in rocky niches in the upper shore. These are all common to the upper sandy and muddy shore as well, and, together with the periwinkle (*M. neritoides*), are more land than sea creatures.

Where there is heavy sedimentation of the shore in sheltered tidal and estuarine flats, there are saltmarshes. These may be narrow strips of salting between shore and land, but are usually flats of closely grazed sheep pasture flooded by the sea at the highest tides. They have erosion features such as pans and creeks, and possess a salt-tolerant flora. The swards are dominated by the saltmarsh grass (*Puccinellia maritima*), thrift

(*Armeria maritima*), sea plantain (*Plantago maritima*), and red fescue grass (*Festuca rubra*). Usually grazing is too heavy to allow the full flowering of the saltmarshes in the Hebrides, but occasionally, when sheep are taken from the machair to the hill land after the lambing in June, the saltings become pink with thrift and greatly enhance the beauty of the coast. In exposed places, scurvy grass (*Cochlearia* spp.) and the sea milkwort (*Glaux maritima*) are common, and in the sheltered places the sea aster (*Aster tripolium*) and the glasswort (*Salicornia europaea*) are also common. The sea milkwort, the rush (*Juncus gerardi*), the early marsh orchid (*Dactylorhiza incarnata*) and the mare's tail (*Hippurus vulgaris*) are found on the transitions to freshwater habitats.

Though the structure and diversity of saltmarshes would appear simple compared with other habitats, on closer examination this is not so. The marshes are a mosaic of plant and animal communities, representing transitions from brackish to freshwaters, from sheltered to exposed sites, and with pioneer and long-established swards (Ratcliffe, 1977; Doody, 1986).

Scurvy-grass on Dun, St Kilda (Photo J. M. Boyd)

Hebridean saltmarshes are generally poor in species, and the frequency of the dominant species can be influenced by grazing; heavy grazing tends to increase the incidence of thrift and plantain, whereas light grazing does the same for red fescue. Nowhere is this more obvious than on the sea-sprayed grasslands of Hirta and Dun, which have saltmarshes on cliff-top slopes. On opposite sides of a sea-filled chasm, Dun, without sheep, has luxuriant fescues, while Hirta, with many sheep, has smooth slopes of thrift and sea plantain.

Saltmarsh habitats are widely distributed in both the Inner and Outer Hebrides. Loch Indaal and Loch Gruinart in Islay, Baleshare and Kirkibost in North Uist, Northton Bay and Luskentyre in Harris, Tong and Gress in Lewis being amongst the most important, but there are many others which provide breeding sites for the oystercatcher, ringed plover, lapwing, dunlin and redshank. In winter, the Hebridean saltings attract large numbers of other waders, and wildfowl.

Middle Shore

This is the area between the average high and average low tides, and on gently sloping, moderately exposed shores contains a welter of marine life. The physical surface open to the settlement of living creatures is enormous; the untold hectares of boulders and pebbles as well as the solid bedrock, the capillary surfaces of sands and muds which hold the microscopic interstitial flora and fauna. Also the external surfaces of the animals and plants themselves provide suitable settlement for many smaller creatures and their internal lumen, acting as a home for diverse, highly specialised parasites.

With such a great choice of surfaces and conditions, competition for living-space might logically be light; yet the exact opposite is the case. Each niche is colonised only by those creatures which have become perfectly adapted to maintain themselves within the specialised conditions of the niche to which they are fitted. Life in rock pools, under stones, on and under weed, on firm or loose rock, in sand and mud, and on the backs of animals is a continuous fight for living space. The entire middle shore is clad with life; the only space for new life is in place of the dead and departed.

Species of the upper shore, mentioned above, extend into the middle shore but are not dominant. Channel and flat wracks are replaced by the bladder wrack (*Fucus vesiculosus*) and the saw wrack (*F. serratus*); the former is recognisable by its 'blistered' and the latter by its 'toothed' fronds, often bearing the small white tubes of the worm *Spirorbis*. The bladder wrack

Beds of wrack showing the main species of Fucus *and* Ascophyllum *typical of the middle shore on sheltered rocky shores (Photo J. M. Boyd)*

floats upward and is spread on the sea's surface, whereas the saw wrack is short and is totally immersed; both have great flexibility and inhabit the exposed rocky coast or areas of strong tidal current, in which the more delicate knotted wrack (*Ascophyllum nodosum*) cannot thrive (Norton, 1986). The latter grows vigorously off sheltered shore, occupies great areas of the middle shore and forms a dense olive-green mat which is floated upwards in the rising tide by its large bladders. It is these extensive areas of dense wrack which have been the harvest fields for alginates. The saw wrack is more sensitive to desiccation than the others and reaches well into the lower shore (Schonbeck and Norton, 1978). Another species *Fucus ceranoides* which grows in brackish water along the rocky and shingle margins of estuaries is often in company with a specialised form of the knotted wrack (*A.n.f. mackaii*) and fresh green *Enteromorpha* spp. Other seaweeds are very sensitive to changes in salinity.

Branched threads (*Cladophora* and *Bryopsis* spp.) grow in dark green tufts underneath the mats of knotted wrack, the appearance of which is often greatly changed by luxuriant festoons of the deep red filamentous alga *Polysiphonia lanosa*. The emerald green sea-lettuce (*Ulva lactuca*) brightens the middle and lower shore, provides food for herbivorous molluscs, is a photosynthesiser of tidal pools and an inhabitant of estuaries. The Hebrides are a meeting ground for northern and southern species of algae. For example the subarctic *Fucus distichus* is found at its southern limit in Lewis and St Kilda; the distinctive southern species *Cystoeeira tamariscifolia* reaches Barra.

There is a fine array of molluscs each beautifully adapted for life on the middle shore. The design of the common limpet (*Patella vulgata*) with its flat, obtuse, conical shell, its massive foot which almost subtends the entire body; its radula or tongue resembling a microscopic band-saw with which it rasps microalgae and tiny sporelings of seaweed from the rock surface, is suited for survival on smooth, exposed rocks. Somewhat different in design and accordingly in distribution are the flat periwinkles (*Littorina littoralis* and *L. mariae*) and the edible periwinkle (*L. littorea*). The former are confined largely to the zone of bladder and knotted wracks upon which the snail feeds. *L. littoralis* is dominant among *Ascophyllum* and *L. mariae* among *F. serratus*. The latter is the most widespread of all the periwinkles on Hebridean shores, ranging from high-water neaps to low-water springs. Living on bare rock surfaces, often in company with limpets and mussels (*Mytilus edulis*) and feeding on algae, it is the only periwinkle to be found below low-water of spring tides.

Zonation of the shore is perhaps more firmly defined by the sessile rather than the mobile animals, particularly the two species of barnacle *Semibalanus balanoides* and *Chthamalus stellatus*. The settlement of these on the shore follows a free-swimming larval life in the sea. They are members of different faunas which meet on the west coasts of Britain; *Semibalanus* is a northern species the spat of which settles on the shore in early summer while the latter settles in autumn and winter; *Semibalanus* occupies the middle and lower shore while *Chthamalus* is on the middle and upper shore. There is an area of overlap but, in the Hebrides, the barnacles on the low shore are likely to be the former and on the high shore, the latter. *Chthamalus* withstands exposure to surf better than *Semibalanus*—on the most sheltered shores it appears in a narrow band about mean high water neaps, always above *Semibalanus*. On exposed faces at St Kilda, *Chthamalus*, of which there may be two species, *stellatus* and *montagui* (Southward, 1976), occurs in the full range of tide and spray zone. *Balanus crenatus*, on the other hand, is sensitive to exposure to air, and is restricted to the lower shore on stones, shells and flotsam. An example of the distribution of barnacles and seaweeds on Goat Island, Jura (Fig. 14) indicates clearly the different sensitivities to wave exposure possessed by the

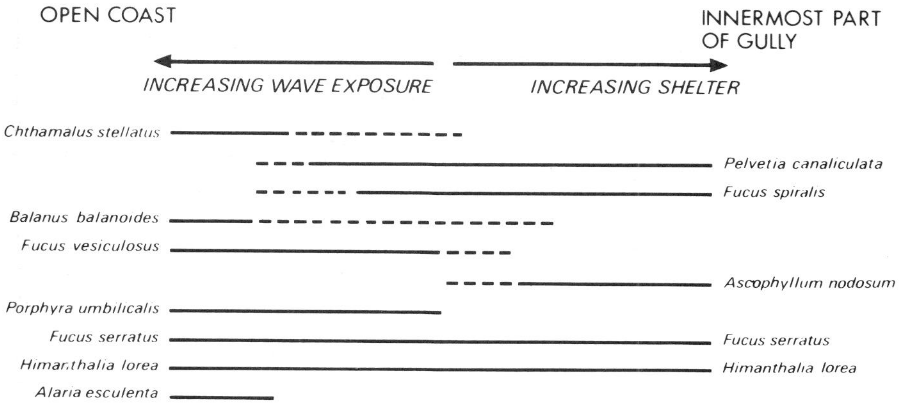

OPEN COAST   INNERMOST PART
                                                                     OF GULLY

INCREASING WAVE EXPOSURE   *INCREASING SHELTER*

Chthamalus stellatus ——————— – – – – – – – – – –

                          – – – —————————————————— Pelvetia canaliculata
                          – – – – – ———————————————— Fucus spiralis

Balanus balanoides ————— – – – – – – – – – – – – – – – –
Fucus vesiculosus ——————————————————— – – – –

                              – – – – ——————————————— Ascophyllum nodosum
Porphyra umbilicalis ————————————————————
Fucus serratus ——————————————————————————— Fucus serratus
Himanthalia lorea ——————————————————————————— Himanthalia lorea
Alaria esculenta —————————

barnacles and seaweeds which give the Hebridean shores their conspicuous zonation.

The top-shells (*Gibbula cineraria* and *G. umbilicalis*) abound on the middle and lower shore, the latter mainly below low-water neaps. A southern species (*G. magus*) was found on the shore at and west of Kyleakin. The painted top-shell (*Callios-toma zizyphinum*) with its red, ribbed and mottled cone, is a common yet always admirable find. The dogwhelk (*Nucella lapillus*) is usually off-white, but possesses a wonderful range of colours and is occasionally vividly striped. It feeds on barnacles and occurs in large numbers usually with mussels and peri-winkles with which it does not compete for food. Whelks gather in the crevices of barnacle-covered, surf-swept rocks, where they lay clusters of up-ended white egg capsules.

Turning to the sandy and muddy shores, we have an entirely different habitat to the rocky shore. Instead of possessing an ability to hold tight against being swept away and battered in the surf and to sustain considerable changes in temperature, aeration, sunlight and salinity, the fauna (there is little flora) escapes by burrowing to depths of 20cms or more where the habitat is in a fairly steady state between tides. The most exposed beaches of the Hebrides are nonetheless very austere, holding sparse communities of a few highly adapted crustacea, mollusca and worms. For example, at west-facing Traigh na Cleavag at Northton, Harris, using a method of coring to a depth of 10cms, Angus (1979) found only 'a few lugworms (*Are-nicola marina*) well below sampling depth and a few sand-hoppers (*Talitrus saltator*)'. However, where the strand is more sheltered on the other side of the isthmus at Scarasta, he found seven species, and where it is yet more sheltered at Seilebost and Luskentyre, at least twenty. The exposed beaches usually

Fig. 14
Distribution of species of animals and plants with relation to varying degrees of wave exposure in Jura (after Kitching, Trans. Roy. Soc. Edinb., LVIII, 368)

hold small numbers of amphipods (*Bathyporeia* sp., *Pontocrates norvegicus* and *T. saltator*), the isopod (*Eurydice pulchra*), a few worms (*Nephthys* sp. and *Nerine cirratulus*) and sand-eels—no molluscs. Moderately exposed beaches (eg Traigh na Berie, Lewis) have as dominants these worms and bivalves (*Tellina tenuis* and *Donax vittatus*). The sheltered beaches (eg Traigh Mhor, Barra) have the bivalves (*Cerastoderma edule* and *Macoma balthica*), the worms (*A. marina* and *Nereis diversicolor*), the urchin (*Echinocardium cordatum*) and on more muddy and brackish shores, the sandhopper (*Corophium volutator*), shrimp (*Crangon vulgaris*), the snail (*Hydrobia ulvae*) and the crab (*Carcinus maenas*).

Life in sheltered sandy mud and fine mud requires some-what different adaptations to those that must be made in sand. Apart from withstanding the changes in salinity in estuarine sediments, the fauna have the problems of feeding and re-spiring in a clogged environment. The cockle and tellins which are abundant in the clean sand are scarce in muddy sand and absent from mud. The thin tellin (*T. tenuis*) is sand-dwelling, while the Baltic tellin (*M. baltica*) thrives in muddy sand.

However, the fine mud has a dense but simple community of the mud-feeding bivalve (*Scrobicularia plana*), the tiny snail (*H. ulva*), the burrow-dwelling amphipod (*C. volutator*) and the rag-worm (*N. diversicolor*), all of which feed on organic detri-tus. The muddy shore is a comparatively rare environment in the Hebrides, occurring in or near the sheltered estuaries of slow-flowing streams from cultivated land, such as at Bridgend and Gruinart in Islay, at Laxadale in Lewis, or in that ramifying system of tidal embayments and channels north of Lochmaddy, North Uist. In the latter, Edith Nicol found that the salinity varied from 30 to three parts per thousand, and the pH, 5.4–7.8–9.9, from the sea to the brackish-waters respectively. In this range there were 59 marine, 25 brackish, 24 freshwater and five euryhaline species, like sea trout which are at home in both sea and freshwaters.

Eel grass (*Zostera* spp.), the only truly marine, flowering plant, and *Enteromorpha* spp. form green mats on the expanses of mud and sand. The eel grass was greatly reduced by disease in the first half of this century but has since recovered and now abounds in favourable habitats such as the Vallay Strand in North Uist and Loch Gruinart in Islay. *Z. angustifolia* occurs on estuary mud in the middle and lower shore and merges with *Z. marina* which is below low watermark but reaches onto the lower shore. These greens are pasture of the fauna of the sandy-mud, of wigeon (*Anas penelope*) and brent geese (*Branta bernicla*) and form eye-catching, flowing shapes upon the spa-cious tidal flats.

Lower Shore

Below mean low tide, most of the inhabitants of the middle and upper shore have either disappeared or are greatly reduced in numbers. Among the seaweeds *F. serratus* still persists and is accompanied by dulse (*Rhodymenia palmata*), *Laurencia* spp., *Gigartina stellata*, carragheen (*Chondrus crispus*), tangle (*Laminaria digitata*) and thong-weed (*Himanthalia elongata*). These can sustain heavy wave action, but in the most exposed faces *Alaria esculenta* is dominant. Bootlace (*Chorda filum*) is almost always attached to shells and pebbles and is easily washed ashore. Limpets, barnacles, periwinkles and top-shells of the middle shore reach well into the lower rocky shore, and are joined by the grey top-shell *G. cineraria* and cowries (*Trivia arctica* and *T. monacha*). The large dog-whelk *Buccinum undatum*, whose empty shells and chitinous egg-shell clusters are common on the shore, lives in the sub-littoral and ventures on to the lower shore when young at spring tides. Similarly, the common lobster (*Homarus vulgaris*) and the squat lobsters (*Galathea* sp.) inhabit the flooded cavities under rocks on the lower shore and present a fierce front to the intruder.

In a survey of polychaete worms, J.D. George (1979) recorded 107 species above and below low-tide; 20 confined

The shore at the estuary of the Ord River, Skye, showing the local brackish-water habitats at the river mouth and the marine seaweed beds beyond (Photo J. M. Boyd)

to the littoral zone; 59 confined to the sub-littoral and 28 occupying both zones. Syllidae were dominant with 17 species, notably *Typosyllis armillaris* and *Eusyllis lamelligera* in the holdfasts of laminarians, and *Brania pusilla* in *Corallina*; 12 were Serpulidae, notably *Pomatoceros triqueter* on stones, *Laeospira borealis* on seaweeds and *L. rupestris* amongst *Lithothamnion* and *Corallina*; 11 were Spionidae, notably *Polydora caeca* on *Corallina* and *Pecten* shells; and eight were Sabellidae, notably *Potamilla torelli* in *Corallina* and holdfasts.

The silted, lower shores also have high densities of bivalves, the occurrence of which relates to the salinity and the proportions of sand and mud. The razor-shells *Ensis* sp., the venuses (*Venus* sp.), the wedge-shell (*Donax vittatus*) and the thin tellin, inhabit clean sand, while the gapers (*Mya* sp.) and the Baltic tellin are in sandy-mud.

Distributed in the shore habitats there are many species of fish adapted to the changeable conditions of the rocky, weedy recesses and the shifting sands of shore and estuary. The tidal pool is a study of still life until, moved by shadow, small fish dart hither and thither between hidey-holes in rock and weed. These are likely to be one of the following:

English	Scientific	Gaelic
black goby	*Gobius niger*	—
spotted goby	*G. ruthensparri*	—
common goby	*G. minutus*	buidhleis
butterfish	*Centronotus gunnellus*	clomhag-chaothaich
3-spined stickleback	*Gasterosteus aculeatus*	biorag-lodain

The last fish has a wide range of salt tolerance and is as happy in a tidal pool as in a freshwater stream. At Loch Bee, which spans South Uist from the sand-silted Atlantic shore to the rocky shores of the Little Minch, the three-spined stickleback is found throughout the salinity range while the ten-spined (*Pungitius pungitius*) and the fifteen-spined sticklebacks (*Spinachia vulgaris*) have a more restricted distribution. Flounder (*Platichthys flesus*), sand smelt (*Atherina presbyter*), eel (*Anguilla anguilla*) (easgann), common goby, trout and pollack also occurred. In the large tidal pools of the lower shore and in the rocky sub-littoral, colourful ballan wrasse (*Labrus bergylta*), lumpsuckers (*Cyclopterus lumpus*) and sinister congers are seldom seen except when landed by a foraging otter or heron. Sheets of tidal water on sandy flats contain the young of sand-eel, plaice, dab and flounder.

Shore Birds and Otters

If the detailed biology of the sea-shore is enjoyed only by a few naturalists, the birds of the shore are a delight to all ornithologists. For to them, the Hebrides, positioned on the edge of Europe and facing the great ocean, has the best of both worlds. Many visitors from central Europe, who live far from the sea, are astonished at the variety and numerical scale of the avifauna of the Scottish coasts. All species are to some extent connected with the sea-shore; some, like the oystercatcher (*Haematopus ostralegus*), ringed plover (*Charadrius hiaticula*), herring gull (*Larus argentatus*) and common gull (*L. canus*), feed, roost and breed on the shore; others, like the cliff-nesting oceanic species, have little contact with the shore *per se* but have a manurial effect on the cliff-base. Between these two extremes there are other species which occupy the shore at some time in their annual life-cycle. In the Hebrides, there are some 37 species which nest on the shore above mean high spring-tide within the spray-zone, and some 82 species which regularly occupy Hebridean shores at some time of the year.

In summer the sound of the breakers is mixed with the piercing calls of oystercatchers, the piping of ringed plovers, the screech of Arctic terns (*Sterna macrura*) (and more rarely of little terns (*S. albifrons*)), and the cries of gulls, all anxious for the safety of eggs or young among pebbles, small jetsam and cushions of thrift. To find the nests with their dappled eggs matching perfectly their stony cup is always a thrill, and to spot the fluffy hatchlings crouching in a shady nook, pretending to be just another pebble, is sheer delight. The tiny, sharp, '*tseep-tseep*' of the rock pipit (*Anthus spinoletta*) and the shrill but delicate '*tschizzik*' of the pied wagtail (*Motacilla alba*) contrast with the harangue of oystercatchers, as they flit back and forth from shore to nesting-sites in the rocks above, often raising two broods under an overhang of thrift or marram grass. Eider ducks (*Somateria mollissima*), red-breasted mergansers (*Mergus serrator*), shelduck (*Tadorna tadorna*) and mallard (*Anas platyrhynchos*) with ducklings, dive and dabble in sheltered weedy inlets. Dunlin (*Calidris alpina*) and redshank (*Tringa totanus*) breed inland and feed on the shore at low tide; in the Uists there are an average of 15 pairs per km^2 of both species on wet machair with over 40 pairs in the densest areas. Small numbers of turnstones (*Arenaria interpres*) and sanderling (*Calidris alba*) which breed in the high arctic, spend the summer on Hebridean shores. Herons (*Ardea cinerea*) nest mostly in trees and occasionally on the ground, but feed on the intertidal, stalking prey in the shallow weedy inlets of the sheltered shores of all the islands.

The shores, particularly of the Uists, attract large numbers of migrant and wintering wildfowl: shelduck, wigeon (*Anas penelope*), teal (*A. crecca*), mallard, pintail (*A. acuta*), shoveler (*A. clypeata*), tufted duck (*Aythya fuligula*), scaup (*A. marila*)— especially in Islay—eider, red-breasted merganser and waders: the oystercatcher, ringed plover, golden plover (*Pluvialis apricaria*), lapwing (*Vanellus vanellus*), sanderling, purple sandpiper (*Calidris maritima*), dunlin, bar-tailed godwit (*Limosa lapponica*), curlew (*Numenius arquata*), redshank, turnstone, and greenshank (*Tringa nebularia*).

To these can be added many rarer species which make the shores of the Hebrides an enchanting place in the bright sharp winter days. Unfortunately the richest areas are shot-over by wildfowlers and the birds take flight at the slightest disturbance except, that is, for the purple sandpipers, which we have had walking between our feet.

The sight of an otter (*Lutra lutra*) on the shore is always exciting; their sleek glistening bodies and elegance of movement in and out of the sea epitomise the beauty of wildlife and the spirit of wilderness. On Hebridean shores the signs of otters are common, and they are often seen. Now fully protected, they are, as Gavin Maxwell described in *Ring of Bright Water*, very confident in their undisturbed habitat on the sea shore, diving and foraging among the weed and often surfacing with and landing a lumpsucker, wrasse, pollack, butterfish or scorpion fish (*Myoxocephalus scorpius*). They are often drowned in eel fyke nets and lobster creels, entering the creels, it is thought, to take pollack, codling and congers which are already trapped. In eighteen months during 1975–76, Jane Twelves recorded the deaths of 20 otters (17 females and three males) in eel fyke nets in South Uist and Benbecula. The damage to local stocks must have been great—one netsman accounted for 13 out of the 20! In 1984, after an eight-year cessation, eel-netting recommenced in the Uists, hopefully with safeguards to the legally-protected otter.

The otter has declined in numbers during the last 30 years in England and lowland Scotland, but it is still numerous in the Highlands and Islands and particularly so in the Hebrides and Shetland. In the 1977–79 survey of otters in Scotland, the highest numbers were recorded from Islay, Colonsay and Oronsay; the largest holts which we have seen were on Eilein Ghaoideamal off Oronsay, Am Fraoch Eilean in the Sound of Islay and at Kylerhea in Skye, where the Forestry Commission has built a hide from which the otters can regularly be seen. The survey showed that the otter is mainly a marine species in the Hebrides, though its spraint and runs are widespread throughout the islands. In the Outer Hebrides 227 sites were

examined and 221 (97%) showed signs of otters. During the
survey, 20 otters were seen by chance in daylight and only two
of these were inland; 18 were in the marine habitat and 12 were
seen in the Hebrides. The east coast of the Outer Hebrides—
uninhabited, sheltered, indented, rocky and weedy—is ideal
otter habitat which is now attractive to fish-farmers. A code of
practice is required for the management of fish-farms and
otters and other protected species of wildlife, and this is now in
hand (see p. 78, H-AML). The fishing otter is often
accompanied at a safe distance by a herring gull keen to
take scraps of food, and in Norway the presence of otters
is often shown by a hovering sea-eagle, ready to swoop
and dispose of any fish the otter might land. The same
may now happen in the Hebrides with the recently
reintroduced sea-eagles (see pp. 287–90).

Of all the habitats possessed by the Hebrides, the sea-shore
is by far the richest in life and the most interesting to the
naturalist. It is also an inspiration to artist and poet alike, and an
unending source of wonder to both old and young. To us the
pellucid 'crab' pools in the surf-polished gneiss in front of our
house are tiny cells, brimming over with life and cupped in the
oldest rock in the world but to children, they are sheer magic!

6 Sand Dunes and Machair

Windblown Sands

In the Hebrides, there are sands of pure quartz such as the Singing Sands of Camus Sgiotaig on Eigg, coral sands at Claigan near Dunvegan on Skye, basalt sands at Carsaig in Mull, heterogeneous mineral sands in many islands, but most of all, there are shell sands formed from the ground-up remains of marine invertebrates and algae. Large geographical structures owe their existence to these sands of organic origin; the large sweeping beaches of the Outer Hebrides, backed by high, extensive systems of dunes and slacks which lead inland to a smooth, flat sea-meadow or machair. The Hebridean machair has no exact equivalent anywhere else. It is similar to links but is richer in calcium carbonate—about 20% on links compared with 80% on machair. This has a concomitant effect on the flora and fauna it supports and, if anything, makes it a richer habitat.

Dry sand begins to move when the wind is travelling at about 16km/10mph or more. Dry, windy weather moves sand on beaches and 'mobile' dunes, while on-shore winds move it inland to become locked up in the terrestrial system. Off-shore winds return the sand to the sea only to be recycled to the beach by tide and wave-action. In the wet, windy weather most prevalent in the Hebrides, rain wets the sand and the hydrogen bonding of water in the thin, wet crust binds the grains and prevents sand-blow.

Behind the beach the land is upswept, usually to an undulating vegetated landscape but, in sheltered places on lee shores, it gives way to a relatively level, green platform. The frontage of slope and scarp varies greatly between and within systems according to their rocky settings, angle to the prevailing winds, and history of coastal and sea level changes. Islands like Oronsay, Tiree, the Monach Isles and Vallay which are encircled by sand have sandy landscapes of great variety. The storm coasts have ramparts of sand raised 10m with extensive, upwind systems of dunes, while those on lee shores have scarpes of 2m with little or no formation of dunes. The contrasts of windward and leeward shores are succinctly seen in

the sandy isthmuses of Eoligarry and Vatersay, Barra and Vaul, Tiree, and Toe Head, Harris. The Eoligarry is a particularly important site to which we will return.

In Chapter 5 we explained the transformation of the Hebrides by blown sand on a front from Luskentyre, Harris to Laggan, Islay with a major lee coast system at Broad Bay, Lewis associated with the local formations of New Red Sandstone. Every system is different, but all are created by the same set of physical and biological forces and man's use of the land. The sand forms a platform, often on top of raised beaches, fluvio-glacial deposits or glacial till, and stretches landward until it strikes bare country rock or blanket peat. In the Uists and Benbecula, the sandy platform sometimes lies upon peat; at Borve in Benbecula, the peat is found below low-water mark. It was apparently placed at that level by a rise in sea level some 5,800 years ago, due to the melting of the ice-sheet.

To understand the dune landscape, the mind's eye traverses the millenia since the islands were rid of the ice, and sees a

The Luskentrye Banks, Harris, possibly the highest shore dunes in the Hebrides (Photo J. M. Boyd)

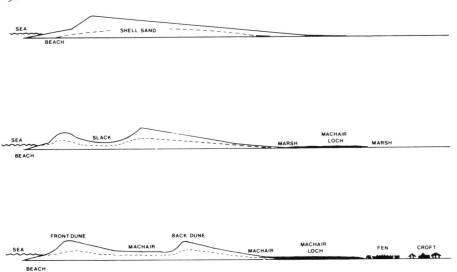

Fig. 15
Three stages in the development of the dune-machair system of the Hebrides showing the accretion of sand and the shaping of the present-day landform. (simplified from Ritchie, 1979)

build-up of high ridges of thinly-vegetated sand above the shore. These ridges were roughly shaped by the wind into wedges of sand possessing a steep seaward scarp, a crest and a long landward slope. However, the simultaneous processes of sand movement, plant colonisation and human settlement have caused large-scale changes in the wedge-shaped profile. The up-sweep of the wind on the scarp above the shore causes not only the build-up of shore sand, but turbulence also serves to disrupt the dune ridge, to form an array of crests and long hollows or slacks. By erosion and deposition, the slack becomes progressively wider and on the landward side, it is bounded by the 'reretreating' scarp of the wedge. This is clad with a gently-sloping grassland on sandy loams stretching inland to fen, cultivation, peatland or bare rock. (This physiographical system has been studied in detail by William Ritchie and colleagues from whose work Fig. 15 has been adapted.)

The dunes and machair are open habitats, spread out for all to see, masked neither by water nor by scrub wood or tall herbs, due to grazing and exposure. There are three main zones; upper beach, dune and machair. If the upper beach has no sand, there are no dunes or machair. However, though most sandy beaches do have associated dunes and machair, Mather and Ritchie (1977) found that almost 22% of the beaches had machair but no dunes. In full development (which is usually achieved only in part at any one site) there is the following zonation from sea to island's core: foredune, mobile dune, fixed dune, machair, old hay-meadow, fen and loch, cultivation and heath. These zones are characterised by their landform, vegetation and fauna.

There are sharp contrasts. The dunes and machair are free-draining and though subject to drought, locally the land is flooded seasonally by the rising water table in deep slacks or by loch margins, and this is faithfully reflected in the flora and fauna. Other contrasts occur between the vegetation of calcareous loams of the machair and the acid, peaty gleys of the heathland known in the Outer Hebrides as 'blackland'. There are also contrasts between tilled and untilled machair and between different stages of natural recolonisation of ploughed ground. Striking contrasts are obtained by leaching of nutrients from the dune humps into the hollows where there is also enrichment by moisture, shelter and the manure of grazing stocks. More subtle effects are caused by induced deficiencies, where the uptake of essential elements by the plants is prevented by the high alkalinity of the soil.

Upper Beach and Foredunes

This is a dry, salty, sand-blasted, habitat between the high spring tide and the front of the main dune. Colin Welch and others have studied the shore beetles living in the rotting, weedy, jetsam of the upper shore at 24 sites in the Outer Hebrides. Twenty-two species were collected from six families of which 16 were Staphylinidae. The hydrophilid *Cercyon littoralis* was taken at 21 sites, and other dominants were the seaweed-frequenting staphylinids *Omalium riparium*, *Atheta vestita* and *Anotylus maritimus* and the weevil *Philopedon plagiatus*, which probably feeds on the roots of marram grass. Fifteen species were taken at Luskentyre, Harris and on the Monach Islands. The wrack-fly *Orygma luctuosa* and the shore-beetles *Cercyon littoralis* and *Micralymma marina* occur on both sides of the Atlantic.

The upper shore rings with the calls of breeding oyster-catchers and ringed plovers. In summer their eggs and young are camouflaged among the sandy shingle, while the parents draw the attention of the intruder with the 'broken wing' display. Arctic and little terns also nest there and greet the visitor with a sudden dive, bill-stab and high whistling *kee, keee-yahor kirri-kikki*. Gulls, hooded crows, starlings, rock-pipits and pied wagtails which nest in neighbouring habitats feed on the rich insect pickings of the upper shore and in the winter there are, amongst other migrants, turnstones, dunlins, sanderlings and curlews, which move in with the floodtide.

The saltmarshes occur in the transition between marine and

freshwater habitats and are often associated with the sand dune-machair landscape, for example, at Luskentyre and Northton, Harris, the Vallay Strand and Baleshare, North Uist, and Iochdar, South Uist. However, saltings are usually just within the reach of the highest spring tides (see Chapter 5).

Well separated clumps of marram grass, *Ammophila arenaria*, trap the beach sand and form isolated shaggy-topped sandhills on the backshore. No other plant can keep company with it in this exposed position. The rhizomes grow both horizontally and vertically to collect moisture from both rain and deep groundwater, and this network of roots also holds the sand fast. Marram thrives in mobile sand with each inundation forcing upward growth and positioning the roots at greater depth of sand with improved moisture. The lyme-grass *Leymus arenarius* is an east and north coast species which is relatively uncommon in the Hebrides, but where it does occur, it reinforces the marram in the mobile dunes. There is no obvious reason for its low incidence in the west, though it is more sensitive to wind-exposure and sand-blast than marram.

A foredune with marram grass at Scarasta, Harris (Photo J. M. Boyd)

In areas where the amounts of blowing sand are moderate to light and which are very occasionally reached by the sea, the flat sand at the foot of the main dune holds a community of sand couch-grass (*Elymus farctus*) and the succulents sea sandwort

(*Honkenya peploides*) and sea rocket (*Cakile maritima*). Orache (*Atriplex* spp.) flourish where the beach pebbles have been blown clear of sand. In one such site in Benbecula we have seen the oysterplant (*Mertensia maritima*) with its spreads of blue-green fleshy leaves and deep blue flowers.

Dunes

The rampart of dunes facing the sea is usually mobile and the scarp face may be rutted by cattle and sheep with slips and slumpings of marram turf. These are the 'yellow' dunes in which the marram grass rises from freshly deposited sand, and nurses a thin plant community including red fescue (*Festuca rubra*), ribwort plantain (*Plantago lanceolata*), lady's bedstraw (*Galium verum*), bird's-foot trefoil (*Lotus corniculatus*) and wild white clover (*Trifolium repens*). Landward of the 'yellow' dune there is the 'grey' dune in which the density of the herb community has increased. The marram, somewhat thinner, rises from immobile sand masked by vegetation in which the sand sedge (*Carex arenaria*), common ragwort (*Senecio jacobaea*) and the moss *Rhytidiadelphus squarrosus* are added (Fig. 16).

The habitat is sufficiently clement for the snails *Helicella itala* and *Cochlicella acuta*, which are found throughout the machair, with the dune snail *Cepaea hortensis*. The 'grey' dune also has a thin community of soil invertebrates, some of which become concentrated in cow-pats which, when wet and fresh, are favourable niches for insect larvae, mostly flies and beetles, and the pioneering earthworms *Lumbricus rubellus* and *Bimastus tenuis*. When dry, red ants *Myrmica rubra* and *M. scabrinodis* are found in the dung. In the dune slacks the damper, more sheltered, and humid conditions support a green sward. These are oases in the austere duneland, often having a richness equal to or surpassing the machair. The slacks attract livestock for shelter, rest and pasture, and are often heavily manured. There is a sense of peace and prosperity in these sheltered hollows, bright with flowers and possessing thriving communities of insects, myriapods (the millipede *Cylindroiulus latestriatus*), snails, slugs (*Arion ater* and *Agriolimax* spp.) and earthworms (such as the *Lambricoides* spp.).

Rabbits (*Oryctolagus cuniculus*) have been introduced to most islands and they thrive in the easily dug, well-drained soils of the dunes. The juxtaposition of excellent burrowing habitat and the rich feeding grounds of the slacks is ideal, providing a short dash for safety from feeding areas when the silhouette of the buzzard (*Buteo buteo*) appears overhead. Rabbits probably have a significant effect on the development of the dunes

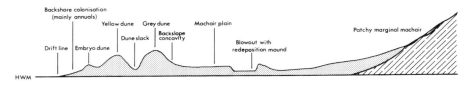

Fig. 16
A transect across dune and machair from the sea's edge to the rock base of the island, showing the range of features described in the text (From Mather and Ritchie, 1977)

because they increase erosion, and they crop the vegetation close to the ground. It is also probable that they affect agriculture. In the Uists and Benbecula it is usual for sheep to be grazed on the dunes and machair whereas on Tiree, where there are no rabbits, cattle are also grazed on the machair, presumably because the lack of rabbits allows the kind of pasture growth more suited to cattle.

These more or less isolated assemblies of plants and animals in a relatively simple ecological setting have attracted biologists in the past. They possess finite resources, can become genetically separated for long periods, and endure different selective pressures resulting in varying frequencies of different morphs of the same species, as happens with the snails *H. itala* and *C. hortensis*. The ecology of each can be subtly different according to such factors as their differential tolerance to seasonal drought or flooding, and parasitism.

Though the dunes are a distinct landscape and ecological zone, they are a patchwork of biological communities some of which have the character of a desert, others of a fruitful land. In the transect of the dunes and the machair, the zonation of vegetation and fauna is as distinct as on the sea shore; the marine influence disappears when, one by one, the salt-tolerant, sandy species vanish from the sward. Landward of the 'grey' dune, there is the backslope (Fig. 16) which may be the clean sweep to a flat grassy plain or a tumult of hillocks, some still topped with wispy marram, which fade into the undulations of the machair plain. On the backslope the characteristic dune community changes to that of the machair, and marram and sand sedge disappear from the sward.

Dry Machair

Beyond the major divisions of upper shore, dunes and machair, there are many minor subdivisions which defeat description here. While marram is dominant in the dunes, it is not on the machair, yet the lady's bedstraw, ribwort plantain, bird's-foot trefoil and white clover are found throughout the entire system. It is therefore only after highly detailed study that the variability of the dune-machair system can be described. However, out of the list of flowering plants (Tables 6.1 and 6.2), there are some species which are constant in all machair systems. In addition to the four species mentioned above these are red fescue, yarrow (*Achillea millefolium*), creeping thistle (*Cirsium arvense*), buttercup (*Ranunculus acris/bulbosus*), eyebright (*Euphrasia* spp.), daisy (*Bellis perennis*) and the moss *Rhytidiadelphus squarrosus*. The dune slacks, which are flooded seasonally, have glaucous sedge (*Carex flacca*), silverweed (*Potentilla anserina*), creeping willow (*Salix repens*), marsh pennywort (*Hydrocotyle vulgaris*) and meadow grass (*Poa pratense*). The machair in June is a floristic idyll. Sunlit, fresh green meadows set by the blue sea are washed with the yellow of buttercup and trefoil and white snowdrifts of daisies and clover. In hay meadows and other ungrazed places there are waving stands of white gowans (*Chrysanthemum leucanthemum*), self-heal (*Prunella vulgaris*), yellow rattle (*Rhinanthus minor*), kidney vetch (*Anthyllis vulneraria*) and red clover (*Trifolium pratense*) among the grasses. The purple milk-vetch (*Astragalus danicus*), normally an east coast species, is found in Tiree hay meadows.

If machair is left ungrazed for a period of years, as it often is in burial grounds and airfields, the red fescue grows deep and rank, and eliminates nearly all other species, though ragwort (*Senecio jacobaea*) and knapweed (*Centaurea nigra*) survive in tall, isolated stalks. Such places demonstrate the importance of grazing in maintaining the diversity of the machair flora, though overgrazing often spoils the beguiling scene. Limited cultivation as happens on the Uists could, on the other hand, provide a valuable seed bed for dune annuals.

The machair flora varies from island to island and from place to place in the same island. Machair plant lists can be found in: Macleod (1948) in Barra; Vose *et al* (1957) in Tiree and Randall (1976) in the Monach Isles. Table 6.1 gives a list of the main species which constitute the floral spectacle and the botanical interest for which the machair is famous.

Table 6.2 gives a summary of the dominant species of plants in the dune-machair habitats in the Uists by Dickinson and Randall (1979). The Nature Conservancy Council (1986) has published details of 39 botanical sites in the Outer Hebrides, which show the rarer species and exemplary machair communities. For example, the one on the small island of Fuday, Barra is especially rich in orchids with uncommon species such as the small white (*Pseudorchis albida*), and at Uig Sands, Lewis the frog orchid (*Coeloglossum viride*) is found. The moss campion (*Silene acaulis*) is also found at Mangersta Sands.

The floristic richness of the machair, however, depends on the flowering opportunities of the pastures in the face of grazing and cultivation. Most plants which are palatable to sheep

Species	Habitats			
	d	dm	wm	fm
Marram grass *Ammophila arenaria*	*	*		
Sand couch-grass *Elymus farctus*	*			
Frosted orache *Atriplex laciniata*	*			
Sea rocket *Cakile maritima*	*			
Curled dock *Rumex crispus*	*			
Silverweed *Potentilla anserina*	*		*	
Daisy *Bellis perennis*	*	*		
Sea sandwort *Honkenya peploides*	*			
Ribwort plantain *Plantago lanceolata*	*	*		
Sea plantain *P.maritima*	*			
Wild white clover *Trifolium repens*	*	*	*	
Red clover *T. pratense*		*		
Lady's bedstraw *Galium verum*	*	*		
Red fescue *Festuca rubra*	*	*	*	
Sea kale *Crambe maritima*	*			
Wallpepper *Sedum acre*	*			
Oyster plant *Mertensia maritima*	*			
Moss *Rhytidiadelphus squarrosus*	*	*		
Liverwort *Peltigera canina*	*	*		
Moss *Hylocomium splendens*		*		
Moss *Thuidium delicatulum*		*		
Moss *Pseudoscleropodium purum*		*		
Moss *Hypnum* spp.		*		
Hogweed *Heracleum sphondylium*		*		
Meadow buttercup *Ranunculus acris*		*		
Bulbous buttercup *R.bulbosus*		*		
Lesser spearwort *R. flammula*			*	
Lesser celandine *R. ficaria*			*	
Wild carrot *Daucus carota*		*		
Lesser meadow rue *Thalictrum minus*		*		
Kidney vetch *Anthyllis vulneraria*		*	*	
Lesser burdock *Arctium minus*		*		
Ragwort *Senecio jacobaea*		*		
Yarrow *Achillea millefolium*		*		
Yellow rattle *Rhinanthus minor*		*	*	
Eyebright *Euphrasia* spp.		*		
Field gentian *Gentianella campestris*		*		
Purging flax *Linum catharticum*		*		
Milkwort *Polygala vulgaris*		*		
Primrose *Primula vulgaris*		*		
Harebell *Campanula rotundifolia*		*		
Frog orchid *Coeloglossum viride*		*		
Creeping bent grass *Agrostis stolonifera*		*		
Crested dog's tail *Cynosurus cristatus*		*		
Sand sedge *Carex arenaria*		*		
Carnation-grass *Carex panicea*		*	*	
Ragged robin *Lychnis flos-cuculi*			*	

Species	Habitats			
	d	dm	wm	fm
Cuckoo flower *Cardamine pratensis*		*		
Pennywort *Hydrocotyle vulgaris*		*		*
Vetches *Vicia* spp.		*		
Violets & pansies *Viola* spp.		*		
Self-heal *Prunella vulgaris*		*		
Marsh bedstraw *Galium palustre*		*		
Creeping willow *Salix repens*		*		
Marsh cinquefoil *Potentilla palustris*		*		*
Amphibious bistort *Polygonum amphibium*		*		
Common sorrel *Rumex acetosa*		*		
Bog stitchwort *Stellaria alsine*		*		
Common spotted orchid *Dactylorhiza fuchsii*		*		
Early marsh orchid *D.incarnata*		*		
Northern marsh orchid *D. majalis* ssp. purpurella		*		
Twayblade *Listera ovata*		*		
Sea pearlwort *Sagina maritima*		*		
Yorkshire fog *Holcus lanatus*		*		
Meadow grass *Poa pratensis*		*		
Jointed rush *Juncus articulatus*		*		
Sweet vernal-grass *Anthoxanthum odoratum*		*		
Field horsetail *Equisetum arvense*		*		
Autumnal hawkbit *Leontodon autumnalis*		*		
Marsh foxtail *Alopecurus geniculatus*		*		
Spike-rush *Eleocharis palustris*		*	*	
Yellow flag *Iris pseudacorus*			*	
Common reed *Phragmites australis*			*	
Mare's-tail *Hippuris vulgaris*			*	
Bulrush *Schoenoplectus lacustris*			*	
Marsh marigold *Caltha palustris*			*	
Water mint *Mentha aquatica*			*	
Bogbean *Menyanthes trifoliata*			*	
Fool's watercress *Apium nodiflorum*			*	
Marsh ragwort *Senecio aquaticus*			*	
Blue water speedwell *Veronica anagallis-aquatica*			*	
Bottle sedge *Carex rostrata*			*	
Greater tussock-panicled sedge *C.paniculata*			*	
Soft rush *Juncus effusus*			*	

Table 6.1 A list of species of plant from the dune-machair system taken from N.C.C. ed. Hambrey (1986), Dickenson & Randall (1979) and showing the distribution in dune (d), dry machair (dm), wet machair (wm) and fen/marsh (fm) habitats.

English	Scientific	Gaelic
1 Dune types		
Active dune front		
Marram grass	*Ammophila arenaria*	*Muran*
Hastate orache	*Atriplex prostrata*	*Ceathramham–caorach*
Sea sandwort	*Honkenya peploides*	
Moribund dune front		
Marram grass		
Red fescue	*Festuca rubra*	
Ribwort	*Plantago lanceolata*	
Lady's bedstraw	*Galium verum*	
Bird's foot trefoil	*Lotus corniculatus*	*Adharc–an–diabhail*
Wild white clover	*Trifolium repens*	*Seamrag–gheal*
Dune back		
Marram grass		
Red fescue		
Lady's bedstraw		
Ribwort plantain		
Wild white clover		
Ragwort	*Senecio jacobaea*	*Buaghallan*
Moss	*Rhytidiadelphus squarrosus*	
Sand hill		
Red fescue		
Marram grass		
Lady's bedstraw		
Ribwort plantain		
Wild white clover		
Moss	*R. squarrosus*	*Coinneach*
2 Grassland types		
Machair grassland		
Red fescue		
Meadow grass	*Poa pratensis*	
Marram grass		
Wild white clover		
Ribwort plantain		
Daisy	*Bellis perennis*	*Neoinean*
Bird's-foot trefoil		
Moss	*R. squarrosus*	
Dune slack		
Carnation-grass	*Carex flacca*	
Meadow grass		
Red fescue		
Silverweed	*Potentilla anserina*	*Brisgean*
Pennywort	*Hydrocotyle vulgaris*	*Cornan–caisil*
Moss	*R. squarrosus*	*Coinneach*

Table 6.2   Summary of the characteristics of machair vegetation in the Uists devised from Dickinson and Randall (1979) and showing the dominant species (in descending order in each habitat) in dune and grassland habitats of the dune-machair system.

The sea-pansy in South Uist (Photo J. M. Boyd)

and cattle have a greatly reduced opportunity of flowering, and thus of advertising their presence. We have walked the machairs of the Hebrides for almost forty years, and in summer the land has almost always been heavily grazed or cultivated pasture. In June 1988, however, while walking on ungrazed machair in Tiree amid countless flowering common orchids (*Dactylorhiza* spp.), we came across our first pyramidal orchid (*Anacamptis pyramidalis*)—a single lonely plant blooming gaily in utter isolation from its own kind. Never had we seen such a luxuriant orchid meadow. Yet, had it been in summer grazing, there would have been few orchids in evidence. Only in ideal flowering conditions which produced hundreds of thousands of the common species, did we see the single, shy rarity.

The fauna of the dune-machair system is nothing like so well-studied as the flora. However, while the ecological distribution of species is largely undescribed, a considerable list has been compiled from pitfall and ultra-violet lamp traps. In the 1950's, one of us described the distribution of earthworms and snails in ten dune-machair areas in the Inner and Outer Hebrides, and made comparisons between grazed and ungrazed machair on Tiree (Boyd, 1957). Sixteen species of earthworm were recorded and the same 16 on grass moor in different proportions, but only seven species on heather moors, all taken by the same methods. Everywhere *Lumbricus rubellus* was dominant over all others. In the dunes the sub-dominant

Machair in Tiree in
June with bloom of
buttercups, daisies and
clovers (Photo
I. L. Boyd)

was *Bimastus tenuis*; in the machair and cultivated soils *Allo-bophora caliginosa, Dendrobeana octohedra* and *L. castaneus* were also prominent; in the moorland *D. octahedra* and *B. eiseni* were the sub-dominants. These are not deep-burrowing worms and they do not raise large casts. They play a vital role in the aeration of the sandy loams without exposing sand on the surface. Locally, populations of *L. terrestris, Octolasium cyaneum* and *O.lacteum* raise large casts which are dispersed by the wind. Machair soils which have not been over blown by sand for centuries and which have never been tilled are organic moulds up to 20cms deep, resting on hard inorganic sand into which earthworms do not penetrate. These shallow, sandy soils are very vulnerable to drying-out, a process which can be accelerated in rainless summers by the activity of earthworms just as it can by the disturbance of rabbits and grazing livestock.

In his list of the non-marine invertebrates of the Outer Hebrides, Rodger Waterston has included species which live mainly or exclusively in sand dunes, but does not specify the habitat preferences—these may be found in the many papers which are cited in the references to his paper. However, in 1976 Dr Colin Welch and others conducted invertebrate surveys using pitfall and ultra-violet light traps from 18 sites situated mostly in the dune-machair habitat in the Outer Hebrides. In the pitfall traps a total of 155 species of beetle were caught of which 30 were Carabidae and of the remainder, half were Staphylinidae. Out of 31,000 beetles recorded about 10,000 were carabids dominated by the genus *Calathus*, especially *C. fuscipes*, with others prominent such as *Serica brunnea*, *Leiodes dubia* and *Silpha tyrolensis*, which are truly representative of a dry habitat, *Megasternum obscurum*, a scavenger of the litter layer, and *Tachyporus chrysomelinus*, a predator of aphids and other small insects which is more commonly found in lush wet habitats.

The data were complex in their interpretation. For example, the staphylinid *Xantholinus linearis* was taken from every site sampled with only 136 specimens, while the dung-beetle *Geotrupes vernalis* was taken from only three sites with 133 specimens. The survey yielded 25 species which were recorded from the Outer Hebrides for the first time, all of which have been recorded in Waterston's list. *Lathridius anthracinus* was recorded at Valtos, Lewis, the most northerly recording in Britain, and *Laemostenus terricola* and *Aleochara cuniculorum*, which live in rabbit burrows, had only been recorded once previously.

Welch (1983) also listed the Coleoptera of the Inner Hebrides. He found 937 species distributed over 15 of the best documented islands, compared with 605 species of beetle on Waterston's list for the Outer Hebrides. The list for the Inner Hebrides is compiled from 78 works, which gives some indication of the ecological background of the species, but again does not identify them to habitat. Our own work in Tiree concerned the dominant species of beetle caught in pitfall traps in grazed and ungrazed machair at Crossapol.

On the grazed ground the most numerous beetles by far were the Chrysomelids (*Longitarsus* spp.), though in biomass the catch was dominated by harvestmen, particularly *Phalangium opilio*. Such groups as *Calathus melanocephalus*, *Tachyporus* spp., *Aphodius* spp. (breed in dung-pats), *Longitarsus* spp., *Sitona* spp., *Apion apricans* and *P. opilio* seem to be favoured by the conditions on the grazed grassland. *Sitona* spp. and *Apion apricans* feed and breed on legumes such as *Trifolium pratense*.

The ungrazed machair had a soil fauna dominated by harvestmen and spiders and the carabid *Pterostichus niger*. Almost all the species caught in the traps showed marked differences between the grazed and the ungrazed ground, the one exception being the spider *Pachygnatha degeeri*. Other spiders were also greatly affected; *Lycosa pullata* was abundant on the ungrazed ground and almost absent from the grazings, while the opposite was the case with *L. tarsalis* and *L. monticola*. The green grasshopper *Omocestus viridulus* was much more abundant on the ungrazed ground. Ants nested and spent the winter in the ungrazed cover and went out onto the grazings in the spring.

The dunes can be an array of suntraps on summer days, giving strong insolation. The slacks can become infested with flies, the larvae of which are found in the soil, dung-pats or as parasites, such as the fly *Sarcophaga nigriventris* or the snail *H. itala*. Other winged insects are the meadow brown (*Maniola jurtina*), common blue (*Polyommatus icarus*), small tortoise-shell (*Aglais urticae*) and grayling (*Hipparchia semele*) butterflies. In the ultra-violet light traps, set mainly in machair areas in the Outer Hebrides, Welch caught 33 of the 367 species of Lepidoptera listed by Waterston for the islands as a whole. The common rustic (*Mesapamea secalis*), and the dark arches moths (*Apamea monoglypha*) were taken at every station, and were the most numerous species of the catch.

The belted beauty (*Lycia zonaria*) is abundant on the machair; the caterpillars feed on legumes and iris and the females are flightless, laying eggs on boulders, driftwood and fence posts. Welch found that numbers fell off dramatically from south to north in the Outer Hebrides. Some lepidopterists have read too much into the distribution pattern of the belted beauty, postulating land connections to explain the presence of the flightless females. However, as Peter Wormell has commented, the affinity of the gravid flightless females for wood has probably taken them to sea on small wooden craft and cargo. There is also the possibility of the females being carried to islands *in copula*. Nonetheless, the distribution in the Outer Hebrides against a constantly high presence of their food plants is interesting and worthy of further study.

The bumble bees *Bombus lucorum magnus*, *B. hortorum* and *B. muscorum liepeterseni* (formerly *smithianus*) are generally common on the machair. *B. distinguendus*, *B. ruderatus* and *B. lapidarius* are patchy in their distribution and possibly still extending their range in the Hebrides. The cuckoo-bee *Psithyrus bohemicus* and the fossorial bee *Colletes floralis* occur in both the Outer and Inner Hebrides, the latter burrowing in firm dune scarps, flying in sunshine and, in dull weather, remaining in its burrow with head protruding. *B. jonellus hebridensis* may be found on the machair, but is more numerous on heather.

Wet Machair

At the landward side of the machair plain the land often becomes marshy, with open water in the Uists, Benbecula and

Tiree forming chains of machair lochs. The seaward shores of these are sandy and part of the machair habitat, while the landward shores are part of the 'blackland' habitat with muddy, sometimes peaty margins often with bare rock and *Phragmites* fens.

Many species of the dry machair are still present in the wet communities. Red fescue and the sedges *Carex panicea* and *C. flacca* are dominant, with other prominent flowering plants such as lesser spearwort (*Ranunculus flammula*), the lesser celandine (*R. ficaria*), ragged robin (*Lychnis flos-cuculi*), cuckoo flower (*Cardamine pratensis*), marsh pennywort (*Hydrocotyle vulgaris*), marsh cinquefoil (*Potentilla palustris*), amphibious bistort (*Polygonum amphibium*), marsh bedstraw (*Galium palustre*), orchids (*Dactylorhiza purpurella* and *D. fuchsii* spp.), lesser twayblade (*Listera cordata*) and the autumnal hawkbit (*Leontodon autumnalis*). The field horsetail (*Equisitum arvense*) and the common spike rush (*Eleocharis palustris*) are also common.

The wet machair is often severely poached by cattle, at the margins of lochs or streams on ground which is seasonally flooded. Such areas may have dense stands of mare's tail (*Hippuris vulgaris*), bulrush (*Schoenoplectus lacustris*) and iris, or a community dominated by the marsh pennywort, common sedge, marsh cinquefoil and water mint (*Mentha aquatica*). The ditches and permanent marshes contain the water speedwells (*Veronica anagallis-aquatica* and *V. catenata*), marsh marigold (*Caltha palustris*), celery-leaved buttercup (*Ranunculus sceleratus*), fool's water cress (*Apium nodiflorum*), marsh willow herb (*Epilobium palustre*), bogbean (*Menyanthes trifoliata*) and others. In some areas the sedges *Carex rostrata* and *C. paniculata* and the rushes *Eleocharis uniglumis* and *Juncus effusus* are dominant. (The vegetation of the open waters is described in Chapter 10.)

The machair idyll is not only floral—in high summer it is full of bird song: the skylark; the cheeping of meadow-pipits; the wheezy *pee-wit, pee-wit* of lapwings; the liquid *toowe, toowe* of ringed plover; the shrill *klee-eep, klee-eep* of oystercatchers; the *tuuu . . . tuuu . . . tuuu* of redshanks; the trill of dunlin; the *chip-per, chip-per, chip-per* of snipe; the screech of terns and cries of gulls. The lapwing, oystercatcher and ringed plover are widespread, but are particularly attracted to nest in a diverse machair habitat of mixed cultivation and fallow stripes. The young are raised on the machair invertebrates and, in closely grazed areas, are particularly vulnerable to predation by gulls. Dunlin, redshank and snipe are hefted to the wet machair, nesting in grassy tussocks raised slightly above the damp substrate, where they find an optimal habitat with plenty of food and good cover in the marshy and trampled ground. The survey of waders on the machairs and blacklands of the Outer Hebrides by the NCC, the Wader Study Group and Durham University in 1983 found about 12,000 pairs of these six species. Lapwings were most numerous (*c.* 3,500) while oystercatchers, dunlin, ringed plovers and redshanks were all found in similar numbers (*c.* 2,000). Snipe were least numerous (*c.* 500) (see Part 3, Table VI in NCC 1986). The overall wader density on the land surveyed was 90 pairs per sq km. Similar data are not available for the Inner Hebrides, though a rather low estimate of 2,000–3,000 pairs of all species was made by Reed, Currie and Love (1983), which reflects the relatively smaller areas of machair in the Inner Hebrides.

In winter the machair is faded like a threadbare tapestry. Gone are the flowers and calling birds, but the apparently dead, buff-coloured flats belie the life within; some of it in hibernation in the soil, and some on the surface. It is a lean time for rabbits in their grazed-out, mossy warrens and hares range further to find food. However, in winter, when the mainland is frozen, the machair is an 'open' habitat for waders, and holds large numbers of lapwings, golden plover, curlew and snipe. In February 1975 an estimate was made of around 4,000 lapwings and 2,000 golden plovers, mostly in machair and blackland, in the Uists and Benbecula. Significant numbers of migrant waders visit the machairs in autumn and spring. Native greylag geese feed on machair and blackland all year round and are joined in winter by barnacle and Greenland white-fronted geese. It is a common sight on a winter's day on Islay and the Uists to see noisy flocks of geese lifting and settling over the sand dunes and machair in the cold watery sunshine.

Crofts and Farms

CHAPTER 7

Inbye and Blackland

In this book we place the agricultural habitats between those of the coast and the moorland, for that is where they are on the islands. Man has found his best opportunities for cultivation where the sandy ground grades into the peat, and his habitations and field systems have interrupted the natural transition from shore to moorland, providing a habitat for wildlife which borrows from each but which is distinct from both. In the crofting townships, the cultivated land, usually close to the crofthouse, is called the 'inbye', and in the Outer Hebrides it is called 'blackland' in contrast with the neighbouring machair, which is 'light' by comparison.

Crofts and farms consist of enclosed and unenclosed land. Generally speaking, the coastal habitats (dunes, machairs, and salt marshes) and the hill pastures are unenclosed; lands situated between these two are enclosed and have been cultivated. These historical patterns of land use (see p. 332) are described for the crofting system in the Uists by Professor J.B. Caird (1979), and for the farming system in Islay by Dr Margaret Storrie (1983). The enclosed lands are tenanted by individual crofters and farmers, whereas the unenclosed lands in the crofting system are the common grazings of the townships, in which each croft has a share, or in farming, are the grazing outruns of individual farms. Since the last war, the enclosed land has increased. Many machairs have been apportioned among the crofters of each township and fenced in separate fields. Also, patches of moorland have been fenced, fertilised and reseeded by both crofters and farmers. The ecology of the agricultural land has therefore been changed, and the more so through a change in practice, from mixed arable/livestock regimes to a grass-intensive/livestock husbandry.

Patterns of Land Use

The boundary between machair with its light sandy soil, and the hill with its dark, peaty gleys and podzols, is sometimes less

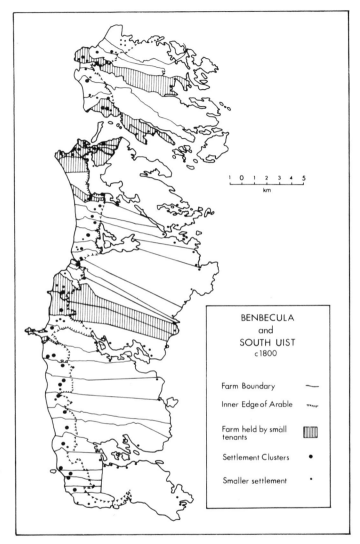

Fig. 17
*Map of South Uist
and Benbecula showing
the boundaries of farms,
c. 1800, transecting the
islands from west to
east (from Caird,
1979)*

than 100 m. More often, it is extended by cultivation. Caird has
shown that around 1800 the farms in South Uist and Benbecula
transected the island from west to east, and each farm possessed the full range of habitats from sandy to peaty, exposed to
sheltered and shore to hill top (Fig. 17). Later, many of these
farms were sectioned into crofts, and in many crofting
townships the land was tenanted in narrow strips aligned from
shore to hill.

On the rocky break of ground between the machair and the

peatland, the croft house was built within the holding—before crofting times the houses were clustered in hamlets on the farms. The low rounded and thatched dwellings of earlier times have now been replaced by upstanding, gavelled, wide-windowed houses, usually built on the same site. The unfenced strips or rigs were worked in a 'run-rig' system of cultivation and husbandry, contained within a substantial dry-stone dyke, beyond which lay the hill grazings. In the growing season of corn and potatoes in rigs, the livestock were either transferred to the hill, enclosed on the inbye ground, or tethered on the rigs out of reach of crops, but from harvest to seed time, livestock had free run of the rigs. Today, fences have been erected between the rigs, and the run-rig system is largely in disuse. The hill ground also has long-disused *feannegan*, spade-

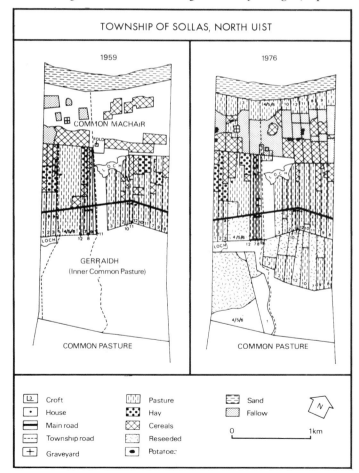

Fig. 18
Diagram of the crofting township of Sollas, North Uist, showing the detailed sectioning of land among the crofter's before and after the apportionment and reseeding of common grazings (from Caird, 1979)

cultivation mistakenly called 'lazy-beds' in English. This form of moorland cultivation, with its ridging and dressing of seaweed, greatly modified the machair-moorland transition, particularly in the Outer Hebrides. Today, only small patches of *feannagan* are worked, but the widespread ecological effects of past husbandry remain.

Caird (1979) has shown how the crofting system has run in the townships of South Boisdale and Sollas in the Uists. We see the sectioning of the habitat which has been wrought over the last two hundred years, and the diversity of use to which the township of Sollas has been put in the production of hay, cereals, old and new reseeded pasture, and potatoes (Fig. 18). While the crofting system was developing in the break-up of the mediaeval farms (Hunter, 1976), a non-crofting landscape of sporting estates and farms with industrial and servicing villages was created in the southern isles. Such a landscape was most highly developed in Islay, with clearance of much cotter settlement from the hill land to the villages, and by emigration. The agricultural habitats in Islay which have become so well known as the wintering grounds for geese which breed in Greenland, date from the mid-nineteenth century. Then the island changed hands, with dramatic reduction in the numbers of tenants, extensive drainage, and reorganisation of the field systems to provide arable land for the growing of barley for distilling and livestock for cheese-making. The new estates became sporting land with game-keepers, and the status of game species changed.

The farmlands around Stornoway in Lewis, on Skye, Raasay, Canna, Muck, Mull, Lismore, Islay, Jura, and Gigha are a different agricultural habitat from the crofts, and are more akin to the west mainland. While the fields of these farms are generally larger and more intensively worked than those in crofting townships, they are smaller than those on the mainland, though the farms in Islay bear comparison with those in Ayrshire and Galloway.

Agricultural Habitats

The inbye land is an integral part of the island ecology which has been neglected in comparison with machair and hill. The agricultural habitats have not attracted the naturalist, lacking as they do the numbers of species and variety of plant and animal communities possessed by the uncultivated land. However, the invertebrates are largely undescribed, and the difference between cultivated and uncultivated habitats in the Hebrides (except Islay) is far less than on the lowland mainland.

Exhaustively surveyed, the inbye would probably yield an inventory of plants and animals comparable to the machair. Many species which are common and of little interest in agricultural habitats on the mainland, are uncommon and of greater interest in the islands. For example, the three common species of white butterfly (*Pieris brassicae, Artogeia rapae, A. napi*) are often rare in the Hebrides and feed on Cruciferae in which the inbye abounds, notably as charlock (*Sinapis arvensis*) the weed of cereal crops. Also, species like bumble bees which feed on the machair, nest in the inbye and *vice-versa* for rock pigeons, which nest on the coasts and feed on the inbye. Buzzards, hen harriers, and short-eared owls breed on the moorland but include the inbye in their feeding range, and swallows may find few nesting sites outside the inbye.

The natural history of the inbye is, therefore, worthy of attention both for what it contains and for the contribution it makes to the ecology of the whole island and the archipelago. It is known for its undulating topography, variable soils, complicated wetland with much open and running water, and mosaics of cultivation and fallow in systems of small fields. Hedges are absent, and hedgerow trees almost unknown except in the sheltered sides of the Inner Hebrides. Nonetheless the inbye is, on the whole, a rich and varied habitat for wildlife.

The inbye has a colourful flora of little botanical interest compared to machair and moor, yet most of the species of both may be found somewhere within the agricultural scene. However, the agricultural character of the land is as attractive to the

Crofts at Tarskavaig, Skye, in September 1988 showing neat modern houses amid meadows of rough grass and rushes where once was cultivation. A view looking to the Cuillin Hills (Photo J. M. Boyd)

artist as it is off-putting to the naturalist. The brilliant daisy and buttercup meadows of lightly grazed pasture contain wild white clover, bird's-foot trefoil, eyebright, self-heal, ladies' bedstraw, harebell, thyme, and grass of parnassus. Among the ungrazed mixtures of tall grasses (*Holcus, Agrostis, Deschampsia, Anthoxanthum, Cynosurus, Dactylis*) of old hay-meadows in early summer, are the swaying heads of hawkbits, gowans, corn marigolds, meadow sweet, yarrow, knapweed, ragwort, devil's bit scabious, wild parsley, wild angelica, iris, ragged robin, cuckooflower, and marsh marigold. The spikes of early and heathspotted orchids are frequent, particularly in the shelter of grassy ditches, and the lesser butterfly orchid is occasionally found in wet meadows.

These and many others wildly but shyly espouse the stands of crofter rye-grass, corn, and barley. A great deal of the wet blackland, which was at one time well drained and cultivated, has become choked with rushes and sedges. On the farms the flora is generally less varied due mainly to the reseeding, fertilising and heavy stocking of permanent grass. The grass-intensive regimes, with a short growing season in the Hebrides, reduce the botanical interest of the farmland, though it does make it more attractive for some birds and mammals, notably geese, starlings, pigeons, rooks, jackdaws, choughs (Islay), rabbits, hares, voles, fieldmice, moles and hedgehogs.

Farmland on Muck showing good grass and livestock with a shelter belt of trees (Photo J. M. Boyd)

The blackland is dotted with the houses of crofters and farmers providing an assortment of man-made niches not generally present in either machair or moor. These are domestic in character, but their insular situation confers a greater interest

upon them, than would be the case in mainland Britain; for example, in the distribution of breeding house sparrows, swallows, bats, and house mice. Mixed noisy flocks of migratory chaffinches, bramblings, greenfinches, twites and redpolls frequent the stackyards, and collared doves are now common. Around the croft and farmhouses there are beds of stinging and purple dead nettles, rose bay willow herb, docks and thistles which are good for birds and insects.

Throughout the year the blackland attracts large numbers of breeding redshank, lapwing and snipe and smaller numbers of oystercatcher, dunlin, curlew and common sandpiper. The wader survey of 1983–84 in the Uists showed about 100 pairs of waders per sq km, with redshank exceptionally numerous. The wetlands form a continuum with the machair and moorland lochs and streams, and have breeding mallard, teal, tufted duck, red-breasted merganser and occasionally shoveller. In winter there are large flocks of lapwing, golden plover and curlew in the bare fields, mixed sometimes with small assemblies of Greenland white-fronted, grey-lag and barnacle geese, and whooper swans (except in Islay, where the white-fronted are numbered in flocks of hundreds and the barnacle geese in thousands—see Chapter 4, H-AMI).

Corncrakes and Corn Buntings

Corncrake

In surveys conducted in 1968–72 and 1978–79, Dr James Cadbury (1980) showed that, between the two, there was a 56% reduction in the number of 10km squares in Scotland possessing breeding corncrakes (*Crex crex*). On the mainland the reduction was 89% in the east and 61% in the West Highlands, while in the Inner and Outer Hebrides, it was 33 and 3% respectively. In 1978–79, the Outer Hebrides held 260 pairs, the Inner Hebrides about 240 pairs, and Scotland as a whole, about 700 pairs (Table 7.1). Thus the Hebrides held about 71% of the Scottish population.

The corncrake breeds in the machair-blackland transition. Its grating call, drifting across the dusky landscape at sunset, is still one of the familiar sounds of mid-summer in Tiree and the Uists. Neighbouring cocks appear to 'talk' to each other; sometimes they call together but often one 'replies' to another. The migratory birds arrive in April from wintering grounds in Africa, and find their breeding habitat in the Hebrides not yet ready to receive them. Their breeding territories are in the grass and cereal crops and in tall mixed stands of weed species

Corncrake and corn bunting habitat among crofts in Tiree with tall, herb-rich hay meadows harvested in mid-late summer (Photo J. M. Boyd)

(see below), which by April have not yet grown long enough to provide sufficient cover for the birds. However, the iris flags are already well grown and receive the corncrakes, holding them until the hay, corn and weed coverts are grown and nesting begins.

In a survey of the habitat occupied by 190 calling corncrakes in the Inner Hebrides, Cadbury (1980, 1983) found 72% in mown grassland, 17% in rough vegetation, and 10% in marshes. Over three-quarters of those in mown grassland were in recent leys, or improved grassland. When nesting, they prefer the taller hay of the 'improved' leys, but when the chicks are at foot, they favour the less dense, herb-rich, 'natural' meadows.

A more recent study of corncrakes in the croftlands of the Uists by T.J. Stowe and A.V. Hudson (1988) has served to confirm many of Cadbury's observations in Tiree, and to define more precisely the habitat requirements of the species. Daily traces of radio-tagged cocks and hens were obtained. These showed that, while the cocks were sedentary in their calling sites at night, they wandered extensively during the day with much overlap; the hens also wandered widely before nesting, but thereafter settled to incubate and raise the brood of 8–12 eggs without assistance from the cock. Breeding lasts from May–August, and early-laying hens may be double-brooded, so a delay in cutting hay until July would therefore not be a ready solution to the problem of destruction of the birds. Stowe and Hudson, however, point to the requirement of the hay meadow beside areas of rough vegetation—beds of iris, hogweed, knapweed, nettles, reeds, rushes, and tall grass and herb communities on field margins, roadside verges, and around fenced installations are all valuable corncrake habitat. These features should be maintained in context with the hay meadow as escape routes for the birds when forced out by mowing *from the centre outwards*, and not as is traditionally done from the edge inwards. However, the greatest threat of all comes from a change in husbandry from hay to silage, and also from cattle to sheep, since spring grazing of nursing ewes in the inbye rather than on machair or hill reduces the nesting cover for corncrakes.

This well-established and successful pattern of behaviour of the corncrake is set in a diverse habitat of small, often rather weedy, unkempt fields (p. 118). Nowadays, however, the pattern is increasingly disrupted by the making of silage. The mowing of leys for silage in June kills corncrakes, and there is no doubt that if silage is generally made in preference to hay, the corncrake will suffer. The changes in agricultural practice which have wrought such damage to the corncrake in mainland Britain and Europe are now showing themselves in the Hebrides. Still, the changes are by no means uniform throughout the islands; the habitat, weather, and farming practice vary

Corncrake (Photo E. Hosking)

a lot from island to island, and there is a bounty scheme whereby crofters and farmers are encouraged to make hay rather than silage.

(a)

Area of Scotland	10km. sq. 1968/72	10km. sq. 1978/79	% Reduc'n occup. sq.
Inner Hebrides	54	36	33
Outer Hebrides	32	31	3
E Mainland	88	10	89
SW Mainland	67	20	70
NW Mainland	61	24	61
Orkney	30	27	10
Shetland	9	2	78
Scotland	341	150	56

(b)

Outer Hebrides		Inner Hebrides	
Lewis	31	Tiree	85
Harris/Bern'y	12	Skye	31–34
South Uist	83	Coll	28
North Uist	75	Islay	22–24
Benbecula	33	Colonsay	20
Other Sth. Is.	26	Small Is.	18–20
		Other Is.	31
Total	260	Total	235–242
Total for the Hebrides		495–502	
Total for Scotland		688–700*	

* +25 recorded on a single occasion and possibly breeding.

Table 7.1 The populations of breeding corncrakes in Scotland in 1968–72 and 1978–79 shown **(a)** by the numbers of 10km. sq. occupied in each survey period and **(b)** the numbers of regularly-calling corncrakes in the Outer and Inner Hebrides (from Cadbury, 1980).

Corn Bunting and Others

The corn bunting (*Miliaria calandra*) is also in decline in Scotland, but the reasons for this are less obvious than for the corncrake. The main breeding areas are in the coastal plains of cereal farming from Berwick to Buchan, and in the Hebrides, and it is scarce in other lowland farming areas along the

Corn bunting (Photo E. Hosking)

Solway, in the Lothians, Perth, Moray, Orkney and Lewis (Thom, 1986). Ideal habitat for both corncrake and corn bunting still exists in Tiree, where calm summer evenings are full of their callings. While numbers of breedings pairs have declined in or disappeared from other Scottish islands and in parts of the mainland, breeding populations still occur in the machair-inbye of Tiree, Coll, Uists and Benbecula, south Harris and north Lewis.

At the turn of the century, the species was plentiful in islands with machair-inbye land, but by the end of the 1930s it had ceased to breed in the Small Isles, was gone from Mull and Colonsay in the 1940s, and from Skye by the 1970s. Cadbury (1983) carried out biennial surveys in Tiree from 1971–79, and found 61–95 singing, mostly in small weedy fields of oats with margins dominated by hogweed. Dr D.B.A. Thompson informed us that in Tiree the corn bunting population declined in the early 1980s to less than 20 males, followed more recently by a slight increase. At present Tiree is the only island in the Inner Hebrides with breeding corn buntings. The ratio of calling corn buntings to corncrakes in Cadbury's survey was about one to one, though in 1971 it was two to one.

Current studies of corn buntings in the Uists and Benbecula by Des Thompson and Terry Burke indicate that the species has not declined: 160–180 singing males have been estimated in North Uist and 80–110 in South Uist and Benbecula. This could be because 'breaking-in' of uncultivated or neglected land under the Integrated Development Programme may have favoured the corn bunting. Fallow land and dunes are the preferred nesting areas, but fledglings occupy the standing cereal crops of the inbye, where there is better cover from predators and ample food.

The corn bunting is thoroughly promiscuous—in its most favoured habitats both males and females can have several partners. In Sussex, a polygamous male may have as many as nine females, yet in North Uist, Thompson and Burke found that the maximum number of females to one male is three, and that only one in three males were polygamous. The cocks are adept at defending their territories by singing from key vantage points, thus at once repelling other males and attracting females, and providing safe escort for them to and from the nest site during incubation. The largest birds have the most forceful songs and possess the richest territories. Peter McGregor and Michael Shepherd have shown that if the recorded songs of corn bunting cocks are played back to another holding territory, the song reaction of the resident is significantly more aggressive to a near neighbour's song than it is to that of a more distant cock (Thompson, pers. comm.). The Hebridean corn buntings in their open habitat, with their lower numbers and less complicated sex life provide especially good opportunities for research in the ecology and behaviour of birds.

Skylarks, meadow pipits, reed buntings and sedge-warblers are common breeding species. In the Outer Isles and Tiree the coverts of gorse and the niches provided by the human habitations offer breeding sites to a range of songbirds, and food and shelter for passerines on migration. In the Inner Hebrides and around Stornoway where there is more scrub and wood mixed within the crofts and farms, the communities of song-birds are enhanced by wren, dunnock, robin, whinchat, blackbird, song thrush, willow warbler, linnet and yellowhammer.

In total, the blackland-inbye of the crofts and the enclosed land of the farms make a major contribution to the natural history of the Hebrides. The invertebrates are largely undescribed, but it is clear from work already done that the fauna is probably as rich and possibly greater in biomass than that on machair and moor.

Woodlands

CHAPTER 8

Tree-growth in the Islands

The windswept nature of the Hebrides together with rain, flying sea spray, the grazing of sheep and deer and the burning of hill pastures means that conditions for the growth of trees are far from ideal. Yet pockets of woodland do occur, mainly in the sheltered glens of the Inner Hebrides. A major gradient of tree-growth occurs from the exposed western rim of the Outer Hebrides, Tiree and Coll to the sheltered glens and eastern aspects of Islay, Jura, Mull, Skye, Rum and Raasay, where conditions are favourable for production forestry. Small semi-natural woods and plantations occur in most of the Inner Hebrides with the exception of Tiree, where tree-growth is restricted to a few clumps of wind-twisted sycamores, elders, willows and hawthorns in the lee of houses or rock crevices. Natural woods occur on islands as small as Garbh Eileach, Bernera (Lismore) and South Rona, but there are none on the Treshnish Isles.

In the Outer Hebrides semi-natural scrub woodlands are usually restricted to islands in freshwater lochs, and in rocky defiles in the rolling country of peat bogs and exposed gneiss rock. The scrub woodlands that occur in lochs, such as at Loch Druidibeg, South Uist, but also on Lewis and Harris, show the potential for tree-growth in the absence of sheep, deer (only recently introduced) and fire, even where the exposure to wind and salt is high (see also p. 173). Before the advent of man and his grazing stocks, the Outer Hebrides probably possessed a wind-shaped scrub-forest of hardy, broadleaved trees to a height of 200m above sea level, and the ecology of the islands would have been different. However, pollen analyses of sediments in western Lewis show that no true woodland has developed in the relatively sheltered district around Little Loch Roag in the post glacial period (Birks and Marsden, 1979). In the Outer Hebrides trees are present on all the major islands, but are rare and usually much reduced in size. St Kilda, the South Barra Isles, Eriskay, Ronay, the Monach Isles, Berneray (Harris), Taransay, Scarp, Scalpay and Great Bernera are all treeless.

Mixed broadleaved and conifer woodland at Kinloch on the sheltered side of Rum. The woods contain Scots and Corsican pines, larch, Norway maple, lime, sweet and horse chestnut with native alder and birch (Photo J. M. Boyd)

'Policy' woodlands have been planted around most of the large houses, and have made a great contribution to the natural history of islands which would otherwise possess little or no woodland. These vary in character from the dwarf, contorted sycamore around such exposed lodges as Grogarry (South Uist) and Newton (North Uist) to the more sheltered, well-grown woods around Stornoway Castle (Lewis), Armadale Castle (Skye), Kinloch Castle (Rum), Canna House, Torosay Castle (Mull) and Islay House. The policy woods of Colonsay have over 200 species of exotic trees and shrubs.

Shelter belts, hedges and parkland have been planted and add much to the wooded aspect of many of the Inner Hebrides, notably on the well-farmed islands of Canna, Muck (p. 116), Lismore and Gigha, where the aesthetic and ecological effects of the trees are striking. Recent efforts to grow trees on a trial basis on the machair of Tiree failed because the trees were killed by wind and salt when they grew taller than the waist-high wind-shielding fence.

Commercial conifer plantations now cover extensive areas of the Inner Hebrides and there are also experimental plantations of spruce and pine on Lewis. Indeed there is probably more forest-covered land in the Hebrides now than since the beginning of man's widespread settlement of the Isles. Over the past fifty years, the spread of this new forestry, which has covered parts of mainland Argyll and West Inverness-shire, has

reached the Hebrides and the western limits of economic growth, and in that short time commercial afforestation has altered the character of Islay, Mull and Skye. Many of the old birch, oak, hazel, ash and willow woods, which have been planted through with conifers, though natural in appearance today, were felled and coppiced in the 17th and 18th centuries to make charcoal for the Lorne Furnace Company. Their furnace at Bonawe, on the shores of Loch Etive, consumed much of the timber yield from natural woodlands around the Firth of Lorne and Sound of Mull. The First Statistical Account (1792–96) mentions the sale of areas of natural woodland in Torosay parish, Mull, for iron-smelting and also woodlands at Portree and Sleat in Skye being coppiced. Fifty years later in the New Statistical Account, the landscapes of Skye, Mull, Islay and Jura were beginning to show the effects of new coppice (presumably from the ravages of iron smelting) and of new plantations of mixed broadleaf and conifer woods. About 1845 the main plantations in Mull were at Torosay, Kilfinichen, Pennycross and Torloisk, and on Skye they were at Portree, Kilmuir, Strath and Sleat. There were others on Raasay.

One of the central questions concerning the history and development of woodlands in the Hebrides is, did any plants survive the last glaciation there, 12,000–13,500 BP (years before present)? A silt deposit from Tolsta in Lewis, carbon-dated to about 27,000 BP, contains the pollen of an open-herb vege-

A native ash-hazel woodland facing the Sound of Sleat, Skye, planted through with conifers, which have now been removed (Photo J. M. Boyd)

tation with willow and juniper. It also contains the Iceland pur-slane *Koenigia islandica*, which is today confined to Skye and Mull and which is a plant of the Arctic. However, the evidence of earliest post-glacial woodland in the Hebrides comes from the pollen analyses by Dr John Birks and his colleagues working in loch-bed sediments in Skye. In the late-glacial period, about 11,500 BP, birch and hazel woods developed in Sleat and Suardal; they may have regressed during the readvance of the ice about 10,000 BP, but progressed again at the beginning of the post-glacial or Flandrian period after 8,000 BP. Birch-hazel scrub was probably the pioneer woodland community in the sheltered areas into which sessile oak, ash, wych elm and holly became established as the climate became drier and warmer. Woodland probably extended its range well into the period of human settlement, which commenced about 5,000 BP, and was probably at its maximum at the end of the climatic optimum in the Sub-boreal about 3,000 BP. At this point, the climate became less favourable for trees, and man had already started to clear the forest from the major islands. Pollen research shows that forest cover in the Hebrides today appears similar to that of 8,000 BP, when much of the land, which has now been commercially afforested in the sheltered islands, held mixed woods of birch, hazel, oak, wych elm, aspen, willow, rowan, bird-cherry and holly, with transitions from wooded to open ground in response to steep gradients or exposure to wind, salt-spray and waterlogging of the soil. There is evidence of past woodland on heather moor, wet heath and shallow blanket mire, where the former forest soils have been converted by long-term waterlogging to gleys, podzols and peats. Since the last war, many such moors have been afforested (see p. 53, H-AHL). The mires which developed on flat ground early in the post-glacial period, such as raised mires, probably never had woodland.

Dean Monro (1549), Sibbald (1684), Heron (1794), Mac-Culloch (1824) and the Statistical Accounts of 1792 and 1843 all mention the presence of woods in the Inner Hebrides contain-ing birch, oak, ash, hazel, rowan, wych elm, holly and willows. During the climatic optimum of the Sub-boreal period (3,000 BP) there were probably two types of woodland below the 200m-contour: oak-ash woods on mixed organic and min-eral soils in Islay and Mull and in local sheltered pockets on Jura, Colonsay, Lismore, Eigg and Raasay; and birch-hazel woods on the more extensive organic soils in the sheltered aspects of the islands. The Hebrides have largely been beyond the western limit of pine, although pine was probably present on Mull, Rum and Skye at one time, and this contrasts with Norway where pine grows close to the sea on outer coasts.

Native Woodland

Today, oak-ash woods in the more favoured areas of climate and soil have oak dominating in the acid soils and ash on the base-rich soils, with hazel, holly, hawthorn, wych elm, willow and alder all common; bird-cherry, aspen, guelder rose (*Viburnum opulus*) and blackthorn (*Prunus spinosa*) are uncommon while juniper is rare and gean is absent. The birch-hazel woods are on acid soils, in exposed situations, higher elevations, and on north-facing and generally wet slopes where oak and ash cannot live. In these arduous conditions they are joined by rowan, alder and willows, of which the rusty (*Salix cinerea* ssp. *oleifolia*) and eared willows (*S. aurita*) are more tolerant of exposure than the others.

The character of the native Hebridean woods (see p. 128–9) is marked aesthetically by their dwarf form as they cling close to valley and scarp, and ecologically by their oceanic and boreal species. To stand in the mature, broadleaved plantations at Bridgend, Torosay, Armadale and even as far west as Stornoway, is to stand in the woods of mainland Scotland, but to stand in native woods of Coille Mhor on Colonsay or Coille Thocabhaig in Sleat is to stand only in the Hebrides. The oceanic element in these woodland types includes flowering

Coille Thocabhaig, the native oak-birch/ash-hazel wood in Sleat, Skye, which is a National Nature Reserve (Photo J. M. Boyd)

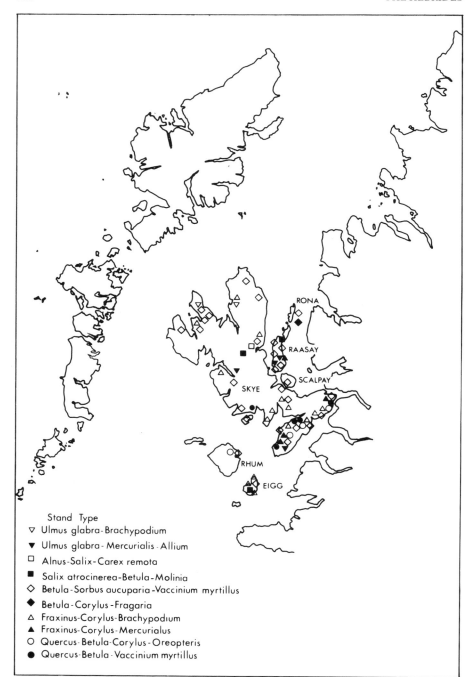

Stand Type
▽ Ulmus glabra-Brachypodium
▼ Ulmus glabra-Mercurialis-Allium
□ Alnus-Salix-Carex remota
■ Salix atrocinerea-Betula-Molinia
◇ Betula-Sorbus aucuparia-Vaccinium myrtillus
◆ Betula-Corylus-Fragaria
△ Fraxinus-Corylus-Brachypodium
▲ Fraxinus-Corylus-Mercurialus
○ Quercus-Betula-Corylus-Oreopteris
● Quercus-Betula-Vaccinium myrtillus

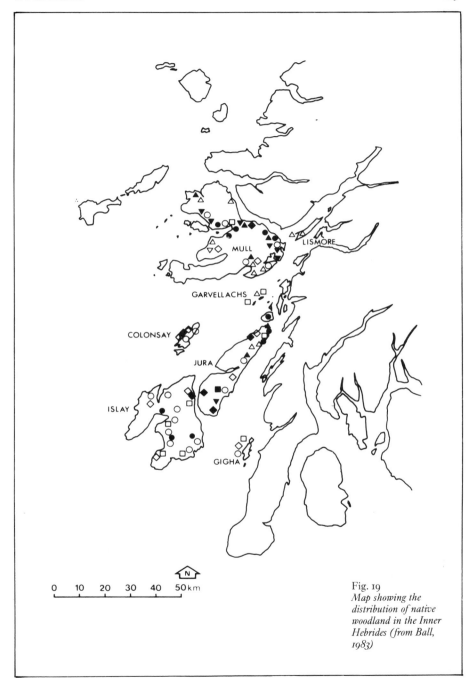

Fig. 19
*Map showing the
distribution of native
woodland in the Inner
Hebrides (from Ball,
1983)*

plants such as the tutsan (*Hypericum androsaemum*), the climbing corydalis (*Corydalis claviculata*), the hay-scented buckler fern (*Dryopteris aemula*), the filmy ferns (*Hymenophyllum tunbrigense*, *H. wilsonii*) and the hard shield-fern (*Polystichum aculeatum*). The boreal element includes the globe flower (*Trollius europaeus*), melancholy thistle (*Cirsium heterophyllum*), enchanter's nightshade (*Circaea intermedia*), marsh hawk's-beard (*Crepis paludosa*), stone bramble (*Rubus saxatilis*), mountain melick (*Melica nutans*), the beech fern (*Phegopteris connectilis*) and the scaly male-fern (*Dryopteris affinis*).

These woods are influenced by the grazing of sheep, cattle and occasionally goats, which encourages growth of bracken, purple moor-grass, sweet vernal-grass, Yorkshire fog, creeping soft grass, bents and fescues with false brome and tufted hair grass on base-rich soils. Other common species are wood sorrel, wood anemone, honeysuckle, common violet, germander speedwell, bugle, yellow pimpernel (*Lysimachia nemorum*), and primrose. Also present are the lady fern (*Athyrium felix-femina*), the narrow buckler fern (*D. carthusiana*) and the lemon-scented fern (*Oreopterus limbosperma*).

The Hebridean woods are festooned with lichens, some holding as many as 200 species. Coille Mhor on Colonsay and Coille Thocabhaig in Sleat have had respectively 132 and 129 species of epiphytic lichens recorded (Rose and Coppins 1983). Coille Mhor has the Lobarion community of many species luxuriant upon oak, and also well developed on hazel and ash, while the Graphidion communities coat the smooth bark of hazel. The acid bark of birch holds the *Parmelietum laevigatae* association of many species, and the Usneion communities, containing five species of *Usnea*, are found on willows.

The damp, mild, oceanic conditions of these native woods favour the growth of mosses and liverworts on the trees and the shaded rocky floor. Barks of oak, birch, alder, hawthorn, rowan and conifers are acid while those of ash, wych elm, sycamore, hazel, willows and elder are alkaline. The spongy bark of elder is particularly favourable to mosses and liverworts, and *Metzgeria fruticulosa*, *Tortula viresens* and *Cryphaea heteromalla* are confined to elder in the Inner Hebrides (Corley 1983), while *Ulota calvescens* and *Zygodon conoideus* are confined to hazel. Several *Orthotrichum* spp. are confined to trees with alkaline bark, and the acid-bark community also includes *U. drummondii* on alder, *Dicranum fuscescens* on oak and *Plagiochila punctata* on sheltered birch stems. Basalt and limestone boulders and scarps provide different woodland substrates from gneiss, granite and Torridonian sandstone for mosses and liverworts, but many species of the genera *Hylocomium*, *Thuidium*, *Dicranum* and *Rhytidiadelphus* are prominent in the woodland floor whatever the substrate, and those of *Hypnum, Isothecium, Frullania* on the tree trunks are also ubiquitous. *U. phyllantha* and *F. dilatata* are salt-tolerant and occur on eared willow close to the sea. Twigs have *U. crispa* and rain-tracks, *M. furcata*.

Ash-elm-hazel woods occur on calcarous soils on Jura, Garbh Eileach, Lismore (Bernera), Mull, Eigg, Skye and Raasay. Two types are recognised; one occurs on base-rich, free-draining soils with false brome, water avens (*Geum rivale*), sweet woodruff, enchanter's nightshade, sanicle and wild strawberry; another grows on alluvial loams with dog's mercury, ramsons (*Allium ursinum*), hedge woundwort, herb Robert, red campion and common nettle. Wych elm is often absent, and the ash-hazel stands have the analogues of the above wych elm woods, one typified by the abundance of false brome and the other by dog's mercury. These have admixtures of hawthorn, holly, bird-cherry, blackthorn and dog rose (*Rosa canina*), and bracken, wood sorrel, wood anemone and wild hyacinth are ubiquitous. In wet areas the ash-wych elm-hazel grade into alder-willow carr.

Alder-willow woods occur on soils developed from alluvium, which is flushed with mineral-rich ground water. Alder grows closely together with rusty willow and the shrubby eared willow on the fringes and in the glades. Where the substrate is more acid and less flushed, the alder may be replaced partially by birch. The wet floors of such woods support the remote sedge (*Carex remota*), in abundance with a characteristic wet com-

Wood anemone (Photo J. M. Boyd)

munity including marsh pennywort, yellow iris, meadowsweet, marsh-thistle (*Cirsium palustre*), marsh hawk's-beard, wavy bitter-cress (*Cardamine flexuosa*), marsh ragwort (*Senecio aquaticus*), hemlock water-dropwort (*Oenanthe crocata*), purple loosestrife and rushes. These woods are seldom extensive but they have a widespread distribution on Gigha, Islay, Jura, Garvellachs, Mull, Skye and Raasay.

Oak-birch woods occur on well-drained brown earths and podzols derived from acid rocks. On low ground where oak has been felled or on higher and north-facing slopes which are too cold and sunless for oak, the woods become birch-rowan on mixed mineral-organic soils and birch-hazel on predominantly organic soils. These woods occur on all the large islands of the Inner Hebrides and, unless they occur within forestry deer-fences, are heavily grazed. The ungrazed birch-oak has a floor of blaeberry and the grazed, of wavy hair-grass, moss carpets and hard fern (*Blechnum spicant*). The woods have a bright-flowering community including common cow-wheat (*Melampyrum pratense*), goldenrod (*Solidago virgaurea*), honeysuckle, tutsan, foxglove, primrose, wood-sorrel, wood-anemone and wild hyacinth. The lightly grazed birch-hazel woods have a ferny floor with *Oreopteris*, *Dryopteris* spp., *Athyrium* and *Phegopteris* spp. When heavily grazed, bracken or a community including sweet vernal-grass, bents, fescues, pignut (*Conopodium majus*), yellow pimpernel, bugle and enchanter's nightshade becomes common.

In exposed and north-facing aspects of mountain and island, where conditions are hard, the ash, oak, wych-elm, hazel, and alder stands are progressively replaced by birch. At the limits of native tree growth, only birch with eared willow and rowan remain, but the gradation to that limit is different depending on the soil type. The birch is mainly *Betula pubescens*; although *B. verrucosa* is present in the Hebrides, its distribution is as yet unstudied.

The leached mineral soils, or podzols, have a birch-rowan association which may contain scattered aspen, hazel and willow, but juniper is rare. The floor is dominated by blaeberry, bracken, purple moor-grass, bents, sweet vernal-grass, tormentil, wavy hair-grass, hard fern and devil's bit scabious. These woods do not occur on soils derived from basalt or in limestone localities but are otherwise widely distributed. The birch-hazel association on the brown earths is the most common native woodland in the Hebrides, and is recorded on all the islands where woodland occurs. It also possesses hawthorn, blackthorn or sloe, holly, aspen, bird-cherry and guelder-rose, though this is rare. The woodland floor is dominated by bracken, or a grass association (sweet vernal-bents-fescues-false brome), with water and wood avens, common valerian, wild strawberry, enchanter's nightshade, lesser celandine, yellow pimpernel, ferns, sedges and the ever-present primrose, sorrel, anemone and bluebell.

On the flushed gleys, peaty gleys and peaty podzols in gneiss, schist, granite, quartzite and sandstone islands, there is willow and birch. The rusty and eared willows are mixed with birch in similar manner to alder in the alluvial soils. This wood can either be a pioneer of new woody cover on moorland or a relict of erstwhile high woodland—the latter still retaining many of the epiphytic lichens, mosses and ferns of native high forest which the former do not possess. The floor is dominated by purple moor-grass, jointed rush (*Juncus articulatus*), and the mosses *Polytrichum* and *Sphagnum*. Many of the species of ground flora in alder-willow woods (above) are also present in these woods which occur on all islands possessing tree-cover. Pioneer phases of the birch-willow woods are particularly well seen in Eigg and Gigha and have many wet-heath plants such as the cross-leaved heath, bog asphodel, bog myrtle (*Myrica gale*), devil's bit scabious, tormentil, marsh cinquefoil, star sedge and flea sedge (*Carex pulicaris*).

In the Outer Hebrides native woodland is confined to islands in lochs and a few rocky ravines. The largest wooded islands occur in the freshwater lochs of South Uist, with smaller stands of low scrub as at Lochs Laxavat, Ard and Iorach and Loch Orasay in Lewis. The most important ravine woodland is at Allt Volagir near the north shore of Loch Eynort, South Uist. This is a dwarf wood which is so sparse as hardly to merit the term 'woodland'. However, in a habitat so exposed and bereft of trees as the Outer Hebrides, these wooded areas have a biological interest well beyond their physical size. The largest of the island woods is in Loch Druidibeg where the canopy consists of birch (*B. pubescens*), rusty and eared willows and rowan and is up to 3–4m tall. One island has a dense cover of *Rhododendron ponticum*, another has planted firs (*Abies* sp.) and there is another tiny birch-rowan wood beside Loch Spotal. These woods have an undercover of the dog rose (*Rosa canina*), brambles (*Rubus* sp.) and honeysuckle. In some of these woods hazel, aspen and juniper are present and there is a fern-rich ground flora.

The Allt Volagir wood is perhaps the most interesting native wood in the Outer Hebrides since it is regarded as a relict of the woodland which was once extensive before the advent of human settlement and animal husbandry changed the face of the islands. There is a canopy of birch, alder, grey willow, hazel, rowan and aspen, with an under layer of eared willow, juniper, holly, bird-cherry, ivy and *Rubus* sp. and a ground flora

A native wood at Allt Volagir, South Uist, containing at least eleven species of tree and a community of woodland plants (Photo J. M. Boyd)

of wood sorrel, wild angelica and bluebells with mosses, lichens and liverworts. An ash sapling has been seen, and over 60 species of vascular plant have been recorded from the wood which has been made a Site of Special Scientific Interest by the Nature Conservancy Council.

Plantations

The only example of high-canopied woodland in the Outer Hebrides occurs at Stornoway, where, about 1850, James S. Matheson began to create wooded policies around the Castle he had built overlooking the town and harbour. As was the custom in the sylvicultural and horticultural enterprises of the 19th and early 20th centuries, soil was imported from the mainland to supplement the poor native peaty gleys and podzols, and a wide variety of exotic species were used. In the Inner Hebrides, on existing brown earths in Skye, Mull and Islay, noble woodlands developed; the woods have grown well as far west as Stornoway and are greatly cherished by Lewis people for their gentle beauty and the relief they give to their otherwise bare landscapes. Peter Cunningham has studied and enjoyed these woods and their birds since the war, and states:

In the course of time and with considerable foresight and planning a magnificent collection of native and exotic trees and shrubs grew up around the castle, so distributed that no part of the woodlands seem ever without leaf and colour.

The plantations include spruces, firs, cypresses, pines, common beech, copper beech, elm, wych elm, sycamore, ash, oak, laburnum, whitebeam, plum, maple, berberis, azalea, fuschia and rhododendrons. To these can be added the native species which have volunteered their presence in the woods and a large and varied ground- and epiflora. The epiflora (mainly lichens) of the Stornoway and Rodel woods is described by Riedl (1979), who found the trees heavily encrusted by at least 58 species of lichen, while the forks of the trees are festooned by many species of moss and the hard fern.

There is a small plantation at Northbay, Barra, containing 13 species of tree and shrub and harbouring breeding goldcrests. It is a fine covert for migrant birds, and the same can be said for small stands at Grogarry, South Uist; Newton, North Uist; Horgabost and Borve, Harris; Voltos Glen and Glen Tolsta, Lewis. Experimental plots of conifers by the Forestry Commission at Balallan and Valtos have been followed by more extensive plantations of lodgepole pine (*Pinus contorta*) and Sitka spruce (*Picea sitchensis*) at Garrynahine (600 ha.) and Aline (200 ha.) in Lewis. In North Uist other experimental plots by J.P. Sutherland of the North of Scotland College of Agriculture have shown that the most successful exotic species of tree were the grey alder (*Alnus incana*), lodgepole pine, mountain pine (*Pinus mugo*), and native goat willow and wych elm. The best exotic shrubs were *Escallonia macrantha*, *Olearia albida*, *O. macrodonta*, *Phormium tenax* and dwarf mountain pine. Strangely, the list does not include sycamore (*Acer pseudoplatanus*) which by its very presence in existing plantations is one of the best trees for shelter in the Hebrides. These plantations give to the Outer Hebrides a range of habitats and species which might otherwise be absent. James Matheson, the Forestry Commission and other landowners who created these woodlands mainly for shelter, amenity and timber, have made a significant contribution to the conservation of nature as well as providing shelter for people and livestock.

The Inner Hebrides have plantations comparable to those of the mainland, again roughly divided into those of long-standing—mainly in broadleaves and conifers in the 'policies'

A spruce plantation at Braes, Skye, showing regeneration of native trees and bushes by the roadside (Photo C. Maclean)

of large houses or around villages—and commercial, coniferous plantations which are now extensive in Islay, Jura, Mull, Skye, Raasay and Scalpay (Skye). The extent of plantation woodland now greatly exceeds that of the native woodland and, though much of the recently-planted land probably carried native woods in the past, the new plantations have substantially changed the environment of the Inner Hebrides. On balance, that change has so far helped to diversify the environment, though the benefit to nature conservation would be enhanced with the greater use of broadleaf species, open space in the plantations of spruce and lodgepole pine, and the retention of old birch, oak, ash, hazel and willow for regeneration within the deer-fences.

The early plantations date back to the first half of the 19th century, and trees of that period still survive in many of the old policy woodlands. The most popular and successful broadleaf was sycamore, but oak, elm, beech (*Fagus sylvaticus*) and Norway maple (*Acer platanoides*) were widely used with the conifers, Norway spruce (*Picea abies*), European larch (*Larix decidua*), Scots pine, Corsican pine (*Pinus nigra*) and Douglas fir (*Pseudotsuga menziesii*). Despite many of these woodlands having been exploited for their best trees, and used over the last century as shelter for game and livestock, many old trees remain, providing habitat for a variety of wildlife. It became fashionable at one time to collect species of exotic trees in arboreta, so many Hebridean policy woods still contain fine specimens of *Thuja, Araucaria, Cedrus, Abies, Chamaecyparis, Tilia, Hippocastanea, Acer* and even palms and bamboos from subtropical regions.

Woodland Fauna

The plantations in Mull and Skye are dominated by lodgepole pine (50%) and Sitka spruce (40%). Larch has been used for amenity and fire protection (9%) and all others, including broadleaf species, amount to 1%. The moorland habitat gradually changes through growth stages of the plantations. In the five years after fencing, planting and cessation of burning, the grasses become rank, and there is often a spread of heather. The moorland waders may have abandoned the plantation, but songbirds such as the meadow pipit, skylark and wheatear may still remain and be joined by the predatory kestrel, short-eared owl, hen-harrier, fox (Skye only), weasel (except on Islay and Jura) and stoat, feeding on the thriving populations of voles in the luxuriant ground vegetation.

Next comes the 'thicket' stage (from 5–10 years), when the moorland birds have been replaced by willow warblers, whinchats, stonechats, robins, dunnocks, linnets, song thrushes and starlings feeding on the enriched supply of seeds, shoots and insects. By the beginning of the 'pole' stage, from 10–20 years, the canopy has completely closed and the thicket species are replaced by those of the 'mature' stage, 20 years or over, including chaffinches, greenfinches, chiffchaffs, siskins, redpols, goldcrests, blue tits, coal tits, great tits, blackbirds, wood pigeons and sparrow hawks. The number of species of bird increases during the growth stages of the forest but declines when the canopy closes tightly, and thinning of the forest at intervals of 10 years enhances the habitat for deer, birds and insects, as does the maintenance of open space with margins of birch, oak, ash, hazel and willow which have a good epiflora and insect fauna. Berry-bearing trees such as rowan, holly, elder, hawthorn, blackthorn or sloe, guelder rose and juniper are attractive to birds in the roadsides, fire-breaks, stream banks, lochsides and glades. Often the forestry fence encloses old broadleaf woodland which is retained unplanted and managed for natural regeneration. A good example of this occurs near Leitir–Fura, in south-east Skye, where a species-rich, ash-hazel wood within the forestry fence is now being cleared of the young coniferous underplantings, and the development of a mixed woodland by the Nature Conservancy Council on Rum, specifically to encourage a wide variety of

Roe deer fawn in the heather of open woodland (Photo J. M. Boyd)

wildlife, is described by Ball (1987). The woods at Stornoway Castle are the main focus of woodland fauna in the Outer Hebrides, and possess the following species of breeding bird:

English	Scientific	Gaelic
Skylark	*Alauda arvensis*	*Uiseag*
Grey wagtail	*Motacilla cinerea*	*Breacan-baintighearna*
Pied wagtail	*M. alba*	*Breac-an-t-sil*
Dipper	*Cinclus cinclus*	*Gobha-uisge*
Wren	*Troglodytes troglodytes*	*Dreathann-donn*
Dunnock	*Prunella modularis*	*Gealbhonn-garaidh*
Robin	*Erithacus rubecula*	*Bru-dhearg*
Whinchat	*Saxicola ruberta*	*Gocan*
Blackbird	*Turdus merula*	*Lon-dubh*
Song thrush	*T. philomelos*	*Smeorach*
Mistle thrush	*T. viscivorus*	*Smeorach-mhor*
Sedge warbler	*Acrocephalus schoenobaenus*	*Uiseag-oidhche*
Whitethroat	*Sylvia communis*	*Gealan-coille*
Chiffchaff	*Phylloscopus collybita*	*Caifean*
Willow warbler	*P. trochilus*	*Crionag-ghiuthais*
Goldcrest	*Regulus regulus*	*Crionag-bhuidhe*
Spotted flycatcher	*Muscicapa striata*	*Breacan-sgiobalt*
Blue tit	*Parus caeruleus*	*Cailleachag-cheann-gorm*
Great tit	*P. major*	*Currac-baintighearna*
Treecreeper	*Certhia familiaris*	*Snaigear*
Buzzard	*Buteo buteo*	*Clamhan*
Corncrake	*Crex crex*	*Traona*
Lapwing	*Vanellus vanellus*	*Curracag*
Snipe	*Gallinago gallinago*	*Naosg*
Wood pigeon	*Columba palumbus*	*Smudan*

English	Scientific	Gaelic
Collared dove	*Streptopelia decaocto*	
Cuckoo	*Cuculus canorus*	Cuthag
Jackdaw	*Corvus monedula*	Cathag
Rook	*C. frugilegus*	Rocas
Raven	*C. corax*	Fitheach
Starling	*Sturnus vulgaris*	Druideag
House sparrow	*Passer domesticus*	Gealbhonn
Tree sparrow	*P. montanus*	Gealbhonn-nan-craobh
Chaffinch	*Fringilla coelebs*	Breacan-beithe
Greenfinch	*Carduelis chloris*	Glaisean-daraich

One of the interesting features of this community of breeding birds is that many of them are at the extreme edge of their range, in particular the whinchat, chiffchaff, willow warbler and treecreeper. Even the garden warbler (*Sylvia borin*) and the wood warbler (*Phylloscopus sibilatrix*) have been recorded in summer. On Lewis many of the moorland birds commute daily or seasonally to and from the Stornoway woods, such as herons, kestrels, merlins, peregrines, hooded crows, ravens and starlings. In winter the dunnocks, robins, thrushes, tits, and finches move from the wood into the gardens of the town; Stornoway with its sycamores and shrubbery is but an urban extension of the neighbouring woodland habitat. The common winter migrants are blackcap (*Sylvia atricapilla*), fieldfare (*Turdus pilaris*), redwing (*T. iliacus*), waxwing, (*Bombycilla garrulus*), brambling (*Fringilla montifringilla*) and a few woodcock (*Scolopax rusticola*), goldfinch (*Carduelis carduelis*) and redpoll (*C. flammea*). No other woodlands in the Outer Hebrides have the same depth and variety of woodland habitat as the Stornoway woods, and few of these species breed elsewhere. However, the long-eared owl (*Asio otus*), the heron and the hooded crow nest on the wooded islands in the lochs.

Bramwell and Cowie (1983) quoting mainly from Taylor (1981), list 42 species of bird, 23 mammals, 3 amphibians and 3 reptiles which are found in the woodlands of Skye, Mull, Jura and Islay. None of these are rare but the distributions on these islands is interesting. Of the 73 vertebrates on this list, 51 were present on all four islands; 6 on three; 10 on two and 6 on one (3 questionable). The last are the brown long-eared bat (*Plecotus auritus*), red squirrel (*Sciurus vulgaris*), fox (*Vulpes vulpes*) and the smooth newt (*Triturus vulgaris*) all on Skye, and the bank vole (*Clethrionomys glareolus*) and polecat/ferret (*Mustela furo*), on Mull.

The nightjar (*Caprimulgus europeus*), which is at the extreme limit of its range in the Hebrides, has declined in Britain and has ceased to breed regularly in the Hebrides. It was last reported from Mull and Jura (1968–72). The great spotted woodpecker (*Dendrocopos major*) has colonised Jura, Mull and Skye since 1953 with single birds seen on Islay and Rum, and the green woodpecker (*Picus viridis*) has bred on Mull since 1979. The robin and redstart (*Pheonicurus phoenicurus*) are restricted to wooded islands but the latter is absent from Raasay, Canna and Eigg. Breeding fieldfares and redwings have not yet been recorded from the Hebrides. Willow warblers are common in all forms of woody cover, but the whitethroat, blackcap, wood warbler and chiffchaff favour extensive scrub or tall, mixed woodland with a scrub understory on Skye, Eigg, Rum, Mull, Jura and Islay.

The goldcrest has colonised the islands that have conifer plantations, as has the coal tit. The goldcrest is the initial coloniser and adjusts its numbers and distribution in the build-up of the dominant coal tit. The blue tit is widespread but the great tit is patchy becoming periodically absent in some of the small islands like Muck. The chaffinch is abundant and widespread in all island woods and the siskin, redpoll, bullfinch and crossbill have all found suitable habitat in the plantations and native woods. The crossbill in the Hebrides depends on maturing spruce plantations and a wide range of size and age classes is to its advantage. The siskin, which was noted as absent from the Hebrides by Baxter and Rintoul (1953), has now also successfully colonised spruce plantations on Skye, Rum, Eigg, Mull, Islay and occasionally Raasay and Canna (Thom, 1986). Bullfinches breed regularly on Skye, Raasay, Mull and Islay and intermittently in Eigg, Rum and Jura. The tree sparrow is not necessarily a woodland bird in the Hebrides, breeding as it has done in the past in treeless habitats such as St Kilda and Tiree; it still breeds sporadically on Islay, Tiree, Canna, Skye, Lewis and North Rona.

The fauna of Hebridean woodlands has not been systematically studied, but the birds, butterflies and moths are reasonably well known. The invertebrates in general are poorly recorded and many rewarding opportunities await the invertebrate biologist in the study of these woodlands. A variety of habitats is present because of the wide range of woodland types, and the new woods created by the Nature Conservancy Council on Rum provide an especially good opportunity to follow the development of woodland communities in the Inner Hebrides over the next fifty years. There is already a good record of colonisation of these woods by Peter Wormell (1977) and others, and on Canna by Dr J.L. Campbell (1984) over the past fifty years.

The wood ant (*Formica aquilonia*) is a recent coloniser of the Hebrides and was recorded at Mudalach Wood, on the Skye shoreline of Loch Alsh, in 1975 and 1984. Arboreal insects are well represented in the Hebrides. Even islands where woodland is restricted to isolated patches of scrub on crags or on islands in lochs, there are relict populations of woodland insects. On Rum, for example, there are 130 species of lepidoptera whose larvae feed on trees. Mull has a number of species of lepidoptera typical of deciduous woodland which are present in ancient woodland relicts on the adjacent mainland, such as the marbled brown (*Drymonia dodonaea*) which is typical of oak woods and the scarce prominent (*Odontosia carmelita*) which is typical of mature birch woods.

Colonisation by insects of newly planted woods occurs continuously. Within eight years of planting oak trees at Harris on the south-west of Rum, three species of gall wasp specific to oaks had colonised—the nearest natural oaks were five miles away. Conifer plantations have also brought colonists with them; the pine weevil (*Hylobius abietis*) and several species of bark and wood-boring beetles, plus the pine beauty moth (*Panolis flammea*), the pine carpets, *Thera firmata* and *T. obeliscata*, and the barred red (*Hylaea fasciaria*) are all present. The tawny-barred angle (*Semiothisa liturata*), another coniferous species, is present in the policy woods of Colonsay, and the giant wood wasp (*Uroceros gigas*) occurs in coniferous plantations in the Inner Hebrides together with its parasite, *Rhyssa persuasoria*, the largest of British ichneumon flies.

The purple hairstreak (*Quercusia quercus*), a true forest butterfly living in the canopy of oaks, is found in Coille Mhor in Colonsay together with the vapourer moth (*Orgyia antiqua*). Relict populations of these insects may have survived in this native wood remote from the charcoal burning which ravaged most other oak woods in the 18th and 19th centuries (Wormell 1983). The speckled wood (*Pararge aegeria*) is now found on Islay, Jura, Mull, Eigg, Rum and Canna and many species are likely to be introduced by the attachment of eggs to imported wood. Wormell (1983) mentions geometrid moths with flightless females from woodland habitats which are found in the Hebrides, such as the mottled umber (*Erannis defoliaria*) in Rum and Canna. However, some may occur naturally in solitary situations, since the larvae of the northern winter moth (*Operophtera fagata*) and the scarce umber (*Agriopis aurantiaria*) moths have been found on isolated birches in remote rocky clefts on Rum.

CHAPTER 9

Moor and Hill

Moorland Habitats

The main road (A865) through the Uists forms the boundary between the blacklands and moorlands over many miles. Travelling north from Daliburgh to Lochmaddy, you see on the right open hill ground rising to the summits of the islands, and on the left enclosed croftland, often known as the blacklands, stretching away towards the machair and the sea. In the previous chapters we have examined all the left-hand area, and now we turn to the right. This embraces the hill-country which stretches from the sea shore to the mountain-tops in some islands. Over most of the coast of the Hebrides there is little or no effect of blown sand and the moorland borders with the upper shore. On the rocky west coasts exposed to the force of the Atlantic, such as on Mull of Oa, Islay; Ceann a' Mhara, Tiree, Tangaval, Barra; Mangersta, Lewis; and Ruaival, St Kilda, the moorland facing the prevailing winds is affected by wind-driven spray, while on the sheltered east coasts this effect is minimal and the peatland, characteristic of the interior of the islands, lies hard upon the shore habitats, as around the east coast sea-lochs of the Outer Isles and the lee coasts of the Inner Isles.

The effect of sea spray on moorland habitats is described in Chapter 5 on salt marshes; here we look in detail at the moorland ecosystem which covers most of the islands and which has been used over the centuries as open-range grazings for sheep and cattle, as a source of peat for fuel, as a sporting range mainly for wildfowl, red deer, salmon and trout and more recently for forestry. The hill ground has its own ecological zonation which relates mainly to the patterns of waterlogging, exposure and altitude. Though bare and barren in aspect, there is in fact considerable variety in a habitat which ranges from the flat expanses of monotonous deep peat in central Lewis to the comparatively dry, thin-soiled slopes of the mountainous islands, especially the base-rich massifs of Skye, Rum and Mull. Lewis is estimated (DAFS, 1965) to have 595 sq km of peat to an average depth of 1.5m while the moorlands of Tiree have no workable peat.

Peat formation depends on rainfall, temperature, topography and country rock. By far the largest land area of the Hebrides has a rainfall, temperature regime, and topography conducive to peat formation, which has continued at different rates during successive climatic periods (see p. 45). The plant communities which have given rise to the peat have also changed. Forest has been very sparse or absent from the Outer Hebrides, Tiree and Canna. The Hebridean peat has therefore been generated by the plant communities of mire, rather than of woodland. Vascular plants and mosses maintain the peat blanket today.

Andrew Currie (1979) has identified the following moor and hill habitats, not all of which are present on each island but which are found throughout all the islands.

Moor	Hill
Sub-maritime heath and grassland	Upland acid heath and grassland
Lowland acid heath and grassland	Upland blanket peat
Lowland blanket peat	Montane flush and snowfields
	Cliff
	Scree
	Boulder field
	Summit

Lowland Heath

Lowland acid heath and grassland is the most extensive habitat of the Hebrides; it merges with other habitats and its dominant species are found over most of the moorland. There are also variants of this acid heath which reflect the degree of waterlogging; the dry areas tend to have more heather while the wet areas have more grass, sedge and rush. Also, in the setting of the Hebrides, species such as red fescue, sea plantain and thrift can be found throughout the altitudinal range of heath from the coast to the mountain tops. Conversely, the arctic-alpine species *Dryas octopetala* occurs on calcareous heaths near sea level in Skye and Raasay.

The plant communities of the acid heaths and grasslands are the main component of the vegetation of the Hebrides which contrast with the calcareous communities of machair and dunes where soil conditions are very different. In general, this is dark country of heather, purple moorgrass, deer grass with

Mountain avens to be found in Skye and Rum (Photo J. M. Boyd)

Sphagnum moss and common cottongrass in the rank wet ground. The proportion of heather to grass is a function of the intensity of grazing and burning as well as the waterlogging of the land. Within the forestry fences on Skye, heather has returned to ground where the land is free from sheep, deer and fire and has generally had better drainage. On the low moorland margins, the influence of sea spray or blown sand brings greenery to the sward with infiltrations of *Festuca-Agrostis-Holcus* communities, which also occur with the moorland around sites of past human settlement such as brochs, derelict crofts, sheilings and sheep folds. Similarly, on the high moorland margins, the effects of altitude, improved drainage and more readily available minerals are shown by spreads of wavy hair grass and mat grass in the moorland patchwork. In the basalt and gabbro country of the Inner Hebrides, where conditions are less acid than on the gneiss, the upper moorlands also possess much sweet vernal, viviparous fescue, and bent grasses.

The following plants determine the character of moorlands:

English	Scientific	Gaelic
Ling	*Caluna vulgaris*	*Fraoch*
Cross-leaved heather	*Erica tetralix*	*Fraoch-frangach*
Bell heather	*E. cinerea*	*Fraoch-a'-bhadain*
Blaeberry	*Vaccinium myrtillus*	*Dearcan-fithich*

English	Scientific	Gaelic
Creeping willow	Salix repens	
Purple moor grass	Molinia caerulea	Fianach
Deergrass	Trichophorum cespitosum	
Common cottongrass	Eriophorum angustifolium	Canach
Star sedge	Carex echinata	
Common sedge	C. nigra	
Pill sedge	C. pilulifera	Seisg
Carnation grass	C. panicea	
Green-ribbed sedge	C. binervis	
Viviparous fescue	Festuca vivipara	Feur-chaorach
Creeping soft grass	Holcus mollis	
Wavy hair-grass	Deschampsia flexuosa	Moin-fheur
Early hair-grass	Aira praecox	
Creeping bent-grass	Agrostis stolonifera	
Common bent-grass	A. capillaris	
Velvet bent-grass	A. canina	
Heath grass	Danthonia decumbens	
Heath rush	Juncus squarrosus	
Soft rush	J. effusus	Luachair-bhog
Sharp-flowered rush	J. acutiflorus	
Bulbous rush	J. bulbosus	
Field wood-rush	Luzula campestris	Learman
Heath wood-rush	L. multiflora	
Common dog-violet	Viola riviniana	Dail-chuach
Common milkwort	Polygala vulgaris	
Heath milkwort	P. serpyllifolia	
Slender St John's wort	Hypericum pulchrum	Achlasan-Chaluim-Chille
Tormentil	Potentilla erecta	Leamhnach
Round-leaved sundew	Drosera rotundifolia	
Long-leaved sundew	D. intermedia	Lus-na-fearnaich
Great sundew	D. anglica	
Sheeps' sorrel	Rumex acetosella	Ruanaidh
Heath speedwell	Veronica officinalis	Lus-cre
Lousewort	Pedicularis sylvatica	Lus-nam-mial
Common butterwort	Pinguicula vulgaris	Mothan
Harebell	Campanula rotundifolia	Butha-mu
Heath bedstraw	Galium saxtile	
Devil's bit scabious	Succisa pratensis	Greim-an-diabhail
Mouse-eared hawkweed	Hieracium pilosella	Lus-na-seabhaig
Bog asphodel	Narthecium ossifragum	Bliochan
Heath-spotted orchid	Dactylorhiza maculata	Urach-Bhallach
Bracken	Pteridium aquilinum	Raineach
Mosses	Sphagnum cuspidatum S. imbricatum, S. rubellum, S. fuscum, S. subsecundum, S. papillosum, S. magellanicum	
Lichens	Cladonia uncialis C. impexa	Crotal

Bog asphodel (Photo
J. M. Boyd)

The zoology of the acid moorland systems is generally less well known than their botany, one exception being the avifauna. The extreme exposure and heavy rainfall, combined with acidic, often waterlogged, soil conditions and a small range of species of plants, limits the diversity of invertebrates living there. However, the species which do occur, such as the midges (*Culicoides impunctatus*), are often present in profusion. Midges are especially abundant on peaty islands where small stagnant pools provide perfect breeding grounds, and clegs, or horse flies (*Tabanidae*), are another biting insect of these areas. Cattle, sheep, deer and, on Rum, ponies are all driven off the moorlands by these insects on still summer days, the red deer and sheep taking to the high ground while the cattle retire to the shore. Six species of clegs are found in the Hebrides, and their larvae are the predators of the larvae of other insects.

Some large and beautiful moths occur on the moorlands. By day, from April to August, the male emperor moth (*Saturnia pavonia*) may be seen flying quickly in an almost straight line over heather moorland. The female, however, which is even larger than the male, flies only at night, and during the day she produces a scent which can attract males from many miles. The caterpillars are equally spectacular and feed mainly on heather. Throughout the spring and summer there is a succession of hairy caterpillars of lasiocampid moths, such as the drinker (*Philudoria potatoria*) on purple moor-grass, fox (*Macrothylacia rubi*) and the northern eggar moths (*Lasiocampa quercus callunae*) on heather, which provide food for the cuckoo (*Cuculus canorus*), a common summer visitor to Hebridean moorlands.

Other day-flying moths on moorlands are the little eye-catching burnet moths with their bright scarlet underwings, which appear to have a somewhat localised distribution. For example, we have never seen burnets on Tiree despite many years of observation, though the six-spot burnet (*Zygaena filipendulae*) is common on the moorlands of most of the Inner Hebrides. We have also seen the Scottish race of the transparent burnet (*Z. purpuralis caledonensis*) on southwest Rum. It is concentrated in the Inner Hebrides, where it occurs on south-facing slopes, with wild thyme (*Thymus drucei*) upon which the larvae feed. It has been recorded from the Tertiary basalt habitats of Skye, Canna, Rum, Eigg, Muck, Mull and also Kerrera. The five-spot burnet (*Z. lonicerae*) occurs on Talisker Point, Skye where it feeds on legumes in the grass heath, and the slender Scotch burnet (*Z. loti scotica*) is confined to the Inner Hebrides with colonies on Mull and Ulva (Wormell, 1983).

Butterflies of the moorland include the meadow brown (*Maniola jurtina*), the small heath (*Coenonympha pamphilus*), the large heath (*C. tullia*), the dark green fritillary (*Argynnis aglaja*) and the small pearl-bordered fritillary (*Boloria selene*). The winter moth (*Operophtera brumata*) is present on moorland on Rum, where its larva has adapted to feeding on heather.

Flies, beetles, moths, butterflies, saw-flies, pondskaters, dragonflies, collembola, harvestmen and spiders sustain low densities of insectivores such as the meadow pipit and skylark, with the wheatear, stonechat and wren on the more broken ground with tall shrubs of gorse, heather and willow and some bare rock. In the spacious, flat mires (see below) the songbird community may be reduced to less than one or two pairs of meadow pipits per hectare. Red-throated and black-throated divers breed on moorland and hill lochs, the latter much scarcer than the former. The red-throat breeds on all the main islands except Colonsay, Tiree and Barra, while the black-throat breeds in Lewis and North Uist. There are also scattered breeding waders on the moors. Most of these feed on the shores and wet machairs and include common sandpipers, dunlin, lapwings, golden plovers, greenshanks, snipe and curlew (Inner Hebrides). Breeding densities of golden plover

Red-throated diver
(Photo D. MacCaskill)

on moorlands of the Outer Hebrides are generally less than one pair per sq km except on Lewis where, locally, they might be twice as numerous. The moorlands of Eigg, Islay, Jura, Mull, Rum, Raasay, Skye, Lewis, Harris and the Uists hold small populations of red grouse with black grouse on Colonsay, Islay and Jura. The raptors include the short-eared owl, hen harrier, sparrowhawk, buzzard, golden eagle, kestrel, merlin and peregrine. Herons, which feed on the weedy sea-inlets, often nest at moorland sites of scrub-covered islands in lochs, and ravens, hooded crows and gulls are common—they scavenge and breed on the moorland which also possesses breeding colonies of Arctic skuas on Coll and Lewis. Frogs occur on Skye and Mull but not on the Outer Hebrides, although they may have been introduced there.

Bogs and Mires

The 1980s will be remembered in the annals of Scottish natural history for the research into peatlands in Caithness and Sutherland, which accompanied the campaign by conservation bodies to safeguard these great mire systems from drainage and afforestation. The resulting publication, *The Flow Country: the peatlands of Caithness and Sutherland* (NCC, 1988) has seven authors, two editors, and fifty other contributors (mostly scientists). It has almost 350 references to other publications and it took 18 months to produce. In Mull, experiments by the Institute of Terrestrial Ecology showed that numbers of grouse could be substantially increased by certain controls of heather burning and sheep grazing (Watson *et al*,

1987). The mire is an organic landscape with features ranging from the bold to the subtle, from the macro- to the micro-habitats. The whole system is termed 'blanket mire complex' and the parts, 'mire units'. However, in the Hebrides, with the exception of central Lewis, the blanket mire complex is not extensive, and we have adopted the established British practice of describing the mire units according to the hydro-morphological features, of which 'blanket mire', 'raised' and 'valley' mires are represented in the Hebrides.

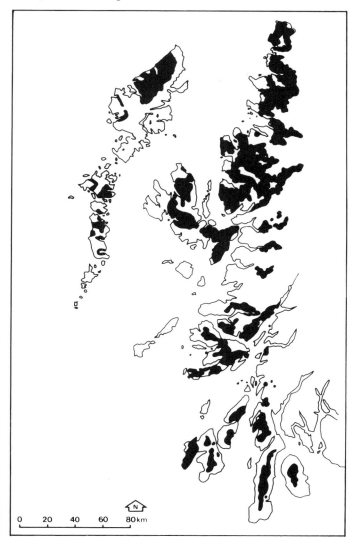

0   20   40   60   80 km

Fig. 20
Map showing the distribution of deposits of deep peat in the Hebrides and west mainland (from The Flow Country—The peatlands of Caithness and Sutherland, *1988, Nature Conservancy Council)*

The Callanish Stones, Lewis (Photo J. M. Boyd)

Within the lowland moorland there are blanket mires and more localised raised and valley mires, which are discrete systems of great interest. About 80% of the Lewisian platform north of the road from Leurbost to Garynahine is covered by deep peat. Peat formation commenced about 6,500 years ago in the 'Atlantic' period, and built-up 5m depth in places such as at Callanish where the megaliths were exposed by clearance of the peat mat in the 19th century. In the remainder of the Hebrides peat is extensive, but is generally neither so deep nor so continuous as on Lewis and is interspaced with tracts of drier heather moorland and bare rock. The inter-relationships of microtopography, water levels and patterns of vegetation of bogs in the Hebrides and comparisons between these and other British bogs are described by Goode and Lindsay (1979); Lindsay, Riggall and Bignal (1983); Ratcliffe (1977).

Blanket and Raised Mires

Blanket and raised mires are ombrotrophic, receiving all their water and nutrients from rainfall on the mire surface. The undisturbed blanket mires have spacious flats, usually of many sq km, which rise by about 1m in 1km from the edge to the crown of the bog. Raised mires are of lesser extent, and are generally flat with boundary streams. These flat surfaces have a

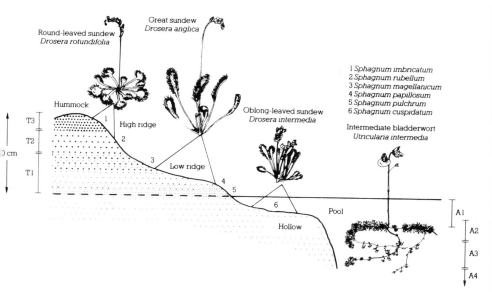

Fig. 21
A section of the pool and hummock showing the zonation of the Sphagnum mosses and the sundews in the microlandform (from The Flow Country—The Peatlands of Caithness and Sutherland, *1988,* Nature Conservancy Council*)*

pattern of communities depending on whether the mire is sloping in one direction (valleyside), or on all sides (watershed); the presence or absence of pool and hummock systems and of hollows; and on the nature of the water table, which about 90% of its time is normally within 5cms of the surface.

Though the entire body of the mire is waterlogged for most of the year, in summer the surface dries differentially causing local changes in the vegetation, which means that the bog vegetation is patterned by the seasonal variation of water levels. Bog biologists describe the habitats as *hummock, high ridge, low ridge, hollow* and *pool* (Fig. 21). In the broad, there are permanently waterlogged hollows and pools dominated by *Sphagnum* spp., mainly *S. cuspidatum*, purple moor grass, white-beak sedge, mud sedge (*C. limosa*), long-leaved sundew (*D. intermedia*), and bogbean. This community contrasts with that on swells of the bog with ridges and hummocks which, though waterlogged in winter, are drier in summer and dominated by tall purple moor-grass, deer grass, heather, cross-leaved heath, bog asphodel, common cottongrass, the hummock-forming *Sphagnum rubellum* and the wooly-fringe moss (*Rhacomitrium lanuginosum*) on the driest parts. There is an intermediate community identified by the growth-form of the moor-grass in clumps, cushions of *Sphagnum magellanicum* and a greater abundance of the white-beak sedge.

At the crown of mires, which have not been drained or otherwise changed by grazing and burning, there are pool and hummock systems. On the surface there seems little pattern, but when viewed from the air such systems are seen to be composed of an infinite variety of shapes. In absolutely flat watersheds in the blanket mire the pools and lochans may be rounded, but in others, on slight slopes of the very shallow 'valleys', the long axes of the pools and hummocks lie along the line of contour. This is due to water flowing at right-angles to the slope towards the edges of the bog where the outflow streams occur. These bog structures are delicate and sensitive to microtopography and changes in hydrostatic conditions within the bog as a whole. If, as often happens, the peripheral areas of a blanket mire are drained, the internal pool systems of the mire might be changed. These subtle widespread effects which sometimes transect ownership boundaries, take years to appear, and in the past have gone unappreciated.

Large cushions of *Sphagnum* are typical of blanket mire conditions, with the frequency of each species differing throughout the wet-dry successions. Bogbean thrives in dense mats in

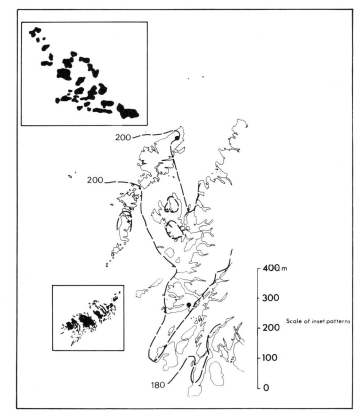

Fig. 22
Diagram showing the pattern of pools and ridges which distinguish the bogs in Lewis and Mull with annual average number of 'wet days' 1951–60 from British Rainfall *(from* The Flow Country—The peatlands of Caithness and Sutherland, *1988, Nature Conservancy Council)*

A bog in Glen Brittle, Skye (Photo I. L. Boyd)

the deep pools in association with sedges, cotton grass and the many-stalked spike-rush (*Eleocharis multicaulis*), while the submerged peat surfaces are covered by filamentous algae (*Batrachospermum* sp. and *Zygogonium* sp.) and the leafy liverwort (*Pleurozia purpurea*). The shallower pools have bog asphodel, sundew and bog pondweed (*Potamogeton polygonifolius*). The *Calluna-Molinia-Narthecium* transitions to the drier areas of the bog have much wooly-fringe moss and antler lichen (*Cladonia* spp.). The driest areas occur on peat mounds and are dominated by heather, crowberry, cotton grass, and the mosses *Pleurozium schreberi* and *Hypnum cupressiforme*. In eroding peat haggs the wooly-fringe moss abounds together with heather, purple moor-grass, common cottongrasses and the fir clubmoss (*Lycopodium selago*).

One of the best examples of blanket mire in the Hebrides is in the flow country at Achmore in central Lewis. This displays the full range of features, with lochans and extensive pool systems. Though grazed and burned for many centuries, these bogs, plus two on Islay, still retain pristine features which elsewhere have largely been destroyed by drainage and peat extraction. We have walked to the pool systems in Duich Moss (Eilean na Muice Duibhe), Islay in hard winter weather, and the frozen lochans at the crown of the bog were spread like white tablecloths. There are other very good examples of near-pristine blanket mire at Glac na Criche, Sanaigmore, Islay— now much reduced from its original size but possessing a striking abundance of black bog-rush (*Schoenus nigricans*)—and at Moineach Mararaulin on the watershed between Glen Brittle and Grunagary Glen, Skye—now almost surrounded by conifer plantations. Glen More, Mull has a fine raised mire between the Coladoir River and the A849 road. The pools and hummocks are well developed on two slightly sloping tongues of mire; as the slope steepens, small drainage channels appear and the pool systems vanish.

Valley Bogs

Valley bogs receive much of their water as run-off from the surrounding countryside, and this carries soil-enriching minerals. This type of bog is particularly frequent on the undulating, loch-studded country between Lochs Roag and Erisort in Lewis. They often merge with blanket mires on neighbouring higher ground, but are usually in small rock basins (<15 ha), and are much wetter than blanket mires because the water moves to the centre of the valley eventually draining away by a water track in the axis of the valley. These tracks are not streams but form definite channels up to 5m wide, sometimes deep and meandering with sparse, open vegetation and a bed of soft, organic detritus often stained red with oxides of iron. Water seeps rather than flows, but there is greater movement and nutrient-loading than in other parts of the bog. The tracks have filamentous algae (*Zygogonium* sp.) and a low, *Carex*-dominated fen with *Sphagnum subsecundum*, mud-sedge, bog pondweed and bogbean. Deergrass, white-beak sedge, slender sedge, sundew and bog-rush are abundant within the water tracks, with common cottongrass on the margins. Table 2 of Goode and Lindsay (1979) shows the changes in the flora of the valley mires in Lewis from the water track to the drier margin. Fifty-four species of bog plant were recorded, 26 in the water track, 25 in the *Carex-Sphagnum* lawns and 42 in the hummock and hollow habitats. The popular impression is of the mire as a dull, wet wasteland when it is in fact a wonderful tapestry whose beauty and interest is open only to those few naturalists who now carry a lens and have knowledge of grasses, sedges, rushes, mosses and lichens. The mire often also acts in the service of man as the sponge which retains the rainfall and regulates the supply of water to stream, river, reservoir, industry and household.

Towards the lower end of the water tracks, the *Carex* fen, dominated by bottle sedge and slender sedge (*C. lasiocarpa*), thickens in response to increased nutrients. The white water-lily, lesser spearwort, marsh cinquefoil, horsetail and the mosses *Sphagnum recurvum* and *Polytrichum commune* thrive in the enrichment. The lower reaches of the water tracks resemble fen hollows with greater diversity of species, particularly on the basalt plateaux of Skye and Mull, where the bedrock is base-rich and of a higher nutrient status than the Lewisian gneiss. *Sphagnum* hummocks in the water tracks usually hold sundews, bog asphodel, deer grass, bottle sedge, common butterwort, occasionally pale butterwort, lesser clubmoss (*Selaginella selaginoides*) and the few-flowered sedge (*Carex pauciflora*). In the dry tops of the hummocks there is heather and bell heather, milkwort and tormentil. On the margins of the tracks the hummocks coalesce, become larger and merge into the context of the mire. White-beak sedge is often characteristic of the margin between the richer valley mire and the surrounding blanket mire which is ombrotrophic. The extreme wetness of the valley mires protects them from the adverse effects of burning and heavy grazing, but they are more vulnerable to drainage than are blanket mires.

Plants which characterise the mires of the Hebrides (wetter (w), intermediate (i), and drier facies (d) of the mire flora) are:

English	Scientific	Gaelic	Facies type
Bog mosses	*Sphagnum palustre*		w
	S. recurvum		w
	S. subsecundum		w
	S. inundatum		w
	S. subnitens		w-i
	S. cuspidatum		w
	S. tenellum		w-i
	S. papillosum		w-i
	S. magellanicum		w-i
	S. rubellum		w-d
Bogbean	*Menyanthes trifoliatus*	*Luibh-nan-tri-bheann*	w
Great sundew	*Drosera anglica*	*Lus-na-fearniach*	i-d

English	Scientific	Gaelic	Facies type
Round-leaved sundew	*D. rotundifolia*	} *Lus-na-fearnaich*	i-d
Oblong sundew	*D. intermedia*		w-i
Deer-grass	*Trichophorum cespitosum*		i-d
Purple moor-grass	*Molinia caerulea*	*Fianach*	i-d
Common cottongrass	*Eriophorum angustifolium*	*Canach*	w-d
Hare's-tail cottongrass	*E. vaginatum*		d
Many-stalked spike-rush	*Eleocharis multicaulis*		w-i
Bog asphodel	*Narthecium ossifragum*	*Bliochan*	i
Common butterwort	*Pinguicula vulgaris*	*Brog-na-cuthaige*	i
Cross-leaved heath	*Erica tetralix*	*Fraoch-frangach*	i
Heather	*Calluna vulgaris*	*Fraoch*	d
Crowberry	*Empetrum nigrum*	*Caora-fithich*	d
Marsh cinquefoil	*Potentilla palustris*	*Coig-bhileach-uisge*	w
Tormentil	*P. erecta*	*Leamhnach*	d
Water horsetail	*Equisetum fluviatile*	*Clois*	w
Lesser spearwort	*Ranunculus flammula*	*Glas-Leumhnach*	w
Bog pondweed	*Potamogeton polygonifolius*	*Linne-lus*	w
Black bog-rush	*Schoenus nigricans*		w-i
Bottle sedge	*Carex rostrata*	}	w
Common sedge	*Carex nigra*		i-d
Bog sedge	*C. limosa*	*Seisg*	w-i
Slender sedge	*C. lasiocarpa*		w
White-beak sedge	*Rhynchospora alba*		i
Mosses	*Polytrichum commune*	}	w
	P. alpestre	*Coinneach*	w
	Pleurozium schreberi		d
	Racomitrium lanuginosum		d
Lichens	*Cladonia impexa*	} *Crotal*	d
	C. uncialis		i-d
Algae	*Zygogonium*	}	w
	Batrachospermum		w

Agricultural development in Britain over the last two millenia has removed much of the widespread, primaeval mire, and in recent years, forestry has also made claims upon the remaining mire systems. The conservation of bogs has thus become a *cause célèbre* in Britain, and Duich Moss in Islay has been at the centre of the public debate. The proposal to extract peat from the bog by Scottish Malt Distillers was opposed by conservation bodies on the grounds that such a development would seriously damage one of the last undisturbed blanket bogs in the Hebrides which is also the winter roost of the rare Greenland white-fronted geese, and the outcome of the controversy was a shift of the peat extraction to another bog in Islay which has no significant interest. It is a good measure of the success of nature conservation in Britain that the safeguard of habitat still popularly regarded as good-for-nothing wasteland has been so successfully accomplished at Duich Moss.

Montane Communities

The lowland heaths with their in-lying mires reach up the
island hills and merge with sub-montane grass heaths of bents,
fescues, sweet vernal and mat grasses on well-drained slopes
with a lot of exposed rock. Variations in the grassy mantle
reflect those of climate and substrate. The mountain tops of the
Hebrides have a limited range of species compared with the
mainland; the Outer Hebrides possess only 29 of the 118
species of montane vascular plants in the British flora, though
the Inner Hebrides has a montane flora similar to the West
Highlands, possessing 93 species. In general, the mountain
tops are too wind-blasted, rugged and limited in summit area to
develop extensive montane communities, though spacious
summits do occur in the larger of the Inner Isles. Often, therefore, the botanically interesting montane communities are
placed on broad terraces or in gullies well below the summits.
Snow-patch vegetation is poorly represented and widely scattered in comparison with the mainland, though it occurs more
frequently on Jura, Mull, Rum and Skye than on North Harris.

The gabbro and basalt summits are more base-rich than
those of granite, gneiss and quartzite, but this difference is not
greatly reflected in the plant communities as it is at the lower
levels, where more mature soils have been generated. The
ultra-basic rocks of Rum, though magnesium-rich, are low in
calcium and have a poor flora. The summit habitats are dominated by a heath of wooly-fringe moss with montane and
Arctic-Alpine sedges, rushes and herbs. These summit habitats are islands within islands; outliers of the Arctic-Alpine
plateau of mainland Scotland which are still being colonised
by the montane species. For example, the lady's mantle
(*Alchemilla wichurae*), rock whitlowgrass (*Draba norvegica*),
Alpine rock-cress (*Arabis alpina*), and rock sedge (*Carex rupestris*) and creeping cudweed (*Gnaphalium supinum*), Alpine
cinquefoil (*Potentilla crantzii*), Alpine pearlwort (*Sagina sagi-
noides*) and *Sibbaldia procumbens* have been found in Skye but in
none other of the Hebrides. Similarly, the spring sandwort
(*Minuartia verna*) is recorded only from Mull, Alpine penny
cress (*Thalspi alpestre*) only from Rum and the bog bilberry
(*Vaccinium uliginosum*) only from Jura.

The thin, wind-clipped, procumbent mantle of plant life on
the rocky summits possesses its own muted beauty when seen
on a fine summer's day. So wonderful are the outward views
from the high-tops of the Cuillins and Paps on such days that
the carpets of moss, lichen and sedge go unnoticed underfoot,
yet this wafer-thin veneer of life is as subtle in its ecology as in
its colours of grey, greens and ochres. The rock surfaces are

encrusted with lichens, and some areas near the summits have especially interesting communities. Take the wet heaths of the endemic mosses *Campylopus shawii* and *Myurum hebridarum* in North Harris, which will only grow where there are over 220 wet days per annum, and the crags of Coire Uaigneich, east of Blaven in the Black Cuillin of Skye, which contain an extensive north-west facing outcrop of Jurassic limestone with a rich flora including tall herbs such as Alpine meadow-rue, mossy saxifrage and Alpine saw-wort. The Cuillin of Rum possesses a maritime grassland with fescues, bents and hair grasses created and maintained by a vast nesting population of burrowing Manx shearwaters. On Rum, the moss-campion (*Silene acaulis*), northern rock cress (*Cardaminopsis petraea*), the two-flowered rush (*Juncus biglumis*) and the arctic sandwort (*Arenaria norvegica*) are to be found on scattered ridges and terraces of the gabbro hills, with the Alpine penny-cress and the snowy saxifrage (*Saxifraga nivalis*) on the basalt, while on the neighbouring granite top of Orval there is a stoney fjellfield holding a heath in which the Alpine-clubmoss (*Lycopodium alpinum*) is locally dominant with wooly-fringe moss, sedges and rushes. The basalt escarpment of The Storr and Quirang in Skye is one of the finest upland botanical sites of the Hebrides with a fine range of species-rich, montane communities on ledges, dry and sunlit rocks, wet and shadowy gullies, steep slopes with screes below cliffs and summit ridges. Both it and the Black Cuillins are SSSIs (Sites of Special Scientific Interest). Saxifrages (*S. hypniodes, S. aizoides, S. oppositifolia, S. nivalis*) and mountain avens occur in a bright

The alpine clubmoss which forms a carpet on the summit of Orval, Rum (Photo J. M. Boyd)

and diverse flora which also includes the rare Iceland purslane *Koenigia islandica*, also found on Mull. There are also fern-rich niches with the green spleenwort (*Asplenium viride*), brittle bladder-fern (*Cysopteris fragilis*), holly fern (*Polystichum lonchitis*) and the mosses *Mnium orthorhynchum* and *Pohlia cruda*.

The species lists for the montane vegetation of the Hebrides are given by Currie (1979) and Currie and Murray (1983). Within the montane elements of the Hebridean flora there are, in addition, the following species which characterise the northern montane (nm), Arctic-subarctic (as), Arctic-alpine (aa) and Alpine elements (a) in both the Inner and Outer Hebrides:

Alpine scurvy-grass	*Cochlearia alpina* nm
Variegated horsetail	*Equisetum variegatum* nm
Interrupted clubmoss	*Lycopodium annotinum* nm
Alpine hair grass	*Deschampsia alpina* as
Eyebright	*Euphrasia frigida* as
Northern yellow rattle	*Rhinanthus borealis* as
Chickweed willow-herb	*Epilobium alsinifolium* aa
Alpine willow-herb	*E. anagallidifolium* aa
Three-leaved rush	*Juncus trifidus* aa
Three-flowered rush	*Juncus triglumis* aa
Trailing azalea	*Loiseleuria procumbens* aa
Alpine meadow-grass	*Poa alpina* aa
Glaucous meadow-grass	*Poa glauca* aa
Alpine bistort	*Polygonum viviparum* aa
Holly fern	*Polystichum lonchitis* aa
Whortle-leaved willow	*Salix myrsinites* aa
Alpine saw-wort	*Saussurea alpina* aa
Scottish asphodel	*Tofieldia pusilla* aa
Mossy cyphel	*Cherleria sedoides* a*

*Requires confirmation from the Outer Hebrides.

The animal ecology of the Hebridean uplands is mainly unknown, though many species have been recorded. The beetles are the best studied group of upland invertebrates, but even so their distribution is still incompletely understood, and even less is known of their ecology. Species once thought typical of the Cairngorm plateau and the highest mainland peaks are now known from the Skye Cuillins, the Paps of Jura and the higher peaks of Mull and Rum. The ground beetle *Nebria nivalis* is one such example, a predator of other invertebrates around the margins of permanent snowfields over which it will forage at night. It is found in company with *N. gyllenhali*, a common and widely distributed upland species. Other typical upland beetles include *Leistus montanus*, *Patrobus septentrionis*, *Arpedium brachypterum*, *Geodromicus longipes*, *Mycetoporus baudueri*, *M. monticola*, *Boreophila islandica*, *Atheta tibialis* and *A.*

nitidiuscula. The flightless weevil, *Otiorhynchus arcticus*, a common montane species, also occurs in the dunes of Kilmory on Rum, but is generally distributed throughout the Outer Isles. Similarly, *Ocypus hibernica*, presently known in the Hebrides only from South Uist, is an example of the many montane species which occur at low altitudes in the Outer Hebrides. At least five species of dung beetles (*Aphodius* sp.) have been found exploiting deer dung in the Hebrides, of which *A. borealis* is a true montane species. There is little information about the spiders of the uplands but *Meioneta nigripes, Theridion bellicosum* and *Entelecara errata* are known to occur.

The Hebrides have a number of rare upland microlepidoptera including *Scrobipalpa montanus*, a leaf miner on the mountain everlasting on Rum, *Nepticula dryadella*, on mountain avens, *Catoptria furcatellus*, on grasses of the high screes and erosion terraces, and *Epinotia nemorivaga*, on bearberry (*Arctostaphylos uva-ursi*) on Coll. However, as with many of the invertebrate groups, this list is probably limited more by the number of expert naturalists who have looked for different species in these parts than by the diversity of the fauna.

The invertebrates on the high tops also include flies and spiders, which are the thinly distributed food of the rock pipit throughout the Hebrides, and ring-ouzel in the Inner Isles. Ptarmigan bred in the Outer Isles until about 1924 and also formerly bred on Rum where it still occurs occasionally. Small breeding populations still survive on Skye, Mull and Jura, feeding on the shoots and fruits of crowberry, bearberry, creeping and dwarf willow and the occasional insect and spider. The raven and the golden eagle occupy the high-top range of all the mountainous islands as well as much of the lower moorland and coastal habitats. Though the eyries are usually at low level, often near the sea—in Skye the golden eagle has been known to nest on flat ground—these birds can rise from their nests and, in a matter of minutes, soar high above the summits on the lookout for prey and carrion. Red deer and sheep occupy the mountain tops of Harris, Skye, Mull and Jura from time to time in settled weather and the carcases of those that die provide food for eagles and ravens. Ptarmigan and mountain hares, although scarce, are also prey of the golden eagle; the mountain hare can be seen on Lewis, Harris, Skye, Raasay, Scalpay and Mull. On Rum, the montane zone contains thousands of breeding Manx shearwaters which have made the tops green and rich in fauna, thus attracting wheatears. The shearwaters provide food for brown rats and both fall prey to the eagle.

Inland Waters

The inland waters of the Hebrides are modest compared with those of the mainland. With the exception of the waters on machair and limestone, the catchments are generally small, of low altitude and poor in nutrients. However, they are a major component of the ecosytem and contribute much to the character and natural history of the islands. The soft bugling of the whooper swans on the machair loch on a still, crisp winter's day is a thrilling sound, while in the long twilight of a summer's day, the sedge warbler calls from the reed bed, its scoldings interspersed with sweet, musical passages. In wet weather the islands' lochs overflow and join the burns rushing downhill in wind-whipped cascades, often ending over a precipice to the sea. This is in sharp contrast to long, warm dry spells when hill streams are reduced to a whisper, and blue damselflies have their courtship on sunny, heathery banks and the red-throated divers perform their high-flying ritual between the hill lochs and the sea.

Physical and Chemical Conditions

On the 1:63,360 O.S. maps, there are some 7,580 lochs in the Hebrides; 1,542 in the Inner and 6,038 in the Outer Isles (Table 10.1). The Outer Hebrides comprise 1.3% of the land area of Great Britain, but have 15% of the area of standing water. Ninety-seven per cent (7,408) of the lochs in the Hebrides are less than 0.25 sq km in area and 98% (5,977) of those in the Outer Hebrides are in nutrient-poor catchments. The largest lochs by area are: Langavat on Lewis (8.9 sq km, 67.6 million cu m); Suainaval, also on Lewis (2.4 sq km, 80.5 million cu m, 65.7 m deep). Lochs are most numerous on the platform of impervious gneiss of the Outer Isles and on the plateau basalts and hard quartzites of the Inner Isles. The landscapes of central and north Lewis and North Uist are a patchwork of lochs and lochans; the sea inlets of North Uist almost connect at high tide with the inland waters while, at the ebb, the frontier between the sea and the fresh waters becomes separated by wide expanses of sand or wrack (see over).

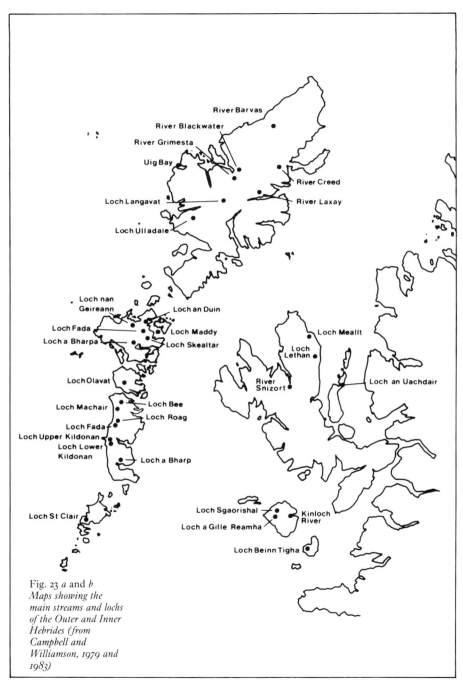

Fig. 23 *a* and *b*
Maps showing the
main streams and lochs
of the Outer and Inner
Hebrides (from
Campbell and
Williamson, 1979 and
1983)

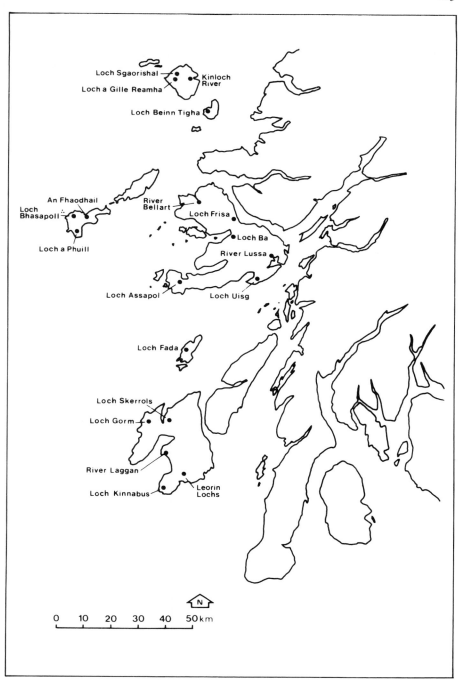

Loch Sgaorishal
Loch a Gille Reamha
Kinloch River
Loch Beinn Tigha
An Fhaodhail
River Bellart
Loch Frisa
Loch Bhasapoll
Loch Ba
Loch a Phuill
River Lussa
Loch Assapol
Loch Uisg
Loch Fada
Loch Skerrols
Loch Gorm
River Laggan
Loch Kinnabus
Leorin Lochs

N

0   10   20   30   40   50 km

Islands	Lochs	Streams
Lewis and Harris	4,136	1,030
North Uist	914	122
Benbecula	325	43
South Uist	650	106
Barra	13	74
Outer Hebrides	6,038	1,375
Skye	307	632
Raasay, Scalpay, South Rona	62	65
Rum, Eigg, Canna, Soay, Muck	129	108
Tiree, Coll, Ulva, Iona	117	66
Mull	226	351
Colonsay, Oronsay	17	34
Lismore, Kerrera, Seil, Luing, Scarba, Shuna	25	65
Jura, Gigha	390	132
Islay	269	162
Inner Hebrides	1,542	1,615
Total for the Hebrides	7,580	2,990

Table 10.1   The numbers of lochs and streams in the Hebrides taken from O.S. maps by Waterston *et al.*, (1979) and Maitland and Holden (1983)

The running waters are short and fast-flowing, except on the flat platforms of mire and through cultivated land and machair. The total number of streams entering the sea, as marked on the O.S. map, is 2,990 (1,375 Outer, 1,615 Inner Hebrides) these are the conflux of 19,347 stream segments (9,240 Outer, 10,107 Inner). In the Inner Hebrides, there are 10,550km of streams covering an area of some 22 sq km.

The rain from the ocean is like very dilute sea water, containing dissolved substances acquired from the atmosphere and the sea, and these find their way into the water system. During its journey through mire, meadow, stream, loch and river back to the sea, the water becomes further charged with substances acquired from the land. Though there are numerous trace substances which enrich these fresh waters, the two which more than any of the others govern their quality as a medium for life, are sodium chloride (salt) obtained from the sea, and calcium carbonate (lime) obtained from shell-sand or alkaline rocks such as limestones. The influence of the sea on the freshwater of the Hebrides is illustrated by Fig. 24, which shows that, while there is little difference in the calcium content of fresh waters from the Outer Hebrides, the Inner

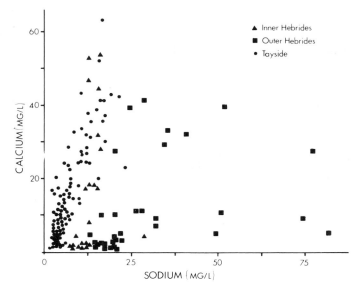

Fig. 24
*Plots of calcium against
sodium values for
various waters in the
Outer Hebrides, Inner
Hebrides and Tayside
to illustrate the
gradient, from the outer
rim to the central
mainland, of ions
derived mainly from
sea spray (from
Maitland and Holden
1983)*

Hebrides and mainland Scotland, the sodium content (indicative of salt) is highest in the exposed Outer Hebrides. The influence of salt and lime on the habitat has already been mentioned in Chapters 5 and 6 respectively, in the descriptions of saltmarshes and machair. Now we deal with the effects of these and other solutes on the biota of inland waters. In this chapter we are concerned with the running and standing waters which lie above the limits of Ordinary Spring Tides but which are still charged with substantial quantities of salt.

Freshwater Vegetation

In Table 20 of *A Nature Conservation Review*, 139 species of vascular plant are listed for open waters in Britain; 86 of these have been recorded from the Outer Hebrides and a greater number from the Inner Hebrides, for which a comprehensive check-list is not available (Currie 1979; Currie and Murray 1983). There is a group of species which is more or less confined to north and north-west Britain: quill-wort (*Isoetes lacustris*), spring quill-wort (*I. echinospora*), the white water-lily (*Nymphaea alba*), awlwort (*Subularia aquatica*), water starwort (*Callitriche hermaphroditica*), creeping forget-me-not (*Myosotis secunda*), marsh bladderwort (*Utricularia intermedia*), water lobelia (*Lobelia dortmanna*), slender-leaved pondweed (*Potamogeton filiformis*) and floating and small bur-reeds

(*Sparganium angustifolium* and *S. minimum*). There are three species rare to the British flora and possessing Irish-American affinities, namely: American pondweed (*Potamogeton epihydrus*) in the Outer Hebrides; slender naiad (*Najas flexilis*) in the Uists, Benbecula, Mull, Colonsay and Islay; and the pipewort (*Eriocaulon aquaticum*), which is confined in the British Isles to Skye, Ardnamurchan and western Ireland. The rare Shetland pondweed (*Potamogeton rutilus*) is found in the Outer Hebrides and Tiree.

Loch Druidibeg (loch of the little starling) in South Uist is at the centre of an inland-water system which embodies most of the estuarine, brackish and freshwater habitats of the Outer Hebrides. Much of this system has been designated an SSSI and National Nature Reserve by the NCC (see also p. 100, H-AHL), and includes alkaline, neutral and acid lochs on machair, blackland and moorland habitats respectively. The range in chemical character of the freshwaters of the Loch Druidibeg NNR is shown in Table 10.2.

Loch	pH	CaCO₃	Na	Ca	Cl	SO₄	Habitat
Stilligary	7.58	104.8	22.6	39.7	29.8	20.8	machair/alk*
a'Mhachair	7.70	62.4	18.9	28.0	33.4	16.8	machair/alk
an Roag	6.60	4.6	21.1	2.6	37.6	11.5	brackish
Fada	6.60	8.4	20.8	3.6	34.1	12.9	blackland/neut**
Eilein	7.63	25.6	15.1	10.5	22.0	12.1	blackland/neut
Rigarry	7.00	14.0	13.3	4.2	20.6	12.1	blackland/neut
Druidibeg (West)	7.23	33.2	18.7	10.9	29.8	10.9	moor/neut-acid
Druidibeg (Mid)	6.30	3.8	12.8	4.4	21.3	9.2	moor/neut-acid
Hamasclett	6.00	0.8	13.6	1.7	22.0	8.0	moor/acid***
A. na h'Achlais	5.82	1.8	13.1	1.3	20.6	10.9	moor/acid
Teanga	5.56	0.6	12.0	1.1	22.0	9.3	moor/acid

*   machair/alkaline = eutrophic/mesotrophic
**   blackland/neutral = mesotrophic
*** moor/acid = oligotrophic

Table 10.2   The range of character in the main lochs in Loch Druidibeg and neighbouring lochs measured by Waterston and Lyster (1979) in April–May 1977:

Fig. 25
Map showing the lochs of South Uist referred to in the text (from Waterston and Lyster, 1979). N.B. Grogarry Loch = Loch a'Mhachair

It is often difficult to categorise Hebridean lochs according to their richness, because of the large influence of the sea on their chemical composition; most are anomalous in whatever trophic category they fall. Probably the only truly eutorphic loch in the Outer Hebrides is Loch a'Chinn Uacraich on Benbecula.

Professor David Spence gave a list of 66 species of macro-phytes from 33 lochs in the north of South Uist (Spence *et al.*,

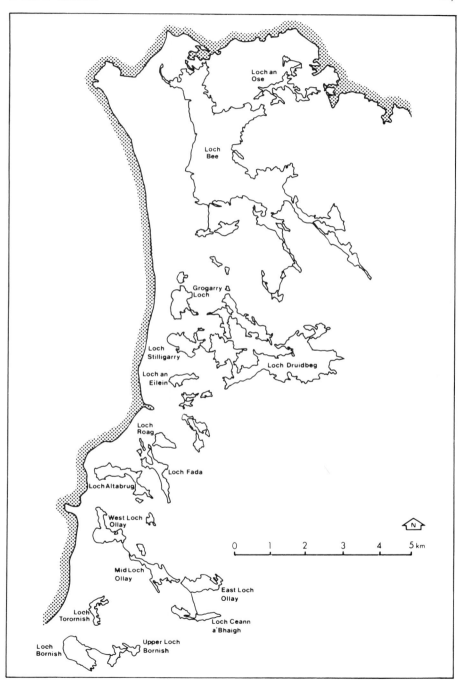

1979) including the widest possible set of ecological conditions from brackish-fresh waters in the Outer Hebrides (Table 10.3).

Species		Lochs	% Freq
Marsh marigold	*Caltha palustris*	10	30
Common sedge	*Carex nigra*	18	54
Stone-wort	*Chara* spp	14	42
Many-stalked spike-rushes	*Eleocharis multicaulis*	9	27
Common spike-rush	*E. palustris*	17	51
Marsh pennywort	*Hydrocotyle vulgaris*	12	26
Quill-wort	*Isoetes lacustris*	14	42
Jointed rush	*Juncus articulatus*	7	21
Bulbous rush	*J. bulbosus*	23	69
Shore-weed	*Littorella uniflora*	27	81
Water lobelia	*Lobelia dortmanna*	21	63
Water mint	*Mentha aquatica*	8	24
Alternate-flowered water milfoil	*Myriophyllum alterniflorum*	27	81
Spiked water milfoil	*M. spicatum*	15	45
Common reed	*Phragmites australis*	7	21
Pondweeds	*Potamogeton gramineus*	23	69
	P. natans	21	63
	P. perfoliatus	11	33
Lesser spearwort	*Ranunculus flammula*	18	54
Unbranched bur-reed	*Sparganium emersum*	9	27
Awlwort	*Subularia aquatica*	9	27

Table 10.3   Twenty-one dominant species found in over six (20 per cent) of the 33 lochs surveyed by Spence *et al.* (1979) in the Uists. The total number of lochs in which each species was found and the percentage frequency are given.

Brackish Waters

Electrical conductivity of water is a function of the amount of dissolved solids in the water; sea water is highly conductive, while rain water is poorly conductive. The quality and quantity of solutes has an effect on the pH and the distribution of living creatures (Table 10.4).

Loch	1	2	3	4
Conductivity	2,573	13,235*	22,490	33,900
pH	8.1	8.8**	8.5	9.6***
Species				
E. palustris	+			
N. alba	+			
P. australis	+			
P. natans	+			
P. perfoliatus	+			
P. praelongus	+			
Callitriche sp.	+			
M. alterniflorum	+	+		
Chara sp.	+	+		
L. uniflora	+	+	+	
P. gramineus	+	+	+	
Enteromopha sp.	+	+	+	
F. ceraniodes	+	+	+	+
R. spiralis		+	+	+
Chaetomorpha sp.		+	+	+
Ectocarpus sp.		+	+	
Polysiphona sp.			+	+
F vesiculosus			+	+
Codium fragile				+
Halidrys siliquosa			+	
A. nodosum				+
Ceramium rubrum				+
Cladophora sp.				+

1   Loch Ceann a' Bhaigh (Ollay-Eynort system)
2   Loch Bee
3   Loch Roag (Howmore system)
4   Loch an-t-Saile (Bee system)
*   Average of range: 9,860–16,610
**   Average of range: 8.5–9.45 pH units
*** Average of range: 9.20–9.95 pH units
+   Found by Spence *et al.*

Table 10.4   The distribution of macrophytes in four lochs in South Uist having conductivities greater than 1,000 Is/cm (at 25°C) arranged in decreasing order (Spence, *et al.*, 1979).

This choice of lochs illustrates well the front between the fresh water and marine systems. The green alga (*Entero-morpha*) occurs at the fresh water-marine interface, because above the level of *Enteromorpha* the species are predominently fresh in character, while below that level they are marine. Indeed a three-tier distribution is detectable in which those above the starworts (*Callitriche*) are positively fresh, those between the starworts and the plant limp (*Ectocarpus*) are brackish, and those below the plant limp positively saline.

Loch Ceann a' Bhaigh is connected to the sea in Loch Eynort. It has remained relatively fresh in character with beds of common reed, white water lily and pondweeds, but *Fucus ceranoides* is a sure indicator of saline conditions. The other extreme is Loch Bee, the largest brackish lagoon in the Hebrides, which is up to four times as salty as Ceann a' Bhaigh and has almost lost its fresh water communities. Around fresh water inlets there are hardy stands of pondweed (*Potamogeton gramineus*), spiral tasselweed, shore-weed, alternate-flowered water milfoil (*Myriophyllum alterniflorum*) and lesser spearwort. Elsewhere, Loch Bee is brackish to marine in character with abundant *F. ceranoides* and bladder wrack. Serrated and knotted wracks, 'bootlace' (*Chorda filum*), sea lettuce (*Ulva lactuca*), *Enteromorpha* sp., and the threads *Codium tomentosum* and *Cladophora glomerata* grow in the vicinity of the sea inlets. Lochs Roag and an-t-Saile are distinctly brackish. Loch Obisary is brackish, with small specimens of the marine mussel (*Mytilus edulis*) on the fronds of the pondweeds in the shallows. This is a very unusual loch because it has a small, shallow inlet from the sea and it is quite large and deep. This means that there is full strength sea water at depth, and almost fresh water at the surface.

Edith Nicol (1936) was the first to describe the brackish habitats of the Hebrides in detail. In twelve brackish water systems, she identified 108 species: 59 marine, 25 brackish and 24 fresh water, as well as seven species of euryhaline fishes; permanently there is the common goby, flounder, fresh water eel, three-spined stickleback and 9-spined stickleback, and occasionally thick-lipped grey mullet and sand smelt. The marine species disappear when the salinity becomes <25 ppt (parts per thousand); brackish communities are centred in salinities of 25 ppt and gradually decline to <5 ppt when fresh water communities become established. The snails, *Lymnaea peregra* and *Skeneopsis planorbis*, are at the fresh and marine ends of the salinity gradient respectively, and the edible mussel occurs throughout. Mysids, gammarids and hydrobiids all have a species in fresh waters and show a remarkable succession of tolerance along the salinity gradient.

The hydroids (*Gonothyrea loveni, Clava multicornis*) and the snails (*Littorina littorea* and *L. mariae*) occur on rocky shores with *Fucus ceranoides*, while the flatworm (*Procerodes littoralis*), the bryozoan (*Bowerbankia gracilis*) and the isopod (*Jaera nordmanni*) live under stones. Other isopods (*Idotea chelipes* and *Sphaeroma hookeri*), the amphipods (*Gammarus duebeni* and *G.*

zaddachi), and spire-shells (*Hydrobia ulvae, H. neglecta, H. ventrosa* and *Potamopygrus jenkinsi*) occur in mats of pondweed, spiral tassel and algae. The ragworm (*Nereis diversicolor*), the cockle (*Cerastoderma glaucum*) and a dwarf form of the sand-gaper (*Mya arenaria*) are widespread in the silt, but the Baltic tellin and the sandhopper (*Corophium volutator*) occur locally. The opossum shrimps (*Praunus flexuosus* and *Neomysis integer*) and the common shrimp (*Crangon vulgaris*) keep company on the silt surfaces.

There are a few freshwater species which reach into the low saline levels of the brackish system. *L. peregra*, water bugs (*Nepa cinerea, Sigara sahlbergi, S. scotii*), dragonfly nymphs (*Ischnura elegans, Enallagma cyathigerum, Sympetrum nigrescens*, and *Libellula quadrimaculata*), beetles (*Gyrinus caspius, G. substriatus, Haliplus confinis, Donacia versicolorea*), caddis larvae (*Leptocerus* sp., *Triaenodes* sp., *Limnephilus* sp.), and the crustaceans (*Eurycercus lamellatus, Daphnia pulex, Cyclops strenuus* and *Diaptomus laticeps*) have been found in salinities of 3 ppt.

Moorland Waters

Loch Druidibeg lies in an ice-hewn saucer in the gneiss platform. Its extensive, complex coastline and small islands are the breeding haunt of native grey-lag geese. Eastward of Druidibeg are Lochs Hamasclett, Teanga, Airigh na h'Achlais and Spotal, filling small valleys in the foothills of Hecla which Waterston reports as having a significant fauna with, among others, bryozoans, hydra, snails and caddises. These are typical

Loch Druidibeg, South Uist, a National Nature Reserve and wetland site of international importance (Photo J. M. Boyd)

of countless little lochs scattered throughout the islands which have brown, acidic waters low in nutrients. Around their margins there is an assortment of water-plant communities whose composition reflects local conditions of exposure, depth of water, texture of the lochbed, inflow of streams as well as the background acidity and poverty of the waters. Shore-weed, water lobelia, water horsetail and spike-rushes grow sometimes in mosaics, sometimes in bands parallel to the margin, while in sheltered, deeper waters there are the pondweeds and the white water lily which, on the dark mirror of Loch Hamasclett, is startling in its beauty. The fine sediments in the deep, quiet waters also support dense beds of the alternate-flowered water milfoil and, in the shallower water near the shore, the quill-wort. E.M. Lind (1952) studied lochs in South Uist and Rum and found that machair and moorland lochs alike were generally poor in phytoplankton with *Eudorina elegans, Botryococcus braunii, Ceratium hirundinella* and *Staurastrum* spp. dominant. (However, machair waters can be so rich in phytoplankton in summer as to possess a 'bloom'.)

Loch Druidibeg itself is bedded on the acid gneiss and fed from the east by streams from a peaty hinterland. In the West, though, it is bounded by green base-rich pastures and there is a distinct increase in acidity from west (pH 7.2) to east (pH 6.0, see above for Loch Hamasclett). Druidibeg also has a great variety of shorelines; some are sheltered and silty, while exposed shores are gravelly, stony and scoured by wave action. In the most sheltered silty places there are boggy margins. These are usually poached by cattle, which graze the stands of common and beaked sedges, carnation grass, bulbous, jointed and spike-rushes and the common reed interspersed with pennywort, brookweed (*Samolus valerandi*) and bog pimpernel (*Anagallis tenella*). This contrasts with the community on the ungrazed margins of the islands with royal fern (*Osmunda regalis*), water horsetail and beaked sedge. The off-shore shallows have submerged stands of shore-weed, water lobelia, lesser spearwort and bulbous rush, and as the water deepens, these are replaced by quill-wort, awlwort and the pondweeds (*Potamogeton gramineus, P. praelongus, P. perfoliatus*). Although the shores are grazed, and wave-action limits the accumulation of organic sediments and the growth of floating and shore vegetation, there is a greater diversity of plant life in Loch Druidibeg than its bleak moorland surroundings suggest. This, however, is in keeping with its large size, complex shape and the neutral to acid range of its waters.

The fauna of moorland waters in the Inner Hebrides is reviewed by Maitland and Holden (1983) and in the Outer Hebrides by Waterston *et al.* (1979). The dominant species of

zooplankton in lochs on Lismore and Rum were the copepods *Diaptomus glacialis, D. laciniatus, Cyclops strenuus*, and the cladocerans *Daphnia hyalina* and *Bosmina coregoni*. Waterston and Lyster (1983) listed and named the zooplankton in a comprehensive list of the invertebrates of the Loch Druidibeg system. *D. hyalina* is probably the most abundant zooplankter, and in Loch Fada, North Uist, R.N.B. Campbell found eight cladocerans and two copepods.

The rocky shores have hydra (*Hydra vulgaris*), a shrimp (*Gammarus duebeni*), sponges (*Ephydatia, Euspongilla* and *Heteromeyenia*), molluscs (*Lymnaea peregra, Armiger crista, Ancylus fluviatilis* and *Pisidium* spp.), bryozoans (*Plumatella* spp., *Fredericella sultana, Cristatella mucedo*), leeches (*Glossiphonia* spp., *Theromyzon tessulatum, Haemopis sanguisuga* and *Helobdella stagnalis*), worms (*Eiseniella tetraedra* and *Lumbriculus variegatus*), caddis larvae (*Polycentropus flavomaculatus, Limnephilus* spp.), bugs (*Salda littoralis, Saldula saltatoria* and *Velia saulii*), beetles (*Haliplus confinis, Hydroporus palustris, Ilybius fuliginosus, Gyrinus substriatus, Orectochilus villosus* and *Dryops griseus*), sponge-fly larvae (*Sisyra fuscata*) and alder-fly larvae (*Sialis lutaria*).

The weedy shores have a similarly diverse but different community with *Gammarus duebeni*, cladocerans, copepods, corixids, beetles, fly (midge) larvae and six species of the bivalve *Pisidium*. The weed beds in deeper water have hydroids

Lochain Dubha beside the A851 east of Broadford, Skye. A fine dubhlochan, *of which there are a great number in the Hebrides, with reedy and sedgy margins and natural, dwarf woods on the islands (Photo J. M. Boyd)*

(*Hydra vulgaris*), worms (*Stylaria lacustris*), cladocerans (*Alona, Alonella, Peracantha, Eurycercus*), molluscs, corixids (*Arctocorisa germari, Sigara* spp.), bugs (*Notonecta glauca* and *Nepa cinerea*), caddis larvae and the larva of the moth *Nymphula nympheata*. The larvae of the beetles *Donacia versicolorea* and *D. simplex* feed respectively on the floating pondweed and floating bur- reed. The main species of fishes in moorland waters are brown trout, eels, three- and nine-spined sticklebacks and occa- sionally sea trout and salmon and on Islay, Skye, Raasay, and Lewis there are lochs containing arctic charr. The common frog, common toad and the palmate newt are widespread in the Inner Hebrides. Grimsay is the only known site where the pal- mate newt has been recorded in the Outer Hebrides and there is also one established toad population on Great Bernera, Lewis. Adult frogs have recently been released on South Uist. Some doubtful records exist for the smooth newt on Scalpay (Skye) and Canna, and the crested newt has been recently introduced to Skye from the mainland.

Machair Waters

West of Loch Druidibeg lies blackland and machair, the eco- logy of which is described in Chapters 6 and 7 respectively. In many islands, freshwater lochs are situated on the shell-sand landward of the dunes, and on the line of contact between the sandy platform and the rocky core of the island (p. 96). Many of these lochs receive their waters from the peaty hinterland and drain to the sea through sand-silted channels, but in some there is little channelled inflow or outflow, and water flux is by seepage. The beds of these shallow, machair lochs are of calcareous sand with some organic silts, and the whole loch is well mixed and aerated by wave-action. Fluctuations of the water table result in the drying out of the shallows in summer and the inundation of wet machair at other times of year. Heavy stocking and cultivation of the surrounding pastures contri- butes to the high nutrient status of these waters, common in the southern Outer Hebrides and Tiree. A pale green 'bloom' on the machair lochs in summer is usually caused by the prolific growth of unicellular algae, possibly caused by the local enrich- ment of nitrogen from agricultural fertilisers and excrement from waterfowl.

In the shallows, stonewort and slender-leaved pondweed (*Potamogeton filiformis*) predominate together with the alternate-flowered water milfoil, maritime water crowfoot (*Ranunculus baudotii*), water mint, marsh cinquefoil, marsh pennywort, bogbean, iris, lesser spearwort and marsh marigold. Dense beds of common reed occur where the swamp is deep and cattle do not have access. Where the reeds grow in standing water with open spaces they are accompanied by common spike-rush (*Epipactis palustris*) and bulbrush (*Schoenoplectus lacustris*). In the outer shallows, there are mixtures of bulbous and spike- rushes and, in the deeper waters, spiked water milfoil, and pondweeds (*P. natans, P. praelongus, P. perfoliatus* and *P. gramineus*). Lochs Stilligary, a'Mhachair, Bornish and Ollay in South Uist are good examples of machair lochs which have been studied (Spence *et al.*, 1979; Waterston and Lyster 1979). The lesser water plantain (*Baldellia ranunculoides*) flowers at the waters edges in Loch a'Mhachair.

No other brackish-fresh water studies in the Hebrides are as comprehensive as those on the lochs in South Uist (R.N.B. Campbell 1986), but studies have been done on the brackish waters of North Uist (Nicol 1936), phytoplankton in five lochs including one on Lismore (Brook 1964), fresh water communities of lochs in Raasay (Heslop Harrison 1937, and Spence 1964), Skye (Vasari and Vasari 1968 and Birks 1973) and Islay (Birks and Adam 1978). There are also many floras for individual islands including inland-water species, but knowledge is patchy, generally thin and in need of integration and extension.

The main zooplankters in the machair lochs are the cladocerans *Daphnia hyalina, D.longispina, Bythotrephes longimanus, Holopedium gibberum, Bosmina coregoni, Polyphemus pediculus, Leptodora kindtii* and *Diaphanosoma brachyurum* and the copepods *Macrocyclops albidus, Cyclops agilis, C. strenuus* and

Loch a'Phuill, Tiree, is a fertile machair loch with a sandy bed and large stocks of invertebrates, trout and wildfowl (Photo J. M. Boyd)

Diaptomus weirzejskii. Neomysis integer, a mysid, can also be found.

On the loch bed there are no sponges or flat worms as in the moorland lochs, but there is a dense and varied fauna, and most of the taxa mentioned above for the moorland waters are also present in the machair lochs, though in greater numbers. In addition to these, *Hydra vulgaris* and the bryozoans are abundant under stones, leeches are common—especially in the haunts of waterfowl—and there are many species of mollusc dominated by *Potamopyrus jenkinsi, Lymnaea peregra* and *Pisidium* spp. distributed in beds of weed or in silt. The larvae of the mayflies *Caenis moesta* and *C. macrura* (also known as the fisherman's curse) are found in the silt and emerge in millions in early summer, providing a surfeit of food for trout. Another, *Cloeon simile*, emerges from the beds of weeds. There are many species of case-bearing caddis larvae, corixids and water beetles, including an aquatic weevil *Litodactylus leucogaster*, amongst submerged water milfoil. Midges (chironomids) are abundant, but only a few have been identified from adults. The dragonflies are *Ischnura elegans, Enallagma cyathigerum, Pyrrhosoma nymphula* and *Sympetrum nigrescens*. Waterston *et al.* (1979) described the free-swimming microfauna over the lochbed, which included 4 species of cladoceran, 9 copepods and 13 ostracods; food in plenty for trout, eels, three- and occasionally nine-spined sticklebacks and flounders.

Rivers and Streams

Most of the plant species mentioned in the description of the Loch Druidibeg system are common and widespread throughout the Hebrides. Accordingly, these surveys provide a wholesome appreciation of the ecology of brackish, machair and moorland waters within the physical and chemical ranges of these islands. However, the highly acid reaches with pH values below five as found in the dark, peaty lochs, or dubh lochans, of the mires are not well represented in the Druidibeg system, nor does it contain the range of running waters found in the Hebrides, which, though possessing a restricted flora and fauna, remain comparatively unstudied except for their migratory fish.

The rivers of Lewis, Harris, Skye, Rum, Mull, Jura and Islay are short, often torrential in character and usually devoid of vegetation. Where the rate of flow declines, the communities resemble those of associated fresh water lochs. Hill streams have a rapid and continuous rise and fall in response to rainfall, and the beds are scoured clean of sediment. The machair

streams also rise and fall, but in more gradual response to the
rise and fall of the water table—the ground water reservoir in
the dune-machair platform. In summer drought, the hill
stream becomes a bare pebble bed linking deep cisterns of
clear rather lifeless water, while the machair streams become
ribbons of sand and pools luxuriantly overgrown with iris,
fool's water cress (*Apium nodiflorum*), alternate water milfoil
and water horsetail. Streams and drains in all parts are often
stained red by the oxides of iron leached from neighbouring
podzolic soil. Many lochs and streams have been modified,
sometimes with disasterous results, to enhance their stocks of
sedentary and migratory fish (see below). The catchments of
the main rivers of Rum, for example, were manipulated last
century to provide a run of sea trout and salmon at Kinloch, but
the scheme was abortive, testimony to man's misjudgment of

*The Ord River, Sleat,
Skye, is typical of the
small, short, unpolluted
streams of the
Hebrides, with runs of
sea-trout and gorges
holding fragments of
native woodland
(Photo J. M. Boyd)*

nature, because a dam ruptured and the Kinloch River was scoured of the gravels necessary for spawning beds.

In the few streams which have been studied in the Hebrides, the fauna was dominated by insect larvae and molluscs. Rodger Waterston described the shallow metre-wide stream running from the hill through arable land and machair to the sea at Borve in Barra: the hill-stream reach had 10 species of water beetle, 5 caddises, a bug, 2 flies, 2 snails and a species of leech. In the mid-reach over rocks with the moss *Fontinalis*, there were limpets (*Ancylus fluviatilis*), midge and caddis larvae, stoneflies (*Leuctra fusca*, *Amphinemura sulcicollis*, *Chloroperla torrentium*), a mayfly (*Baetis rhodani*) and a beetle (*Dryops griseus*). The silted, slow-flowing stretches overgrown with water cress, water crowfoot, marsh-wort and water milfoil had abundant *Gammarus duebeni*, molluscs, water beetles, midge and crane-fly larvae, caddises and corixids, including the minute water boatman *Micronecta poweri*.

Balfour-Browne (1953) recorded 23 species of water beetles from 12 streamlets in Lewis and Harris: (*Haliplus* spp., *Hydroporus* spp., *Agabus* spp., *Helophorus* spp., *Ilybius* and others) of which only *A. paludosus* and *A. guttatus* were regarded as true stream species. The pearl mussel (*Margaritifera margaritifera*) occurs in some of the rivers, and Loch Cravadale, of Harris, where it was first noted by Martin Martin (1703).

Fish

There are seven indigenous species of fresh water fish in the Hebrides: Atlantic salmon (*Salmo salar*), trout (*Salmo trutta*), arctic charr (*Salvelinus alpinus*), three-spined stickleback (*Gasterosteus aculeatus*), nine-spinned stickleback (*Pungitius pungitius*), European eel (*Anguilla anguilla*) and brook lamprey (*Lampetra planeri*), though this last may be absent from the Outer Hebrides. Four species have been introduced to the Inner Hebrides: rainbow trout (*Salmo gairdneri*), American brook charr (*Salvelinus fontinalis*), pike (*Esox lucius*) and perch (*Perca fluviatilis*). Attempts to introduce the American brook charr and the rainbow trout to the Outer Hebrides have been unsuccessful, and rainbow trout populations in the Inner Hebrides are maintained by stocking only. The flounder (*Pleuronectes flesus*), sand smelt (*Atherina presbyter*)—which often shoals with sticklebacks—and the thick-lipped grey mullet (*Crenimugil labrosus*) are found in brackish waters and, temporarily, in fresh waters, with the flounder sometimes going far upstream. Sturgeon (*Acipenser sturio*) and the allis and twaite shads (*Alosa alosa* and *A. fallax*), sea bass (*Dicentrarchus labrax*) and the common goby (*Potamoschistus microps*) are also recorded from fresh waters in the Inner Hebrides (Maitland and Holden 1983).

The inland fish stocks of the Outer Hebrides are probably more representative of the original colonisers of the islands in the melt-waters of the Pleistocene ice. Only migratory, euryhaline species could live in both salt and fresh waters and run upstream from the sea as the land emerged from the ice-sheet, held back only by unscalable waterfalls (except for eels). Salmon have remained anadromous (spawn in fresh waters and feed at sea), trout have become divided into an anadromous form, the sea trout, and a non-migratory form, the brown trout, and the fresh water eel is catadromous (spawns at sea and returns to fresh waters). In contrast, the arctic charr, which must have arrived in the Hebrides as an anadromous species, is now confined to a few fresh water lochs with no migratory stock. Three-spined sticklebacks have also formed anadromous and non-migratory stocks.

The fish of the inland waters of the Hebrides are described by Campbell and Williamson (1979 and 1983), (Table 10.5).

Island/Fish	1	2	3	4	5	6	7	8	9	10	11	12	13	14	15	16	17
Skye	*	*	*	*		@	*	*		*			*				
Scalpay		*	*				*										
Raasay		*	*				*	∴		*							
South Rona							*										
Soay						@	*										
Rum	*	*	*				*	*		*	*						
Canna							*										
Eigg			*		*		*										
Muck							*										
Coll			*				*	*	*	*	*						
Tiree			*				*	*	?	*	*						
Mull	*	*	*		*	@	*	*	*	*	*						
Lismore			*				*	*									
Kerrera			*				*					?					
Seil		*	*			@	*	*		*							
Easdale						?	?										
Luing						@	*										
Scarba						@	?										
Shuna							*										
Colonsay			*				*	*		*							
Garvellachs							*										
Jura	*	*	*				*	*		*	*						
Islay	*	*	*	*		@	*	*	*	*		?	*	*			
Gigha			e			@	*			*							
North Rona							?										

Island/Fish	1	2	3	4	5	6	7	8	9	10	11	12	13	14	15	16	17
St Kilda							*										
Harris	*	*	*			@	*	*									
Lewis	*	*	*			@	*	*			?						
Pabbay (Harris)						@											
Monach Isles							*	*									
North Uist	*	*	*	*		@	*	*	*	*	*	?					
Benbecula	*	*	*				*	*	*	?	*						
South Uist	*	*	*			@	*	*	*	*	*						
Barra	*	*	*				*	*	?								
Berneray (Harris)			o				*	*		*							
Totals																	
Outer Hebrides	*	*	*	*		@	*	*	*	*	*	?	?				
Inner Hebrides	*	*	*	*	*	@	*	*	*	*	*	*	*	*	*		
Mainland+	*	*	*	*	*	@	*	*	*	*	*	*	*	*	*	*	*

1 Salmon   2 Sea trout   3 Brown trout   4 Arctic charr   5 American brook charr   6 Rainbow trout   7 European eel   8 3-spined stickleback   9 Spined stickleback   10 Flounder   11 Thick-lipped grey mullet   12 Sea or river lamprey   13 Brook lamprey   14 Pike   15 Perch   16 Minnow++   17 Common carp

* present;   @ an introduction, not an established population;   + Lochs Morar, Shiel and Awe, carp in Kintyre;   ++ *Phoxinus phoxinus*;   e recently extinct;   o introduced into Loch Bhruist in 1988.

Table 10.5   The distribution of brackish-freshwater fish is given by Campbell and Williamson, (1979 and 1973) for the Outer and Inner Hebrides and it has been supplemented by information on the distribution of fish in the Outer Hebrides supplied by R.N.B. Campbell.

Salmon 'run' (return to the rivers) in the Outer Hebrides from late February into the summer, with a peak in July, although this will depend on the level of the rivers. The main river-loch systems are the Rivers Barvas, Blackwater, Grimersta and Laxay in Lewis, Amhuinsuidhe, Laxadale and Obbe in Harris, Skealtar in North Uist, and Howmore, Kildonan and a'Bharp in South Uist. There is a spring run of salmon in two systems of the Outer Hebrides which are more typical of the much larger Scottish east-coast rivers than the summer runs in the West Highlands and the Inner Hebrides. In the Skealtar, angling can begin in late February, and by the end of May over 40 salmon can be landed at an average weight of 6.5kg with some individuals over 13kg. Grilse, the early maturing phase of the salmon which have probably spent only one year at sea before returning to the spawning river, weigh from 2 to 5kg and run from late May onwards. Peak angling catches of grilse on the Skealtar occur in late July-early August, averaging 2.7kg in weight. However, salmon farming on this river has recently affected catches.

In the Outer Hebrides between 3,700 and 5,900 salmon are caught by anglers every year. There are small bag-net salmon fisheries in the Inner Hebrides, particularly off Skye, which to some extent will affect the catches of salmon in the river-loch systems, yet substantial catches have been recorded from some of these systems. During the 1970s, for example, between 1,200 and 5,000 salmon were caught each year in the systems of the Sligachan and Snizort district of Skye. Slightly greater numbers have been recorded from the Ba, Pennygowan and Lussa districts of Mull, and many fewer from Islay, where good catches are still recorded from the River Laggan but not on the River Sorn.

Mills and Graesser (1981) briefly described the rivers in the Hebrides which have stocks of salmon for angling. In the Inner Hebrides these are confined to the larger islands, and they do not have as high a sporting reputation as those of the mainland or the Outer Hebrides. This is reflected in the relatively poor information given about their stocks. Menzies (1938) tagged and released 94 salmon at bag nets off Soay; of the 22 recaptures, one was taken on Skye, 3 on the west coast of Scotland and 18 on the north and east coasts. This indicates that stocks of fish frequenting the west coast may be in passage to the north and east coasts. However, other tagging at Ardnamurchan showed that the majority of fish recaptured were caught within 64km of the tagging point. The salmon disease Ulcerated Dermal Necrosis (UDN) has been known in the Hebrides in the past, occurring when salmon and sea trout were held back in the sea by drought and low stream flows. A few outbreaks of UDN have been reported from the River Aros, Mull and the River Sorn on Islay, but it is believed that the disease does not flourish in the acid fresh waters that characterise the major river-loch systems in the Hebrides.

The lochs of Harris and the Uists used to have excellent sea trout angling, and the fish are larger and more numerous in the fertile machair waters than in moorland habitats. This is easily seen by comparing the stocks of the Lower Kildonan and Howmore situated on the machair with Loch a'Bharp in the moorland, all in South Uist. Nall (1930) suggested that the Howmore-Lower Kildonan sea trout are typically fast-growing, short-lived and spawn few times, compared with those elsewhere on the west coast, which grow slowly, live longer and spawn more often. The spawning performance of the Howmore sea trout resembles more that of the distant River Tweed than it does that of the much nearer River Ewe in Wester Ross. Nall (1932, 1934) also found that the growth of sea trout in North Uist was similar to the fast-growing Howmore stock and that those from Harris and Lewis resembled the slow-growing Loch a'Bharp stock.

Though sizable runs of sea trout do not occur until July, the angling season opens in February, when good fish occupy estuaries and tidal races feeding on sand-eels, young herring and elvers in season. There has been a dramatic decline in catches of sea trout, with fairly constant angling on the three South Uist lochs, compared with salmon which have remained fairly steady in numbers:

Years	sea trout	salmon
1962–66	564	50
1967–71	236	41
1972–76	81	66

The average weight of sea trout in these years was 1.13kg with the largest fish usually weighing between 3.5 and 4.5kg, though the largest sea trout caught was 6.4kg.

Brown trout are widespread, but unlike eels are not present on many smaller islands such as St Kilda, Mingulay, Canna, Muck and Scarba, because these islands do not possess sufficiently permanent or extensive enough stream and loch systems to support a population. They have a highly varied diet. Small and large trout have roughly the same dietary range, except the smaller trout take the smaller-sized end of the spectrum of prey including cladocerans, copepods and other micro-crustacea, insect larvae, pupae and nymphs, amphipods, molluscs, small fish and in the few waters in which they occur, palmate newts. In moorland systems with acid waters and very low stocks of invertebrates, such as those on the gneiss, granite, Torridonian sandstone and quartzite in the Outer Hebrides, Jura and Islay, the few trout which survive are large and almost entirely piscivorous, feeding on charr. This sometimes leads anglers to seek the large cannibalistic 'ferox' trout to be found in some of these dark lochs, which have ample spawning beds, poverty of invertebrate food, but shoals of charr. In the Outer Hebrides 'ferox' occur in Loch Langavat, Lewis, where conditions are right for piscivorous trout.

The status of the brown trout populations in lochs depends, therefore, on the balance which is struck between the rate or recruitment of young fish to the population, and the amount of food available. The balance is achieved differently even in somewhat similar lochs. For example, in both the main machair lochs on Tiree, Lochs a'Phuil and Bhasapol, there are high stocks of invertebrates, but the former has much more extensive spawning beds than the latter. This results in Loch a'Phuil having a large population of medium-sized, rather thin fish while Loch Bhasapol possesses fewer larger-sized fish in good condition and the same comparison can be obtained in South Uist between the rich Lochs a'Mhachair and Upper Kildonan.

Rainbow trout have been introduced to the Hebrides but have been unsuccessful in permanent establishment. The rapid growth of trout-farming on the west coast of Scotland has resulted in escapes from netted pens in lochs, including at least one loch on Mull, and American brook charr introduced late last century to Loch Beinn Tighe on Eigg and a few small lochs on Mull are still extant. None of these lochs have trout, however.

Arctic charr occur in Lochs Fada, a'Bharpa and the Loch Skealtar system on North Uist, Lochs Langavat and Suainaval on Lewis, an Uachdair on Raasay, Mealt on Skye and Kennabus on Islay. However, there are still other suitable waters on Lewis and Skye in which charr might be found where they may be sympatric with brown trout feeding almost exclusively on plankton. In Loch Mealt though, there are no trout and the allopatric charr feed on organisms normally taken by trout including sticklebacks and stickleback egg clumps.

The three-spined stickleback is widely distributed and occurs in three forms, roughly associated with tidal pools, open waters, and streams and ditches. There are several forms: *trachurus* the rough-tailed, which is found in brackish habitats and is anadromous, *leiurus* the smooth-tailed and the intermediate *semiarmatus* which are all found throughout the Hebrides. However, *anomalus*, which lacks pelvic spines and has a varying number of dorsal spines, has been found only on North Uist. The nine-spined stickleback is less widely distributed than the three-spined and is restricted to shallows with abundant aquatic vegetation; they are much more common in the Outer Isles than in the Inner, where they have been found on Islay, southwest Mull and in Loch Claid on Coll.

Elvers born in the Sargasso Sea in the western Atlantic make the astounding journey to the fresh water systems of Europe, arriving in the Hebrides in April and May. They are ubiquitous in inland waters, even in small systems such as on St Kilda and the Monach Isles which contain no other fish, with the possible exception of sticklebacks. The movement of eels into the estuaries and stream systems is often marked by the appearance of predatory herons, gulls and otters. The eels, which may spend over 30 years in fresh water before migrating to spawn and die, feed on molluscs, crustaceans, insect larvae and nymphs. Apart from a few eel traps, which killed otters as well as eels (see p. 92), there has been no large scale exploitation of eels in the Hebrides.

Brook lampreys have only been reported from the Inner Hebrides, although both the river lamprey and the sea lamprey are probably more widespread than the records show. The only record of a river or a sea lamprey is from a small stream on Kerrera, but the presence of these primitive fish is only readily recorded during the spawning season in the spring or early summer. Otherwise, tell-tale marks on salmon in Skye which have been parasitised by lampreys suggest their presence— though this does not tell us where the parasitism occurred during the long migrations of the Atlantic salmon—and parts of a lamprey were also recently recorded in North Uist in the regurgitated meal of a heron.

Perch and pike occur only as introduced species to a few lochs in northern Islay and form the only populations of coarse fish in the Hebrides. Pike feed on young trout, and efforts have been made to eliminate them from Loch Skerrols by treating the loch with a piscicide.

Reptiles and Amphibians

Like coarse fish, reptiles and amphibians have also found great difficulty in bridging the marine barrier (Table 10.6). Although the reptiles—adder, slow worm and common lizard—depend on fresh waters only to a very small degree, the amphibians— palmate and smooth newts, common frog and common toad—require fresh waters for breeding and live in moist, fresh habitats.

Island/Species	1	2	3	4	5	6	7	8
Skye	*	*	*	@	@	*	*	*
Raasay	*	*	*		*	*	*	*
Scalpay	*		*		*		*	*
Soay							*	*
Eigg			*			*	*	
Rum			*			*		
Canna					?	*		
Coll			*					
Tiree								
Mull	*	*	*			*	*	*
Kerrera							*	*
Iona							*	
Lismore			*					
Jura	*	*	*			*	*	*
Garvellachs			*			*	*	

Island/Species	1	2	3	4	5	6	7	8
Luing		*			N	N	*	*
Scarba	*							
Seil								
Shuna								
Islay	*		*				*	*
Colonsay		*	*					
Gigha						Y	*	*
South Uist							*	
North Uist			*					
Lewis	?	*						
Harris	?	*						
Inner Hebrides	*	*	*		*	*	*	*
Outer Hebrides		*				*	*	
West Mainland	*	*	*		*	*	*	*

1 Adder   2 Slow worm   3 Common lizard   4 Crested newt
5 Smooth newt   6 Palmate newt   7 Common toad   8 Common frog

* present;   @ introduced but not established;   N newt of unknown species;   Y young (tadpole).

Table 10.6   The distribution of amphibians and reptiles in the Hebrides compiled by R.N. Campbell.

Many species predate the populations of toads, frogs and newts. These include fish, gulls, herons, mergansers, crows, otters and feral mink. In 18 years of study of brown trout food in north Scotland, Niall Campbell has not found tadpoles in the stomachs, though frogs were commonly found in spring. It is therefore all the more remarkable that American brook charr have been found gorged on both tadpoles and small frogs in Mull.

Waterfowl

The inshore, coastal and inland waters of the Hebrides are a rich and varied habitat for many species of water bird. The wildfowl (swans, geese, ducks, grebes and divers) are described in greater detail in *A Mosaic of Islands*, since they have had a special place in the natural history of the islands for well over a century, and today hold much that is of special interest in science and conservation. Many species commute between the shore and inland waters, or between the rich machair lochs, which are feeding and nursery areas, and the poor moorland lochs which provide sequestered breeding sites. In winter, the communities of waterbirds are different from those in summer and spring, and autumn sees migrants—particularly on the busy, weedy shallows of protected shores, and the machair lochs, often still 'open' when mainland fresh waters are frozen. The maintenance of sufficiently high water levels in the machair lochs, particularly in dry summers, is vital for the waterbirds. These levels are affected by drainage for agriculture and therein lies a conservation problem.

Mammals

In the Hebrides the otter is mainly a marine species and is widespread on all the islands except perhaps distant outliers like St Kilda and North Rona, where it has not so far been recorded. It is described in Chapter 5. Mink (*Mustela vison*) has recently been introduced to Lewis and Harris, possibly as escapes from mink farms at Steinish and Dalmore, which were both closed in 1961. They are thought to have spread through the islets in the Sound of Harris and are now colonising the southern Outer Hebrides. The water vole (*Arvicola terrestris*) has been recorded in Skye and Islay, and the water shrew (*Neomys fodiens*) in Skye, Raasay, Pabay (Skye), Mull, Kerrera, Garvellachs and Shuna.

The inland waters of the Hebrides are probably second to none in Britain as a refuge for wildlife. Unlike many parts of mainland Britain, the waters are unpolluted from agricultural seepage or industrial effluent, and they possess many unique features. However, they are fragile, and require careful and sympathetic management if they are to maintain their diverse qualities.

The general distribution of mammals in the Hebrides is tabulated in the companion volume *The Hebrides—A Habitable Land?*

A young heron on the nest among nettles on the Dun in Loch Iosal an Duin, North Uist in 1954. (Photo: J. M. Boyd)

Epilogue
by J. M. Boyd

In that milestone of Scottish natural history, *The Influence of Man on Animal Life in Scotland* (1920), James Ritchie, writing in the dawn of modern ecology, stated that no influence has been more potent in changing the face of Scotland and in altering relationships of wild life of the country, than the care of domesticated animals. This has resulted in levelling of forests, draining of swamps, and turning the wilderness of mountain and moor into fertile grazings. Remote though the Hebrides have been in history, they have not escaped these human influences. In the traumatic history of the Hebridean people over the last three centuries, few, if any, islets holding a few acres of pasture have been left ungrazed or uncultivated. The stark, treeless character of the islands is in great part due to the grazing of livestock, and the seasonal burning of the hill pastures, which is part of sheep husbandry. However, human influence need not always be damaging to Nature, and indeed, when moderately applied, it is often beneficial. For example, without grazing animals in limited numbers there would be no flower-bespangled machairs for which the Hebrides are famous.

Thin, depleted pastures, severely trampled land, and widespread erosion are the symptoms of overgrazing (p. 189). They have been prevalent for at least two centuries and are common today throughout the islands, especially where rabbits are present. On the other hand, if machair is left ungrazed, it loses its natural diversity of flora and fauna, and usually becomes a rank grassland, possessing none of the beauty and interest of the neighbouring grazed swards. Machair is at its best for both man and animal when used as a winter grazing, and left during the summer to grow, flower and set seed.

The end of the Second World War was a time for new beginnings. A new regard emerged for our quality of life, and for the world we live in. This found many outlets—one of which was the conservation movement, driven partly by a sheer love of country, and partly by a desire to protect it against what might be the worst excesses of a new industrial age. However, while the seeds of the 'environmental' ethos were generated in philosophy and science and broadcast by the media as a theme of growing popularity in the 1950s, it fell on ground already fully

possessed by more powerful political, social and economic organisms. The conservation message came rather late in the day; the industrial revolution had all but run its course in Britain by the time the people became sufficiently aware of the enormous irreversible change that they had wrought upon their environment. In *The New Environmental Age*, Max Nicholson (1988) gives an effervescent commentary on the struggle that the movement has had to find its rightful place in the public life. The conservation message was widely known, poorly understood, reluctantly recognised, and grudgingly acted upon. Viewing the world scene, he writes:

Erosion of the machair plain at Crossapol, Tiree, caused by cattle seeking shelter from the wind in an otherwise exposed pasture. The dark band is an old over-blown soil. A picture of the 1950s; the erosion platforms have now disappeared (Photo J. M. Boyd)

The spectacle of many groups of intelligent people doing their utmost to destroy the vital life support systems of their posterity on earth, and angrily opposing efforts by more enlightened groups to mitigate or prevent the mischief, is a truly remarkable phenomenon of our age, and one which we can be sure our successors, if they are permitted to survive on earth, will find difficult to credit.

Fortunately, the dramatic effects of human exploitation that evoke such a view are in much lower profile in the Hebrides than they are in mainland Britain, and much less so than in the Third World. In the age of industrial pollution, gone is the notion of pure, clean air and sea; yet the Hebrides is the part of Britain least affected by acid precipitation, and marine pollution by PCBs. Gone in the leisure age is the notion of solitude and peace; yet the Hebrides is also the part of Britain least affected by tourism and recreation. Gone in the age of the welfare state and social services is the image of the thatched

A cottage at Elgol, Skye, sheltered by a wind-shaped sycamore and looking to Loch Scavaig and the Black Cuillins with Loch Coruisk hidden in the glaciated horseshoe of peaks (Photo J. M. Boyd)

cottage and the peat stack—'the lone shieling on the misty isle'; yet the Hebrides retains its mystique and unique life style.

Today conservation, as part of the wider environmental or 'green' movement, has become a cardinal force in human affairs which is felt deeply in the Hebrides, particularly when the local people are asked to change their ways for the sake of wildlife. The struggle for human survival is innate in the island communities, which have a long memory of privation and exodus, and an equally long history of economic use of limited natural resources. The islands have been greatly changed by man, and locally they have been devastated. Nonetheless, they have remarkable powers of natural regeneration and today, when compared with the rest of Britain and Europe, they are remarkably natural and free of industrial spoil and pollution.

But what of the future? In hindsight we know that there have been great changes in the islands over the last ten thousand years which have resulted from changes in climate and in sea-level, and the portents of change in the near future are some-what alarming. What it has taken Nature 300 million years to achieve in the build-up of the coal, oil and gas fields in the earth's crust, man will substantially combust in 300 years. In so doing, he will change the balance of atmospheric gasses, surface temperatures and sea levels. Such physical changes are likely to be accompanied by widespread biological changes, and archipelagos like the Hebrides are likely to be greatly affected.

One of the major scientific endeavours of the next decade will be researching these changes caused by the burning of fossil fuels, the dramatic reduction over the last century in the earth's forests, and the use of chlorofluorocarbons (CFCs), since they relate to the well being and possibly to the survival of mankind. The effects of acidification of freshwaters and soils by atmospheric precipitation of the oxides of sulphur and nitrogen, the 'green house' effect — the warming of the earth's surface due to higher concentrations of carbon dioxide in the upper atmosphere — and the damage to the ozone layer in the upper atmosphere (a protective shield against solar radiation) by CFCs, are already evident. What is not yet known though, are the 'knock-on' effects that these changes will have on climate, marine hydrography, and the seasonal growth of vegetation and fauna, including crops of all sorts. The water balance between atmosphere and hydrosphere will be crucial in determining weather patterns, especially in the storm belt of the North Atlantic. The Hebrides might become somewhat warmer, but such warming might be off-set by increased cloud cover and higher rainfall. Higher sea-levels would inundate much low-lying terrain; islands would change their shapes, reefs would disappear and the charts would require to be redrawn. Higher winds would further inhibit the growth of woodland. On the other hand, if the warming is accompanied by a drier, less windy climate, the Hebrides might become much more clement for people than they are today, with better growth of crops, and an extension of woodland. If such changes do occur, this book will require to be rewritten and a new set of objectives will be required for nature conservation.

In the early days, conservation did not possess the strong statutory and financial backing from Government that it does today. When Rum was acquired by the Nature Conservancy in 1957, there was an angry outcry from sheep farming interests in the north of Scotland about the withdrawal of sheep stocks from the island. Since then there have been no sheep on Rum and, without any significant loss to the hill-sheep industry, the island is now a celebrated Nature Reserve known throughout the world. Today, in spite of considerable adverse pressures over the last thirty years, the vision of the founding fathers of the Rum Reserve has survived. In contrast to this, in that same

The rose-root and primrose blooming together in the solitudes of Glen Mor, St Kilda (Photo J. M. Boyd)

year, St Kilda was included in the Guided Weapons Range, Hebrides, and there was great concern about the future of that jewel of Nature. Would it be flawed for ever? But for the timely intervention of the National Trust for Scotland and the Nature Conservancy, it might well have been irreparably damaged. Instead of which, it is now the first natural site in the United Kingdom to be declared under the World Heritage Convention, and the greatest possible care is required in its management. The introduction of rats, particularly from the army vessels breaching on Hirta and in contractors' cargo, would pose a great threat to the seabirds and the St Kilda field-mouse.

The crofters of Grogarry, Stilligarry and Howmore were highly suspicious of the overtures of the Nature Conservancy in the setting-up of the Loch Druidibeg National Nature

Reserve in South Uist. The task of getting a favourable opinion for this new proposal from three crofting townships and grazing clubs in a community possessing both Roman Catholic and Presbyterian congregations was difficult, yet these problems were overcome, and today Loch Druidibeg is a site of international importance under the Ramsar Convention. This reserve was indeed the forerunner of many conservation projects in crofting and farming areas in the Hebrides, culminating in the Integrated Development Programme (IDP) in the Outer Hebrides (1981–86), the Agricultural Development Plan in the Inner Hebrides (1987–1992), and the goose conservation and farming issue in Islay, all of which we describe in this book.

The Wildlife and Countryside Act (1981) and the heated debate that accompanied it changed the whole complexion of conservation in Great Britain. It put 'teeth' into the mechanism of safeguard of species and habitats, and resulted in greatly increased funding to compensate farmers and others for any reasonable loss they might sustain in conserving wildlife. It also made nature conservation more bureaucratic and caught-up in business than ever before, changing the lives of all who were professionally or voluntarily employed in nature conservation. It changed the leadership of the conservation movement with the appointment of administrators, industrialists, planners, media persons, and others from the wider scene of public affairs, to fill positions previously occupied by natural scientists, amateur naturalists of high standing, agriculturalists, and foresters.

The traumas endured by the Nature Conservancy in becoming a component body of the Natural Environment Research Council (NERC), and then becoming split into the Nature Conservancy Council and the Institute of Terrestrial Ecology, caused the scientists to divide. Those who went to the NCC, mainly as managers of the new nature conservation enterprise, were not accorded a high standing in science. Since the passing of the Act, the main echelons of natural scientists in conservation have been given new directives, just as those in agriculture and forestry had been given long ago. Now good naturalists and aspirant practitioners in botany, zoology and geology have the role of local administrators and managers, while the science of conservation is vested in a group of specialists at headquarters. This may be an inevitable development if nature conservation is to take its proper place in society. It is far better for conservation that scientists should accept an administrative role by which sites and species can be effectively safeguarded, than would otherwise be the case if each had a research role. However, the science of the local administrator is vital to the success of conservation among local people, and it should be continuously enhanced. The conservation catechism which is issued from the centre should encourage and not stifle the gifted, experienced naturalist, acting successfully as an administrator or manager. In the Hebrides, where there are few resident naturalists, the need for scientific field work by the resident staff of professional conservation bodies is much greater than in more densely populated parts of the country.

In 1992 the NCC was partitioned into separate bodies for Scotland, England and Wales. A small fourth body was retained to co-ordinate scientific research in nature conservation throughout Great Britain and deal with international conservation affairs. The Scottish and Welsh parts were amalgamated with the respective Countryside Commissions. In Scotland the new combined NCC–CCS body was named Scottish Natural Heritage (SNH).

The young naturalist I. L. B., as a boy, passes through a natural arch on the north shore of Rum (Photo J. M. Boyd)

A main change in SNH from the old system was the delegation of authority and accountability from headquarters in England and Edinburgh to Regional Boards and Headquarters secretariats in Glasgow, Edinburgh (later Perth), Aberdeen and Inverness. The aim was to give local communities a much greater say in the conservation of nature and the countryside. An advisory Committee was later set up to deal with objections on scientific grounds to the notification of SSSIs. Another major change saw the role of science in the make-up of SNH reduced, as compared with the NC/NCC. Few distinguished scientists were appointed to Main and Regional Boards, and science was accorded an advisory role only through a Scientific Advisory Committee and a Research and Advisory Services Directorate. At present there is no scientist on the Main Board.

The cost of SNH has been high. Against some twenty-five *unpaid* members of the NCC/CCS board/committee system for Scotland with about 200 members of staff, there are now some sixty *paid* board/committee members, and well over 500 staff. Compensations of tens, and hundreds, of thousands of pounds have been paid to landowners and their tenants for not cultivating, afforesting, extracting minerals, storing and extracting water, and peat cutting, on their land. There is an outward show of progress, but has the benefit to the natural heritage, *per se*, been proportionate to this greatly increased cost? Of that there may be doubt, but one thing is certain. The increased cost has provided benefit to people, particularly those who are employed by, or in various ways funded by SNH, and those who are in receipt of compensation through the management agreements of SSSIs. The probity of such compensation (sometimes seen as payment for doing nothing) is now being publicly challenged. The Scottish Office should appreciate more that it is from its science that SNH ultimately receives its identity and credibility. SNH should demonstrate beyond reasonable doubt that its endeavours are primarily directed towards the conservation of nature and the countryside, for the benefit of all the people, and not of itself or those with whom it enters into an agreement.

The publication of this book and its two companions follows upon the centenary of Harvie-Brown and Buckley's *Vertebrate Faunas of the Outer Hebrides* (1888) and of *Argyll and Inner Hebrides* (1892). We salute these naturalists of the last century who provided such a fine series of books, which, though now collectors' items, are still mines of information which are drawn upon by historians. We hope that this book will continue to stimulate the interest in the natural history of the Hebrides that was initiated by Harvie-Brown and Buckley, and later kept alive by James Ritchie, Seton Gordon, Fraser Darling, James Fisher, F. Balfour-Brown, John Lorne Campbell, Rodger Waterston and others who followed them.

The gannet's majestic outlook upon the future of the world. (Photo: J. M. Boyd)

Bibliography

Anderton, R. & Bowes, D. R. (1983).
Precambrian and Palaeozoic rocks of the
Inner Hebrides. *Proc. Roy. Soc. Edinb.*
83B, 32–45.

Angus, I. S. (1979). The macrofauna of the
intertidal sand in the Outer Hebrides.
Proc. Roy. Soc. Edinb. 77B, 155–171.

Atkinson, R. (1940). Notes on the botany
of North Rona and Sula Sgeir. *Trans.
Proc. Bot. Soc. Edinb.* 30, 52–60.

Balfour-Brown, F. (1953). The aquatic
coleoptera of the Western Scottish Islands
with a discussion of their sources of
origin and means of arrival. *Entomologist's
Gaz.* 23, 1–71.

Ball, M. E. (1987). Botany, woodland and
forestry. In *Rhum,* ed. T. H. Clutton-
Brock & M. E. Ball. Edinburgh
University Press.

Baxter, E. V. & Rintoul, E. J. (1953). *The
Birds of Scotland.* Oliver & Boyd,
Edinburgh.

Bennett, A. (1905). Supplement to
Topographic Botany 2nd ed. *J. Bot. Lond.*
48, Suppl.

Bennett, A., Salmon, C. E. & Matthews,
J. R. (1929–30). 2nd Supplement to
Topographic Botany 2nd ed. *J. Bot. Lond.*
62 & 63, Suppl.

Berry, R. J. (1969). History in the
evoloution of *Apodemus sylvaticus* at one
edge of its range. *J. Zool. Lond.* 159,
311–328.

Berry, R. J. (1979). The Outer Hebrides:
where genes and geography meet. *Proc.
Roy. Soc. Edinb.* 77B, 21–43.

Berry, R. J. (1983). Evolution of animals
and plants in the Inner Hebrides. *Proc.
Roy. Soc. Edinb.* 83B, 433–447.

Berry, R. J. & Tricker, B. J. K. (1969).
Competition and extinction: field mice of
Foula, Fair Isle and St Kilda. *J. Zool.
Lond.* 158, 247–265.

Birks, J. H. B. (1970). Inwashed pollen
spectra of Loch Fada, Isle of Skye. *New
Phytol.* 69, 807–820.

Birks, J. H. B. (1973). *Past and Present
Vegetation of the Isle of Skye—a
paleoecological study.* Cambridge
University Press.

Birks, J. H. B. & Adam P. (1978). Notes on
the flora of Islay. *Trans. Bot. Soc. Edinb.*
43, 37–39.

Birks, J. H. B. & Marsden, B. J. (1970).
Flandrian vegetation history of Little
Loch Roag, Isle of Lewis, Scotland.
J. Ecol. 67, 825–842.

Birks, J. H. B. & Williams, W. (1983). Late
quaternary vegetational history of the
Inner Hebrides. *Proc. Roy. Soc. Edinb.*
83B, 293–318.

Bland, K. P., Christie, I. C. & Wormell, P.
(1987). The lepidoptera of the Isle of
Coll, Inner Hebrides. *Glasg. Nat.* 21,
309–330.

Bowes, D. R. (1983). Geological
framework of the Inner Hebrides. *Proc.
Roy. Soc. Edinb.* 83B, 25–29.

Bowes, D. R., Hopgood, A. M. &
Pidgeon, R. T. (1976). Sources and ages
of zircons in an Archaean quartzite,
Rona, Inner Hebrides, Scotland. *Geol.
Mag.* 113, 545–552.

Boyd, A. (1986). *Seann Taighean Tirisdeach.*
Cairdean nan Tiaghean Tugha.

Boyd, I. L. (1981). Population changes in
the distribution of a herd of feral goats
(*Capra* sp.) on Rhum, Inner Hebrides.
J. Zool. Lond. 193, 287–304.

Boyd, J. M. (1957). The ecological
distribution of the Lumbricidae in the
Hebrides. *Proc. Roy. Soc. Edinb.* 66B,
311–338.

Boyd, J. M. (1960b). Studies of the
differences between fauna of grazed and
ungrazed grassland in Tiree, Argyll, *Proc.
Zool. Soc. Lond.* 135, 33–54.

Boyd, J. M. (ed.) (1979). The Natural
Environment of the Outer Hebrides. *Proc.
Roy. Soc. Edinb.* 77B, 561pp.

Boyd, J. M. (1983a). Natural Environment
of the Inner Hebrides: an introduction.
Proc. Roy. Soc. Edinb. 83B, 3–22.

Boyd, J. M. (1983b). Two hundred years of biological sciences in Scotland. Nature Conservation. *Proc. Roy. Soc. Edinb.* 84B, 295–336.

Boyd, J. M. & Bowes, D. R. (eds.) (1983). The Natural Environment of the Inner Hebrides. *Proc. Roy. Soc. Edinb.* 83B, 648pp.

Bramwell, A. G. & Cowie, G. M. (1983). Forests of the Inner Hebrides—status and habitat. *Proc. Roy. Soc. Edinb.* 83B, 577–597.

Bristow, W. S. (1927). The spider fauna of the Western Islands of Scotland. *Scot. Nat.* 1927, 88–94, 117–122.

Brook, A. J. (1964). The phytoplanton of the Scottish freshwater lochs. In *The Vegetation of Scotland* ed. J. H. Burnett. Oliver & Boyd, Edinburgh.

Burnett, J. H. (1964). *The Vegetation of Scotland.* Oliver & Boyd, Edinburgh.

Cadbury, C. J. (1980). The status and habitats of the corncrake in Britain 1978–79. *Bird Study* 27, 203–218.

Cadbury, C. J. (1988). Corncrake and corn bunting status and habitats on Tiree and Coll, Inner Hebrides. In *Birds of Coll and Tiree* (ed. D. A. Stroud). Nature Conservancy Council, Peterborough.

Caird, J. B. (1979). Landuse in the Uists since 1800. *Proc. Roy. Soc. Edinb.* 77B, 505–526.

Campbell, J. L. ed. (1958). *Gaelic Words and Expressions from South Uist and Eriskay.* Dublin Institute for Advanced Studies.

Campbell, J. L. (1970 et seq.). Macrolepidoptera Cannae. *Entomologist's Rec.* 82, 1–27.

Campbell, J. L. (1984). *Canna—the story of a Hebridean island.* Oxford University Press, Oxford.

Campbell, M. S. (1945). *The Flora of Uig (Lewis).* Buncle, Arbroath.

Campbell, R. N. & Williamson, R. B. (1979). The fishes of the inland waters of the Outer Hebrides. *Proc. Roy. Soc. Edinb.* 77B, 377–393.

Campbell, R. N. & Williamson, R. B. (1983). Salmon and freshwater fishes of the Inner Hebrides. *Proc. Roy. Soc. Edinb.* 83B, 245–265.

Campbell, R. N. B. (1986). Surveys of 61 lochs in the Outer Hebrides, mainly on national Nature Reserves and Sites of Special Scientific Interest, June–Sept.

1986. Nature Conservancy Council NW Region Report, Inverness.

Carmichael, A., Watson, J. C. & Matheson, A. (1900 et seq.) 6 vols. *Carmina Gadelica.* Edinburgh.

Clapham, A. R., Tutin, T. G. & Warburg, E. F. (1975). *Excursion Flora of the British Isles.* Cambridge University Press.

Clutton-Brock, T. H., Guinness, F. E. & Albon, S. D. (1988). Red deer in the Highlands. Blackwell, Oxford.

Cockburn, A. M. (1935). Geology of St Kilda. *Trans. Roy. Soc. Edinb.* 58 (21), 511–548.

Corley, M. F. V. (1983). Ecology and phytogeographical affinities of the bryophytes of the Inner Hebrides. *Proc. Roy. Soc. Edinb.* 83B, 373–401.

Craig, G. Y. (1983). ed. *Geology of Scotland.* Scottish Academic Press.

Cunningham, W. A. J. (1983). *Birds of the Outer Hebrides.* Methuen, Perth.

Currie, A. (1979). The vegetation of the Outer Hebrides. *Proc. Roy. Soc. Edinb.* 77B, 219–265.

Currie, A. (1988). West Highland Free Press 22 July, 5 Aug.

Currie, A. & Murray, C. (1983). Flora and vegetation of the Inner Hebrides. *Proc. Roy. Soc. Edinb.* 83B, 293–318.

Darling, F. F. (1944). *Island Farm.* Bell, London.

Darling, F. F. (1945). *Crofting Agriculture.* Oliver & Boyd, Edinburgh.

Darling, F. F. (1947). *Natural History of the Highlands and Islands.* Collins, London.

Darling, F. F. (1955). *West Highland Survey: an essay in human ecology.* Oxford University Press.

Darling, F. F. & Boyd, J. M. (1964). *The Highlands and Islands.* Collins, London.

Delany, M. J. (1964). Variation in the long-tailed field mouse (*Apodemus sylvaticus* L.) in north-west Scotland. A comparison of individual characters. *Proc. Roy. Soc. Edinb.* B161, 191–199.

Delany, M. J. (1970). Variation in the ecology of island populations of the long-tailed field mouse (*Apodemus sylvaticus* L.). In *Variation in Mammalian Populations* eds. R. J. Berry & H. N. Southern, pp. 283–295. Academic Press, London.

Dennis, R. W. G. & Watling, R. (1983). Fungi in the Inner Hebrides. *Proc. Roy. Soc. Edinb.* 83B, 415–429.

Dickenson, G. & Randall, R. E. (1979). An interpretation of machair vegetation. *Proc. Roy. Soc. Edinb.* 77B, 267–278.

Dobson, R. H. & Dobson, R. M. (1985). The natural history of the Muck Islands, N. Ebudes. 1. Introduction and vegetation with a list of vascular plants. *Glasg. Nat.* 21, 13–38.

Dobson, R. H. & Dobson, R. M. (1986). The natural history of the Muck Islands, N. Ebudes. 3. Seabirds and wildfowl. *Glasg. Nat.* 21, 183–199.

Donaldson, C. H. (1983). Tertiary igneous activity in the Inner Hebrides. *Proc. Roy. Soc. Edinb.* 83B, 65–81.

Doody, J. P. (1986). The saltmarshes of the Firth of Clyde. *Proc. Roy. Soc. Edinb.* 90B, 519–531.

Druce, G. C. (1993). *The Comital Flora of the British Isles.* Buncle, Arbroath.

Duncan, U. K. (1968–70). Botanical studies in Coll & Tiree. *Proc. Bot. Soc. Br. Isles* 7, 298–299, 636–637; *Trans. Bot. Soc. Edinb.* 40, 482–485, 653–655.

Dwelly, E. (1977). ninth ed. *The Illustrated Gaelic-English Dictionary.* Gairm, Glasgow.

Eggeling, W. J. (1965). Check list of the plants of Rhum after a reduction or exclusion of grazing. *Trans. Bot. Soc. Edinb.* 40, 60–69.

Ellett, D. J. (1979). Some oceanographic features of Hebridean waters. *Proc. Roy. Soc. Edinb.* 77B, 61–74.

Ellett, D. J. & Edwards, A. (1983). Oceanography and inshore hydrology of the Inner Hebrides. *Proc. Roy. Soc. Edinb.* 77B, 61–74.

Emeleus, C. H. (1980). *1:20,000 Solid Geology Map of Rhum.* Nature Conservancy Council.

Emeleus, C. H. (1983). Tertiary igneous activity. In *Geology of Scotland.* ed. G. Y. Craig. Scottish Academic Press, Edinburgh.

Emeleus, C. H. (1987). The Rhum volcano. In *Rhum,* ed. T. H. Clutton-Brock & M. E. Ball, Edinburgh University Press.

Evans, P. G. H. (1980). Cetaceans in British waters. *Mammal Review* 10, 1–59.

Evans, P. G. H. (1982). Association between seabirds and cetaceans: a review. *Mammal Review* 12, 187–206.

Ewing, P. (1887–95). A contribution to the topographic botany of the west of Scotland. *Proc. Trans. Nat. Hist. Soc. Glasg.* 2, 309–321; 3, 159–165; 4, 199–214.

Ewing, P. (1892, 1899). The Glasgow catalogue of native and established plants; etc. 1st & 2nd eds. Ewing, Glasgow.

Farrow, G. E. (1983). Recent sediments and sedimentation in the Inner Hebrides. *Proc. Roy. Soc. Edinb.* 83B, 91–105.

Ferreira, R. E. C. (1967). Community descriptions in field survey of vegetation map of the Isle of Rhum. Unpubl. report to Nature Conservancy.

Fletcher, W. W. & Kirkwood, R. C. ed. (1982). Bracken in Scotland. *Proc. Roy. Soc. Edinb.* 81B, 1–143.

Forbes, A. R. (1905). Gaelic names of beasts (mammalia), birds, fishes, insects, reptiles, etc. Oliver & Boyd, Edinburgh.

Forest, J. E., Waterston, A. R. & Watson, E. V. (1936). The natural history of Barra, Outer Hebrides. *Proc. Roy. Soc. Edinb.* 22, 41–96.

Fuller, R. J., Wilson, R. & Coxon, P. (1979). Birds of the Outer Hebrides: the waders. *Proc. Roy. Soc. Edinb.* 77B, 419–430.

George, J. D. (1979). The polychaetes of Lewis and Harris with notes on other marine invertebrates. *Proc. Roy. Soc. Edinb.* 77B, 189–216.

Gimmingham, C. H. (1964). Maritime and sub-maritime communities. In *The Vegetation of Scotland* ed. J. H. Burnett, Oliver & Boyd, Edinburgh.

Glentwoth, R. (1979). Observations on the soils of the Outer Hebrides. *Proc. Roy. Soc. Edinb.* 77B, 123–137.

Goode, D. A. & Lindsay, R. A. (1979). The peatland vegetation of Lewis. *Proc. Roy. Soc. Edinb.* 77B, 123–137.

Goodier, R. & Boyd, J. M. (1979). Environmental science, planning and resource management in the Outer Hebrides. *Proc. Roy. Soc. Edinb.* 77B, 551–561.

Gowen, R., Brown, J., Bradbury, N. & McLusky, D. S. (1988). Investigations into the benthic enrichment, hypernutrification and eutrophication associated with mariculture in Scottish coastal waters, 1984–88. Report to the HIDB, CEC, NCC, CCS & SSGA.

Grant, J. W. (1979). Cereals and grass production in Lewis and the Uists. *Proc. Roy. Soc. Edinb.* 77, 527–534.

Grant, J. W. & MacLeod, A. (1983). Agriculture in the Inner Hebrides. *Proc. Roy. Soc. Edinb.* 83B, 567–575.

Green, F. H. W. & Harding, R. (1983). Climate of the Inner Hebrides. *Proc. Roy. Soc. Edinb.* 83B, 121–140.

Green, J. & Green, R. (1980). *Otter Survey of Scotland 1977–79.* Vincent Wildlife Trust, London.

Gribble, C. D. (1983). Mineral resources of the Inner Hebrides. *Proc. Roy. Soc. Edinb.* 83B, 611–625.

Hallam, A. (1983). Jurassic, Cretaceous and Tertiary sediments. *Geology of Scotland* (ed. G. Y. Craig) pp. 334–356. Scottish Academic Press, Edinburgh.

Hambrey, J. (1986). *Agriculture & Environment in the Outer Hebrides.* Nature Conservancy Council, Edinburgh.

Harvie-Brown, J. A. & Buckley, T. E. (1888). *A Vertebrate Fauna of the Outer Hebrides.* Douglas, Edinburgh.

Harvie-Brown, J. A. & Buckley, T. E. (1892). *A Vertebrate Fauna of the Inner Hebrides.* Douglas, Edinburgh.

Heron, R. (1794). *General View of the Hebudae or Hebrides.* Patterson, Edinburgh

Heslop-Harrison, J. W. (1937 and 1939). In *Proc. Univ. Durham Phil. Soc.* The flora of Raasay and adjoining islands, etc. 9, 260–304; the flora of Rhum, Eigg, Canna, Sanday, Muck, Eilein nan Each, Hyskeir, Soay, Pabbay, 10, 87–123; *et al.* (1941) the flora of Coll, Tiree & Gunna, 10, 274–308.

Hewer, H. R. (1974). *British Seals.* Collins, London.

Hewson, R. (1954). The mountain hare in the Scottish islands. *Scot. Nat.* 67, 52–60.

Hiscock, S. (1988). Hidden depths. *Scottish Marine Life,* 1988, 55–58.

Hogan, F. E., Hogan, J. & Macerlean, J. C. (1900). *Irish and Scottish Gaelic Names of Herbs, Plants, Trees, etc.* Gill and Son, Dublin.

Hudson, J. D. (1983). Mesozoic sedementation and sedimentary rocks in the Inner Hebrides. *Proc. Roy. Soc. Edinb.* 83B, 47–63.

Hudson, G. & Henderson, D. J. (1983). Soils of the Inner Hebrides. *Proc. Roy. Soc. Edinb.* 83B, 107–119.

Hunter, J. (1976). *The Making of the Crofting Community.* John Donald, Edinburgh.

Institute of Terrestrial Ecology (NERC) (1979). *The invertebrate fauna of dune and machair sites in Scotland.* 2. vols. Report to the Nature Conservancy Council.

Jeffereys, J. G. (1879–84). On the mollusca procured during the 'Lightning' and 'Porcupine' expeditions. *Proc. Zool. Soc. Lond.* Parts III to VIII.

Jehu, T. J. & Craig, R. M. (1923–24). Geology of the Outer Hebrides. *Trans. Roy. Soc. Edinb.* 53, 419–441, 615–641; 54, 467–489; 55, 457–488; 57, 839–874.

Jenkins, D. (1986). *Trees & Wildlife in the Scottish Uplands.* Institute of Terrestrial Ecology, Banchory.

Jewell, P. A., Milner, C. & Boyd, J. M. eds. (1974). *Island Suvivors: the ecology of the Soay sheep of St Kilda.* Athlone Press, London.

Kerr, A. J. & Boyd, J. M. (1983). Nature conservation in the Inner Hebrides. *Proc. Roy. Soc. Edinb.* 83B, 627–648.

Kruuk, H. & Hewson, R. (1978). Spacing and foraging of otters (*Lutra lutra*) in a marine habitat, *J. Zool. Lond.* 185, 205–212.

Lewis, J. L. (1957). An introduction to the intertidal ecology of the rocky shore of a Hebridean island. *Oikos.* 8, 130–160.

Lewis, J. R. (1964). *The Ecology of Rocky Shores.* English Universities Press, London.

Lhuyd, E. (1707). *Archaelogia Britannica.* London.

Lightfoot, J. (1777). *Flora Scotia.* White, London.

Lind, E. M. (1952). The phytoplankton of some lochs in South Uist and Rhum. *Trans. Bot. Soc. Edinb.* 36, 35–47.

Lindsay, R. A., Riggall, J. & Bignal, E. M. (1983). Ombrogenous mires in Islay and Mull. *Proc. Roy. Soc. Edinb.* 83B, 341–371.

Lockie, J. D. & Stephen, D. (1959). Eagle, lambs and land management in Lewis. *J. Anim. Ecol.* 28, 43–50.

Lodge, E. (1963). Bryophytes of the Small Isles parish of Inverness-shire. *Nova Hedwigia* 5, 117–148; 6, 57–65.

Lovell, J. P. B. (1977). *The British Isles through Geological Time—a northward drift.* George Allen & Unwin, London.

Mackie, E. W. (1965). Brochs and the Hebridean Iron Age. *Antiquity* 39, 266–278.

Macleod, A. M. (1948). Some aspects of the plant ecology of the Island of Barra. *Trans. Bot. Soc. Edinb.* 35, 67–81.

MacLeoid, R. & MacThomais, R. (1976). *Bith-Eolas.* Gairm, Glaschu.

MacCulloch, J. (1819 & 1824). *A Description of the Western Isles of Scotland.* London.

Maitland, P. S. & Holden, A. V. (1983). Inland waters of the Inner Hebrides. *Proc. Roy. Soc. Edinb.* 83B, 229–244.

Manley, G. (1979). The climatic environment of the Outer Hebrides. *Proc. Roy. Soc. Edinb.* 77B, 47–59.

Marshall, J. T. (1896–1912). Additions to 'British Conchology'. *J. Conch. Lond.* Vols. 9–13.

Mason, J., Shelton, R. G. J., Drinkwater, J. & Howard, F. G. (1983). Shellfish resources in the Inner Hebrides. *Proc. Roy. Soc. Edinb.* 83B, 599–610.

Mather, A. S. & Ritchie, W. (1977). *The Beaches of the Highlands and Islands of Scotland.* Countryside Commission for Scotland.

Maxwell, G. (1952). *Harpoon at a Venture.* Hart-Davis, London.

Maxwell, G. (1960). *Ring of Bright Water.* Longmans, London.

McIntosh, W. C. (1866). Observations on the marine zoology of North Uist. *Proc. Roy. Soc. Edinb.* 5, 600–614.

McVean, D. N. & Ratcliffe, D. A. (1962). *Plant Communities of the Scottish Highlands.* Nature Conservancy Monograph No. 1. HMSO, Edinburgh.

McVean, D. N. (1958). Flora and vegetation of the islands of St Kilda and North Rona. *J. Ecol.* 49, 39–54.

Menzies, W. J. M. (1938). The movement of salmon marked in the sea, II—Island of Soay and Ardnamurchan in 1938. *Rep. Fishery Bd. Scotl. VII.*

Meteorological Office (1989). *Scotland's Climate.* Meteorological Office, Edinburgh.

Miller, H. (1858). *The Cruise of the Betsey.* Nimmo, Edinburgh.

Mills, D. H. & Graesser, N. (1981). *The Salmon Rivers of Scotland.* Cassell, London.

Mitchell, B., Staines, B. W. & Welch, D. (1977). *Ecology of Red Deer.* Institute of Terrestrial Ecology, Banchory.

Mitchell, R., Earll, R. C. & Dipper, F. A. (1983). Shallow sublittoral ecosystems in the Inner Hebrides. *Proc. Roy. Soc. Edinb.* 83B, 161–184.

Monaghan, P., Bignal, E., Bignal, S., Easterbee, N. & Mackay, A. G. (1989).

The distribution and status of the chough in Scotland in 1986. *Scot. Birds* 15, 114–118.

Monro, D. (1884). Description of the Western Isles of Scotland (Circa 1549). Thomas D. Morrison, Glasgow.

Mowle, A. D. (1980). *The use of natural resources in the Scottish Highlands, with particular reference to the island of Mull.* PhD Thesis: University of Stirling.

Murray, J. & Pullar, L. (1910). Bathymetrical survey of the Scottish freshwater lochs. *Rep. Scient, Results Bathymetr. Surv. Scot. Freshw. Lochs* 2, 183–221; 6, 68–69.

Nall, G. H. (1930). *The Life of the Sea Trout.* Seeley Service, London.

Nall, G. H. (1932). Notes on the collections of sea trout scales from Lewis and Harris and from North Uist. *Salm. Fish. Edinb.* 1932, 1.

Nall, G. H. (1934). Sea trout of Lewis and Harris. *Salm. Fish. Edinb.* 1934, 4.

National Trust for Scotland (1979). *St Kilda Handbook* ed. A. Small. NTS, Edinburgh.

Nature Conservancy Council (1974). *Isle of Rhum National Nature Reserve Handbook.* NCC, Edinburgh.

Nature Conservancy Council (1988). *Flow Country: the Peatlands of Caithness and Sutherland* ed. D. A. Ratcliffe & P. H. Oswald. NCC, Edinburgh.

Nethersole-Thompson, D. & Nethersole-Thompson, M. (1986). *Waders: their breeding haunts, and watchers.* T. & A. D. Poyser, London.

Newton, I. & Krebs, R. H. (1974). Breeding greylag geese (*Anser anser*) on the Outer Hebrides. *J. Anim. Ecol.* 43, 771–783.

Nicholson, E. M. (1988). *The New Environmental Age.* Cambridge University Press.

Nicol, E. A. T. (1936). The brackish water lochs of North Uist. *Proc. Roy. Soc. Edinb.* 56, 169–195.

Nicolaisen, W. F. H. (1976). *Scottish Place Names: Their Study and Significance.* Batsford, London.

Norton, T. A. (1972). The marine algae of Lewis and Harris in the Outer Hebrides. *Br. Phycol. J.* 7, 375–385.

Norton, T. A. (1986). The ecology of macroalgae in the Firth of Clyde. *Proc. Roy. Soc. Edinb.* 90B, 255–269.

Norton, T. A. & Powell, H. T. (1979). Seaweeds and rocky shores of the Outer Hebrides. *Proc. Roy. Soc. Edinb.* 77B, 141–153.

Ogilvie, M. A. (1983a). Wildlife on Islay. *Proc. Roy. Soc. Edinb.* 83B, 473–489.
Ogilvie, M. A. & Atkinson-Willes, G. W. (1983). Wildlfowl of the Inner Hebrides. *Proc. Roy. Soc. Edinb.* 83B, 491–504.
Ogilvie, M. A., Atkinson-Willes, G. W. & Salmon, D. (1986). *Wildlfowl in Britain* (2nd edit). Cambridge University Press.

Peacock, J. D. (1983). Quaternary geology of the Inner Hebrides. *Proc. Roy. Soc. Edinb.* 83B, 83–89.
Pearsall, W. H. (1950). *Mountains and Moorlands*. Collins, London.
Perring, F. H. & Randall, R. E. (1972). An annotated flora of the Monach Isles NNR, Outer Hebrides. *Trans. Bot. Soc. Edinb.* 41, 431–444.
Poore, M. E. D. & Robertson, V. C. (1949). The vegetation of St Kilda in 1948. *J. Ecol.* 37, 82–89.
Powell, H. T., Holme, N. A., Knight, S. J. T., Harvey, T., Bishop, G. and Bartrop, J. (1979). *Survey of the littoral zone of the coast of Great Britain, 3, Report on the shores of the Outer Hebrides.* Report to the Nature Conservancy Council.
Powell, H. T., Holme, N. A., Knight, S. J. T., Harvey, T., Bishop, G. and Bartrop, J. (1980). *Survey of the littoral zone of the coast of Great Britain, 6, Report on the shores of Northwest Scotland.* Report to the Nature Conservancy Council.

Rae, B. B. & Wilson, E. (1953–61). Rare and exotic fishes recorded in Scotland. *Scot. Nat.* 65, 141–153; 66, 170–185; 68, 23–38, 92–109; 70, 22–33.
Rae, B. B. & Lamont, J. M. (1961–64). Rare and exostic fishes recorded in Scotland. *Scot. Nat.* 70, 34–42, 102–119; 71, 29–36, 39–46.
Randall, R. E. (1976). Machair zonation of the Monach Isles NNR, Outer Hebrides. *Trans. Bot. Soc. Edinb.* 42, 441–462.
Ratcliffe, D. A. (ed.) (1977). *A Nature Conservation Review.* Cambridge University Press.
Red Deer Commission (1961–75). *Annual Reports.* RDC, Inverness.

Reed, T. M., Currie, A. & Love, J. A. (1983). Birds of the Inner Hebrides. *Proc. Roy. Soc. Edinb.* 83B, 449–472.
Riedl, H. (1979). Phytogeographical and ecological relations of epiphytic lichens from Lewis and Harris with notes on other cryptogamic epiphytes. *Proc. Roy. Soc. Edinb.* 77B, 295–304.
Ritchie, J. (1920). *The Influence of Man on Animal Life in Scotland.* Cambridge University Press.
Ritchie, J. (1930). Scotland's testimony to the march of evolution. *Scot. Nat.* 1930, 161–169.
Ritchie, J. E. (1932). Tertiary ring structures in Britain. *Trans. Geol. Soc. Glasgow* 19, 42–140.
Ritchie, W. (1966). The post-glacial rise in sea level and coastal changes in the Uists. *Trans. Inst. Br. Geogr.* 39, 79–86.
Ritchie, W. (1976). The meaning and definition of machair. *Trans. Proc. Bot. Soc. Edinb.* 42, 431–440.
Ritchie, W. (1979). Machair development and chronology in the Uists and adjacent islands. *Proc. Roy. Soc. Edinb.* 77B, 107–122.
Rose, F. & Coppins, B. J. (1983). Lichens of Colonsay. *Proc. Roy. Soc. Edinb.* 83B, 403–413.

Schonbeck, M. & Norton, T. (1978). Factors controlling the upper limits of fucoid algae on the shore. *J. Exp. Mar. Ecol.* 31, 303–313.
Seebohm, H. (1884). New species of British wren. *Zool.* 8, 333–335.
Sharrock, J. T. R. (1976). *The Atlas of Breeding Birds of Britain.* T. &. A. D. Poyser, Berkhamstead.
Sibbald, Sir R. (1684). *Scotia Illustrata.*
Simkin, T. (1984). Geology of the Galapagos. *Biol. J. Linn. Soc.* 21, 61–76.
Sissons, J. B. (1983). Quaternary. In *Geology of Scotland* ed. G. Y. Craig, pp. 399–424, Scottish Academic Press.
Skene, W. F. (1886–90). *Celtic Scotland,* 3 vols, Edinburgh.
Smith, D. I. & Fettes, D. J. (1979). Geological framework of the Outer Hebrides. *Proc. Roy. Soc. Edinb.* 77B, 75–83.
Smith, S. M. (1979). Mollusca of rocky shores: Lewis and Harris, Outer Hebrides. *Proc. Roy. Soc. Edinb.* 77B, 173–187.
Smith, S. M. (1983). Marine mollusca of Islay and Skye. *Proc. Roy. Soc. Edinb.* 83B, 195–217.

Southward, A. J. (1976). On the taxonomic status and distribution of *Cathalamus stellatus* (Cirripedia) in the north-east Atlantic: a key to the common intertidal barnacles of Britain. *J. Mar. Biol. Ass. UK* 56, 1007–1028.

Spence, D. H. N. (1964). The macrophytic vegetation of lochs, swamps and associated fens. In *The Vegetation of Scotland* ed. J. H. Burnett, 306–425, Oliver & Boyd, Edinburgh.

Spence, D. H. N., Allen, E. D. & Fraser, J. (1979). Macrophytic vegetation of fresh and brackish waters in and near the Loch Druidibeg National Nature Reserve, South Uist. *Proc. Roy. Soc. Edinb.* 77B, 307–328.

Spray, C. J. (1981). An isolated population of *Cygnus olor* in Scotland. *Proc. 2nd Int. Swan Symp. Sapporo* 1980, 191–208.

Statistical Account of Scotland (Old) (1791–99). Edinburgh.

Statistical Account of Scotland (New) (1845). Blackwoods, Edinburgh.

Steel, W. O. & Woodraffe, G. E. (1969). The entomology of the Isle of Rhum National Nature Reserve. *Trans. Soc. Brit. Entomol.* 18, 91–167.

Storrie, M. C. (1981). *Islay: Biography of an Island.* Oa Press, Isle of Islay.

Storrie, M. C. (1983). Landuse and settlement history in the southern Inner Hebrides. *Proc. Roy. Soc. Edinb.* 83B, 549–566.

Stowe, T. J. & Hudson, A. V. (1988). Corncrake studies in the Western Isles. *RSPB Conservation Review.* 1988, 38–42.

Stroud, D. A. ed. (1989). The birds of Coll and Tiree: status, habitats and conservation. Scottish Ornothologists Club/Nature Conservancy Council, Edinburgh.

Sulloway, F. J. (1984). Darwin and the Galapagos. *Biol. J. Linn. Soc.* 21, 29–60.

Swann, R. L. (1984). Birds of Canna. *Canna—the story of a Hebridean Island,* J. L. Campbell, pp. 265–277.

Sykes, E. R. (1906–25). In the mollusca procured during the 'Porcupine' expeditions 1869–70. *Proc. Malac. Soc. Lond.* Parts III, IV, V.

Tansley, A. G. (1949). *The British Islands and their Vegetation.* Cambridge University Press.

Taylor, C. S. (1981). *Status and habitats available for invertebrates in forests in the Inner Hebrides.* (Report to the Forestry Commission).

Thom, V. M. (1986). *Birds in Scotland.* Poyser, Calton.

Thompson, D. S. (1983). *The Companion to Gaelic Scotland.* Blackwell, Oxford.

Thomson, D'A. W. (1928). On whales landed at Scottish whaling stations during the years 1908–14 and 1920–27. *Sc. Inv. Fish. Bd. Scot.* 3, 1–40.

Trail, J. W. H. (1898–1909). Topographical botany of Scotland (followed by additions and corrections). *Ann. Scot. Nat. Hist.* 1898–1900; 1905–1909.

Twelves, J. (1983). Otter (*Lutra lutra*) mortalities in lobster creels. *J. Zool. Lond.* 201, 285–288.

Vasari, Y. & Vasari, A. (1968). Late- and post-glacial macrophytic vegetation in the lochs of northern Scotland. *Acta. Bot. Fenn.* 80, 1–120.

Vose, P. B., Powell, H. G. & Spence, J. B. (1957). The machair grazings of Tiree, Inner Hebrides. *Trans. Bot. Soc. Edinb.* 37, 89–110.

Waterston, A. R. (1981). Present knowledge of the non-marine invertebrate fauna of the Outer Hebrides *Proc. Roy. Soc. Edinb.* 77B, 251–321.

Waterston, A. R., Holden, A. V., Campbell, R. N. & Maitland, P. S. (1979). The inland waters of the Outer Hebrides. *Proc. Roy. Soc. Edinb.* 77B, 329–351.

Waterston, A. R. & Lyster, I. H. J. (1979). The macrofauna of brackish and freshwaters of the Loch Druidibeg National Nature Reserve and its neighbourhood, South Uist. *Proc. Roy. Soc. Edinb.* 77B, 353–376.

Watling, R., Irvine, L. M. & Norton, T. A. (1970). The marine algae of St Kilda. *Trans. Proc. Bot. Soc. Edinb.* 41, 31–42.

Watson, A., Moss, R. & Parr, R. (1987). Grouse increase in Mull. *Landowning in Scotland*, 207, 6.

Watson, H. C. (1873–74). *Topographic Botany.* 1st ed. London. 2nd ed. 1883.

Watson, J. (1983). Lewisian. In *Geology of Scotland* ed. G. Y. Craig. Scottish Academic Press, Edinburgh.

Watson, W. J. (1926). *The History of the Celtic Place-names of Scotland.* Blackwood, Edinburgh.

Welch, R. C. (1979). Survey of the invertebrate fauna of sand dune and machair sites in the Outer Hebrides during 1976. *Proc. Roy. Soc. Edinb.* 77B, 395–404.

Welch, R. C. (1983). Coleoptera in the Inner Hebrides. *Proc. Roy. Soc. Edinb.* 83B, 505–529.

Williamson, K. & Boyd, J. M. (1960). *St Kilda Summer*. Hutchinson, London.

Williamson, K. & Boyd, J. M. (1963). *Mosaic of Islands*. Oliver & Boyd, Edinburgh.

Wormell, P. (1977). Woodland insect population changes in the Isle of Rhum in relation to forest history and woodland restoration. *Scott. Forest.* 31, 13–36.

Wormell, P. (ed.) (1982). The entomology of the Isle of Rhum National Nature Reserve. *Biol. J. Linn. Soc.* 18, 291–401.

Wormell, P. (1983). Lepidoptera in the Inner Hebrides. *Proc. Roy. Soc. Edinb.* 83B, 531–546.

Wormell, P. (1987). Invertebrates of Rhum. In *Rhum* ed. T. H. Clutton-Brock and M. E. Ball. Edinburgh University Press, Edinburgh.

Yonge, C. M. (1949). *The Sea Shore*. Collins, London.

Index

adder 184-185
Agricultural Development Programme 51
agricultural improvement 51-52, 56, 156
agriculture 29, 35, 38, 51-52, 59, 111-117, 186
amphibians 184-185; also see frog, toads and newts
Ardnamurchan 15, 24-28
Armadale Castle 124
Arran 24-28
Atlantic Current 46
Atlantic Period 45, 150

Barra 16, 38, 43, 47, 54, 142, 147; Eoligarry 95; Vallay 94
Barra Head 19, 47, 50
Barra Isles 51, 123
bees 108, 115
Benbecula 19, 34, 41-42, 52, 92, 95, 108, 110, 112, 121-122, 166
Berneray (Harris) 123
biomes 4
birds 97, 115-117, 122, 156; also see seabirds; buzzard 99; corn bunting 120-122; corncrake 117-120; heathland 147-148; machair 109-110; St Kilda wren 5; sea shore 84, 91-92, 97; starling 5; upland 160; waterfowl 185-186; woodland 137-140
blackland 97, 109, 111, 166
Blackstones Bank 24
bogs 45, 123, 126, 143, 148-156; blanket and raised 150-154; valley 154-156
Boreal Period 45, 127
brackish water 88, 168-171, 175
bryophyte 45, 130, 133-134, 143, 145, 151-156
butterflies 108, 115, 140-141, 147

Caledonian Orogeny 7, 13-14, 16, 20
Cambrian 13-14, 21
Cambro-Ordovician 12, 15-16, 20
Canna 15, 17, 24-26, 29, 43, 114, 124, 140-141, 143, 147, 174, 182, 184; House 124
Carboniferous 16
cattle 100, 146
charcoal 42
climate 23, 28, 30-46, 78, 152, 191;

ecological effects of 32-35; historical 45-46
Coastal Current 47-49
coral 7
Coll 7, 16, 18, 20, 27, 37, 54, 121, 123, 183-184
Colonsay 16-17, 20-21, 27, 28, 37, 46, 53-54, 68, 121, 126-127, 130, 141, 166, 185
conservation 57, 92, 136, 140, 156, 189-196
copepods 63, 69, 75
Corryvreckan, Gulf of 49-50
Countryside Commission for Scotland 194
Cretaceous 17, 22-24
crofting 51-54, 111-122, 144
crops 35, 38, 51, 113-114, 118
crustaceans 81-82, 84-89, 170-171, 173, 183; also see shellfish
cultivation 51-52, 88, 96, 111-117

Dalradian Supergroup 12, 14, 16
Darling, F. Fraser 2, 71
Darwin, Charles 3
Devensian 28
Devonian 16, 21
drainage 54
dunes 7, 94-100, 122
Durness limestone 18; also see rocks
dykes 19, 24, 26-27

earthquakes 27
earthworms 105-106
Eigg 15, 17, 19, 22, 24-26, 57, 126, 140-141, 147-148, 183-184
Eocene 17, 24
Eriskay 123
erosion 38, 51, 57

farming see crofting
faults, Camasunary-Skerryvore 17, 19; Great Glen 17, 18; Highland Boundary 17; Moine Thrust 17-18, 20; Outer Hebrides Thrust Zone 17-19
fauna 4-5, 57, 97; marine 60-76; woodland 137-141; see also molluscs, crustacea, invertebrates, birds and mammals
fen 96; also see bogs
fertilizer 51-52, 111
fire 123, 148, 155